NIKI GOLDSCHMIDT:
A LIFE IN CANADIAN MUSIC

Niki Goldschmidt, Conductor, c 1985. NG's private collection.

Niki Goldschmidt
A Life in Canadian Music

GWENLYN SETTERFIELD

UNIVERSITY OF TORONTO PRESS
Toronto Buffalo London

© University of Toronto Press Incorporated 2003
Toronto Buffalo London
Printed in Canada

ISBN 0-8020-4807-2

Printed on acid-free paper

National Library of Canada Cataloguing in Publication

Setterfield, Gwenlyn
    Niki Goldschmidt : a life in Canadian music / Gwenlyn Setterfield.

    Includes bibliographical references and index.
    ISBN 0-8020-4807-2

    1. Goldschmidt, Nicholas, 1908–   2. Concert agents – Canada –
Biography.   3. Conductors (Music) – Canada – Biography.
I. Title.

ML429.G623S49 2003   782.1′092   C2002-905195-9

University of Toronto Press acknowledges the financial assistance to
its publishing program of the Canada Council for the Arts and the
Ontario Arts Council.

University of Toronto Press acknowledges the financial support for its
publishing activities of the Government of Canada through the Book
Publishing Industry Development Program (BPIDP).

To my daughters

Contents

viii   Contents

Illustrations follow p. 128

Foreword

'So yooo arrr Terreza Strratas. They tell me you are *eemmensely* talented. Is this trooo?' The voice was like a gentle song.

It was the autumn of 1956. I was standing in the Royal Conservatory of Music in Toronto, having just enrolled in the school days before. I was in a world so different from my familiar world at home. I was just sixteen and under five feet tall. I now calculate that he was forty-eight and definitely over six feet tall. I looked up and thus began my first of many encounters with Niki Goldschmidt. I remember thinking that he was the tallest man I had ever met. Now, almost half a century later, having travelled and sung around the globe many times over, and having met all sorts of people, including kings and saints, I can still say that Niki is truly a very tall man.

He was a most striking man, and if not for the radiance of his smile he would have frightened me. Yes, I would have thought him fierce-looking with that dark forest of bushy eyebrows, under which laser-blue eyes pierced me in place. But then, almost in the same moment they twinkled as if he knew a secret and was about to burst into laughter – a secret about me, about him, about life, and about the mysterious musical world he inhabited. Indeed he was a strange amalgam of Bugs Bunny, Nosferatu, and Peter O'Toole. Bugs Bunny, because he was ever moving and mischievous, Nosferatu because of a haunting, gaunt, and angular quality, and Peter O'Toole because, well, because Niki was handsome and, as I was to find out later, very charming too.

Niki Goldschmidt was one of the first three people to ever acknowledge my talent (actually within days of each other). The first person was Arnold Walter, a catalyst in Niki's life and in my own. Dr Walter was the head of Senior School and had brought Niki to Canada from the United

States to help him form Canada's first opera school, having hired him in the capacity of conductor, coach, and music director in 1946. Ten years after that, Arnold Walter heard me sing and gave me a full scholarship to begin my studies of classical music and singing.

Along with Herman Geiger-Torel, the talented stage director of the opera school, these three powerful men had the foresight to recognize my talent even though it must have been very raw at that time, and to pave a secure road of learning along with opportunities that allowed me to grow as a young artist. Under the guidance and encouragement of these three people (and with voice lessons from the lovable and excellent Madame Irene Jessner, who by the way didn't think I had any talent at all that first year), I was trained in the great traditions of Europe and encouraged to have my own ideas about music and singing. Three years later, I won a contract with the Metropolitan Opera where I would sing leading roles for the next thirty-seven years. Great teachers – great schooling. I've written these things about myself to show how bound up a part of my life has been with Niki Goldschmidt and I am only one of thousands of people on whose life he has had an impact.

I wonder now, did Niki have an office then? He just seemed to always be there when I needed direction. He would materialize in front of me, prodding and encouraging me and then his head would turn as if he had received an international communication of great musical importance and had to respond quickly. Off he went, vanishing as quickly as he had appeared ... but not before he had imbued me with a sense of hope and excitement of wonderful things to come.

In the next year, Niki conducted me in *Gianni Schicchi*, an opera school production that was the first complete opera I had ever sung. A few years later he hired me to sing *Butterfly*, with him as conductor at the Vancouver International Festival, which he had established the year before. I have sung under the baton of many conductors good and bad over the years, but Niki was one of the few whose face radiated the very essence of music as he conducted his singers and musicians. It is all too rare to encounter this quality in a conductor.

Niki would visit me from time to time in New York. We would sit in my apartment and discuss music and life and he would tell me of his various projects with great enthusiasm. Never once did I ever feel he was promoting himself. This too is a very rare quality. His enthusiasm was for the music, the project, the musicians and singers of the project and the people and the city where it would take place. Though his hair had greyed over the years, his spirit and love for the talented young people he worked with remained undiminished.

The extraordinary quality of being absolutely delighted with some wonderful secret he knew always remained. Is it humour about life? Is it effervescence for living? I don't know. I wish I did. Did he live a charmed life? Everything always seemed to fall into place for Niki. Or was it his great capacity to get immediately back on his feet when something didn't turn out quite right and know that next time, things would work out much better? He didn't dwell. He always moved on. How I admire this capability and I wish I had it.

He was so proud to tell me of the many achievements of Canadians in music. Whenever I returned to Canada to receive an award he was always there, enthusiastic and happy for me. The last time I saw him was the autumn of 2000. I had flown to Ottawa to receive the Governor General's Performing Arts Award for lifetime achievement. There he was, his hair now pure white, wearing his many medals – including his own lifetime achievement award – and with his beautiful wife Shelagh at his side. (Their love story and how inseparable these two have always been are integral to Niki's life.) His vivacity and focus were as they had always been. As he regaled me with stories of his Music Canada Musique 2000 project, composers, conductors, directors, and singers came up to him and greeted and kissed him. He would introduce them to me: 'This one was composing such and such *splllendid* piece and this *eemmensely* talented one was singing in another *splllendid* project.' It was fascinating to watch him in action with these artists. I think that though he has been a teacher to so many, he remains childlike in his eagerness to learn. A student at heart, he cares profoundly about music and all the arts.

Niki is not only loved and admired by his peers. Jon Vickers and I often spoke of how supportive and enthusiastic he was and has always been to us, and now a whole new generation of artists is hanging on Niki's every word. He inspires young artists to know the great traditions of the world and to build on them and to find their own new voices with that solid foundation in place. I believe this to be one part of his enormous contribution to Canada.

Many years ago he came to Canada. He brought Europe's musical culture and great traditions with him. Fortunately for us he remained. He encourages Canadian artists to surpass the borders of limited thinking to become voices for the enrichment not only of Canada's artistic life but the artistic life of the world. Niki is a visionary. Whether helping to build the first opera school in Canada, conducting some of its first performances, helping to establish the first Canadian opera company, conducting his great choral festivals, or building singers, conductors, and composers, he has been Canada's Pied Piper, diplomatically leading us to the power of internationalism through music making. His work with young people and his various projects, not least of all Music Canada Musique 2000, helped put Canada on the world's musical map. He is esteemed the world over as an important force behind Canadian music.

The following pages are a much-deserved chronicle and tribute to a life superbly lived. Simply, clearly, yet lovingly, Gwenlyn Setterfield sets forth an inspiring chronicle of a maverick and visionary whose life has been, and continues to be, an astounding adventure. It is a pleasure to introduce a book that makes his fascinating story available for the first time. We are indebted to Niki Goldschmidt for living the life and to Gwenlyn Setterfield for writing this book.

Teresa Stratas, New York City, 28 February 2003

Acknowledgments

I first want to express my gratitude to Maria Muszynska and Susan Hayes, who had the foresight to sit down with Niki, recording his recollections and thoughts on his life and career. They generously made those tapes available to me, providing abundant material from which to begin filling out this story. Their dedication and understanding of Niki's importance in the development of the arts in Canada set the tone for my work.

Thanks are due to Hon. Henry N.R. Jackman, and to the J.P. Bickell Foundation, through David Windeyer, for their financial support of this project. They are among the few in Canada who understand the costs involved in telling our nation's stories and how scarce are the resources available to offset those costs. Without their help I could not have committed myself to this task.

Librarians and archivists are the foundation on which rests the essential research for a project of this kind. To Timothy Maloney, head of the Music Division of the National Library of Canada, and to his staff, in particular Maureen Nevins, I extend my deepest thanks. They were unfailingly helpful, always knowledgeable and provided invaluable direction to the relevant material. Thanks also to Ian Wilson, Canada's National Archivist.

Thanks are due also to the staff of the Archival and Special Collections division of the University of Guelph Library, who guided me through their collections, especially the Guelph Spring Festival Archives. Similarly, Birthe Joergensen, archivist of the Joan Baillie Archives of the Canadian Opera Company, provided invaluable assistance and access to material. The Metropolitan Toronto Reference Library and the Archives and Records Management Services of the University of Toronto Library both offered extensive resources and answers to many questions. Additional assistance was received from the New York Public Library, the Vancouver, BC, Archives, the Vancouver Public Library, the Archives of Columbia University, Lisa Philpott at the University of Western Ontario Music Library, and the San Francisco Performing Arts Library and Museum.

Uncatalogued 'surprises' are treasures for a biographer. Thanks to Michael Patrick Albano, who looked into an old trunk at the University of Toronto Faculty of Music and suggested I should sort through the papers he saw there. I did, and found those surprises. Similarly, Jennifer Kersley welcomed me to Sault Ste Marie, where the staff of the Algoma Fall Festival left me to go through their files and memorabilia and discover the importance of that festival to their region. Robert Creech provided extensive records from Niki's summers at Courtenay.

Daniel Janke and everyone associated with the Longest Night Festival in Whitehorse, Yukon, were welcoming, and helped immeasurably to give this book its beginning.

John Friesen deserves special mention for the voluminous material he supplied regarding Niki's years in Vancouver, at the university and with the Vancouver International Festival. John was generous with his time, his invaluable recollections of people and events, and with Mrs Friesen's special chocolate chip cookies!

I thank all of the individuals who willingly responded to my requests for interviews and additional information. I appreciate their openness, their efforts to find documents, and their hospitality: William Lord, William Littler, George Crum, Moira Johnson, Jean Latrémouille, Alberta Nokes and Vision TV, Colin Graham, Brian Macdonald, Robert Missen, Robert Cooper, Naomi Lightbourne, Harvey Olnick, Vincent Tovell, Mary Morrison, Victor Feldbrill, Patricia Rideout, Janet Stubbs, Carl Morey, John Beckwith, Ezra Schabas, Cathryn Gregor, Jon Vickers, Teresa Stratas, Leopold Simoneau, Walter Taussig, David Leighton, David Catton, Murdo MacKinnon, Edwina and Noel Carson, Marilyn Crooks, John Cripton and Linda Sword, James Norcop and Charlotte Holmes, Catherine Belyea, Gloria Dent, Leo Goldschmidt, Suzanne Bradshaw, John Godfrey, and the late Senator Godfrey and Mrs Godfrey, John Hobday, Mavor Moore and Alexandra Browning, Joy Coghill, Tim Porteous, Barbara and Carl Little, Charles Wilson, George Zukerman, Brian Gooch, Leon Major, Lee Willingham, Barry Cole, Walter Pitman, Heather Clark, and Barbra Kršek. Thanks to Lidie Krupakova for her patience, to Nalini Stewart for her encouragement, and unlimited gratitude to Jocelyn Harvey for her information, friendship, and a comfortable home away from home.

I am particularly grateful to my editor, Suzanne Rancourt, for her patience, her wise advice and support throughout the writing of this book.

Finally, thanks to Shelagh Goldschmidt for her gracious hospitality, wisdom, and good humour. She and Niki gave me many happy hours, as I uncovered the details of this story.

NIKI GOLDSCHMIDT

Prologue

The Longest Night Society of Whitehorse, in Canada's Yukon Territory, is rehearsing for its annual festival. In the far north this is a time for celebration, for music and singing and storytelling. It's the time of the winter solstice, the turning of the year, when the sun begins its long journey back from the southern sky. These performers, struggling over lines and lighting cues, know that this year's show, 21 December 1999, is special. Not only does it mark the last festival of the century, but also it has brought important visitors from the south. *The Longest Night* is to launch the country's pre-eminent artistic millennium project, Music Canada Musique 2000. During the coming year concert halls from east to west will ring with the sounds of dozens of premieres, many featuring world-famous performers. But Whitehorse is first, and sitting in the darkened auditorium of the Yukon Performing Arts Centre, fresh off the plane from Toronto, is the man who started it all, the artistic director of Music 2000, Nicholas Goldschmidt.

Elbows resting on his knees, hands tucked under his chin, he watches the rehearsal intently. His sixty-plus years of experience in the performance business tell him that the complex multi-media music drama, *Time Pieces*, the centrepiece of this festival, is a formidable challenge for the technical and musical resources available in this small community. His standards are high and he is anxious that it all come together perfectly for tomorrow's premiere. After all, it marks the realization of Niki Goldschmidt's latest dream, which started, like most of the inspirations in his long life, with a question to himself: 'What can we do that will be marvellous, to celebrate the millennium in music?' New musical sounds, written and performed in communities across Canada, that was the unlikely answer. Never inclined to step back from a challenge, especially one posed to himself, he went to work, pulling and pushing, putting all the pieces in place, gathering the patrons, cajoling the politicians, negotiating with the presenters. He made the dream sing, and the opening chords will be heard right here in this hall.

Outside, the late afternoon is cold. The rising moon, close to the earth this December, shines brighter than the low-lying sun, its light reflecting luminously off the surrounding snow-covered mountains. This is a place as different from the estate where Niki Goldschmidt began life almost a century ago as the Orient Express is from a paddle-wheeler. This is a place of empty spaces, and spectacular natural beauty, a place that, although the first Native people arrived over twelve thousand years ago, still feels like a frontier.

In contrast, Niki was born in a castle set in the lush orderly landscape of Moravia, in the last glory days of the Austro-Hungarian Empire. He studied music in bustling Vienna surrounded by grand palaces and concert halls. In the Yukon they were mining for gold, in Vienna they were using it to gild their buildings. Tourists in Vienna take pictures beside statues of the city's great historical figures, political, military, and artistic. In Whitehorse the pre-eminent statue stands in the modest square in front of the government building. It features a man, Everyman, dressed in frontier costume with a floppy hat, carrying a shovel, dog by his side. The dedication reads, 'To all who would follow their Dreams.'

And this is perhaps where the contradictions are resolved, where the divergent themes of Nicholas Goldschmidt's life come together. This is a man who has followed his dreams, using his talents and the tools at hand. Whitehorse may be far from the Central Europe of his upbringing, in time and form, a spaceship voyage away it seems, but it overflows with stories of adventure and challenge, two of the elements that have defined Niki's life and have brought him here for the Longest Night. Like the performers, he is looking forward to the moment when the curtain goes up, to hearing the music and how it will blend with the narration and dance and film to create a seamless dramatic voyage to another dimension. He has always loved sitting in the audience and feeling the pleasure in the shared encounter. It's an experience Niki Goldschmidt has had hundreds, if not thousands, of times. More often than not he has been the catalyst for what happens on the stage. But each time is new for him, and he comes to each town and each theatre with undiminished enthusiasm that infects everyone around him.

However, at this moment in the Yukon Performing Arts Centre, with his wife, Shelagh, at his side, as she has been for over half a century, Niki is nervous. The rehearsal has a chaotic feel to it; the director from Toronto arrived only hours ago and must quickly pull together the complex elements in this show where many of the participants have 'day jobs' and cannot be available exactly on demand. Niki is not expecting a grand classical musical work like those he heard regularly in his student days; this is jazz mixed with elements of folk and rock, a new sound. That's all right with Niki; all kinds of musical and dramatic forms attract his interest. But he does expect every performance to be as polished as it can be, a professional job, in which the performers can take pride and from which the audience can derive real pleasure. He is not absolutely certain at this point that this show will meet that standard.

And it is important. Governments and private patrons have heavily supported Music Canada Musique 2000 (relative to the level of arts funding generally). Many of these officials will be present at the opening, including the prime minister's parliamentary secretary, territorial officials, and board members from Music Canada. Niki wants them to be impressed, to leave with the feeling that it was all worthwhile, money and effort well spent. Contemporary music is not always an easy sell; patrons and performers alike are known to groan aloud about the obligatory 'Canadian piece' on a concert program. It took all of Niki's persuasive ardour to raise the money for this celebration. Success here will reinforce his reputation as an instigator of exciting musical ventures, and, most significant, will support his deep conviction that the arts, especially music, bond people together, and that Canadians should enter the new millennium hearing the sounds of their own music.

The rehearsal ends with many problems unresolved. 'They'll be sorted out later,' says Daniel Janke, composer and musical director, but now it's time to eat. Will Mr and Mrs Goldschmidt and friends join the cast, crew, and their families in the green room for a potluck supper? And will Mr Goldschmidt do a couple of interviews with the press? The answer is an enthusiastic yes from this couple who have travelled the world together, been entertained at elegant banquets and candlelit salons. In this backstage room, furnished with practical chairs and tables and fluorescent lights, they serve themselves from the buffet of homemade dishes, old-fashioned casseroles, salads, vegetarian mixes, and moose curry. The room buzzes with excited performers and even more excited children and babies. It's a good old-fashioned get-together, friendly and casual. Shelagh talks to everyone, her Upper Canada style contrasting vividly with the casual group. But she is comfortable, asking questions and attending to the answers.

What part do they have in the show? How long have they lived here in the Yukon? What brought them here? Her interest is genuine; she has always had a natural curiosity about the world around her, and people warm to it. Meanwhile, Niki is off doing his interviews, and attending quietly to other details. He is concerned about the printed program. Will it include appropriate acknowledgment of the 'man from Ottawa' and the Millennium Bureau? Is someone meeting the dignitaries at the airport? What about the speeches at the reception? Have they been carefully arranged so everyone knows who introduces whom? His experience with festivals and productions around the world has taught him that the most trivial matter, if neglected, can tarnish an otherwise shining success.

Business finished for the moment, Niki joins the party. He moves across the room at once to introduce himself to one particular young woman, Ann-Marie MacDonald, actor and writer from Toronto whose reading of excerpts from her award-winning novel, *Fall on Your Knees*, has been woven into *Time Pieces*. For Niki, she is a discovery. He has never encountered her before, either in print or on the stage, but he is excited about her compelling text and her performance. As a student at the academy in Vienna he learned an important lesson about language and enunciation by which he has measured singers and actors wherever he has travelled and worked. 'I was taught to mould the word,' he says, 'to sing the melody of the language.'[1] To him, MacDonald's speech is perfect in diction and rhythm and tone; the instruction given to him decades ago is perfectly realized on this Whitehorse stage.

The final rehearsal is called, and this time Niki is not invited to stay. He and Shelagh thank their hosts with genuine grace for a delightful supper and go together, arm in arm, to the waiting car. They stop outside the theatre to admire the glowing night sky, but they do not linger. It is cold, and it has been a long day. Tomorrow the festival will open, and it will please; *Time Pieces* will unfold without a hitch, a solid performance. Everyone will be taken care of, Music Canada Musique 2000 will be applauded for its assistance in bringing this new and uniquely northern piece to life. Niki will smile happily. 'It's marvellous,' he will tell everyone.

That is tomorrow. For now, Niki wants to return to the hotel, where before sleeping he might just watch a favourite video he has brought along: *Der Rosenkavalier*, by Richard Strauss, in this case starring the legendary Elisabeth Schwarzkopf. While he will always feel that Lotte Lehmann was the definitive Marschallin, he nevertheless enjoys this particular production and its stars. This is music from that other time and place in his life, music that gives him continuing pleasure for its beauty and craftsmanship.

Music in its many forms has been essential to his life since he was a small boy, collecting butterflies in the fields of his father's estate. They say, in chaos theory, that when a butterfly flutters its wings on one side of the world, a storm will blow on the other. Niki Goldschmidt is like that butterfly; a living energy field. Formed in a Europe surviving on old nineteenth-century dreams, he was propelled across oceans and borders into a new world, making things happen wherever he landed. He profoundly affected the development of music in Canada in the second half of the twentieth century, and continues to spark new projects in the twenty-first.

His story is one of many successes and a few disappointments, but always there has been a forward momentum, with an optimism that comes at least in part from advice his father gave him decades ago and that he likes to quote. 'If something doesn't come off the first time as expected, there must be a reason, so move on to the next.'

1

'Tempi passati'

Moravia, next to Bohemia in what is now the southernmost part of the Czech Republic, belonged to the Austrian portion of the Habsburgs' empire. It was a region of pleasant villages and rural estates on which stood elegant residences, neoclassical and baroque castles. It was on such an estate, on the edge of the village of Tavíkovice and not far from the city of Brno, that the fifth of six sons was born to Robert and Margarete Goldschmidt on 6 December 1908. The new arrival was named after the special saint of that day, St Nicholas, patron saint of children (and of pawnbrokers), a saint with a cheerful and positive image who makes things happen as if by magic, a good sign for young Niki.

His father, born in Berlin in 1868, moved to Brussels with his family when he was still a child, establishing contact with the Belgian line of his family that would have an important influence later on the life of his son. When he was twenty-two, Robert undertook the management of two estates for his elderly aunts, Mrs Schnapper and Mrs Dormitzer. Lying just 120 kilometres north of Vienna with a combined expanse totalling nearly thirty thousand hectares, the estates would have provided a considerable challenge for the young man, but evidently he was a capable and reliable overseer; the aunts later willed him the properties, a spectacular legacy by almost any standards.

In 1899 Robert married a distant cousin, Margarete von Goldschmidt, who came from a distinguished Viennese family; the newlyweds took up residence on the country estate where all of their six sons were born.

It was an opulent and leisurely life that the family enjoyed in those last glorious imperial years before the political fallout from the First World War obliterated it forever. Their neighbours were all members of the Austrian aristocracy, the Lichtensteins, the Kinskys, old and powerful

families. It was a world that seems as fanciful as the setting for an operetta. Niki says, 'When I think back on that life now, it is like recalling a
dream.'

Robert was occupied daily with the details of being a landlord, while
Margarete, known affectionately as Daisy by her family, supervised the
household and the demanding task of raising six boisterous boys. Life
was not always serene with so many children, and young Nicholas was
not an easy baby. Years later Mathilde, the maid who looked after him,
wrote to the family recalling that Nicholas was a baby with a truly disturbing cry, a real screamer, happy with nothing except when Mathilde
rocked his cradle and sang him an old Tyrolean folk song that would
calm him almost at once. The maid, writing with the benefit of hind-
sight, was convinced that the baby's response to her song was a sure sign
of things to come, that he already had decided on his future, and that 'if
only everyone could know their true calling so early in life, there would
be far less trouble in the world.'

Certainly, there was little trouble in the family's world during Niki's
early years. From the windows of the splendid residence the boys could
watch the comings and goings in the central courtyard, including the
gatherings for great hunting parties and opulent picnics, scenes that we
now know only in Merchant-Ivory films. Each estate held its big day to
which the landowners were invited in turn. They set out to hunt the
local game, partridge, pheasant, and hare. Carriages, six or eight at a
time, lined up in procession, horses at the ready to take the visitors out
to some particularly picturesque spot, while behind came the carts
laden with food and wine, tables, silver, china, and linen with liveried
servants to organize and serve the magnificent al fresco luncheon feast.
And later came the dinner that Niki can picture vividly to this day:
'There were dinner parties galore, especially at hunting season. All the
neighbours came, and of course everyone dressed up formally. There
would be as many as twenty-four at the table with the butler and maids
serving. It was unforgettable.'[1]

Christmas was another occasion for what now seem to Niki like magical celebrations:

> In the dining room six tables were set out around the edge, by the wall, one
> for each of the children, the six brothers. They were for our presents, and
> of course we each counted up what was on the other table to see if anyone
> got more. I think the older ones always received the most! But first, on
> Christmas Eve, before presents, we assembled with the family and servants

in my mother's drawing room where we boys had to sing some Christmas songs or play something on the piano together, four hands. Then, the butler came and said that the tree had been lit. It was always enormous, freshly cut from our forest and lit with candles. So we went in to the tree, then opened our gifts, which usually were things to wear, or some music or a briefcase, things of that sort. And then we all sat down for the late supper. It was beautiful.[2]

Niki loved the country, spending hours roaming across the fields and the long valley of the Rokytná River that flowed through the estate. Robert Goldschmidt had the foresight to install a generator on the river, about five kilometres from the castle. It supplied the entire village with electric power, a rarity in rural areas at that time.

Niki covered long distances on his forays across the countryside, on foot or on horseback. In the large stables behind the house the family kept several horses, and one of Niki's older brothers was an excellent horseman who taught him how to ride. 'I was often sent on horseback to bring news to my father of the harvest. The valley was several kilometres in length and not all cultivated, so it was a challenging ride, jumping over creeks, and up and down hillsides. I was very proud of that.'[3]

Most often young Niki was out hunting, not for game but for butterflies and moths. With the commitment and enthusiasm that have remained his most remarkable characteristics, the youngster built a substantial collection of over five hundred different species, each one mounted, labelled with the correct Latin name, and placed in a cupboard especially built by the gardener. Niki still remembers the giant green Oleander butterfly that was a particularly exciting find. His uncle in Vienna was a friend of Dr Rebel, director of Vienna's Museum of Natural History and an expert on butterflies. He came to visit the family estate and young Nicholas was summoned to present his collection for examination. The knowledgeable visitor attested to the rarity of some of the specimens, including one that had never been discovered before in Central Europe. The boy and the scientist discussed butterflies and their habitat just like two colleagues, a treasured experience for the young collector.

Niki's ability to infuse others with his own enthusiasm was evident even then. His brothers were often convinced to assist in the collecting, and they did so with enthusiasm, showing their ingenuity in the process. They helped Niki hang white cloths and lamps along the castle windows to attract the night moths, and later, when the family acquired a car, they just turned on the car lights to achieve the same result. Residents of the village and workers on the estate were inspired by the boy's devotion to his hobby and came with specimens, asking if they were interesting enough to be added to the collection. Niki says, 'I always told them it was wonderful, although generally it was very ordinary!'

More exciting was his acceptance as an official member of the Lepi-dopterology Society of Frankfurt on Main, an honour in which he still takes pride. One edition of the society's monthly newsletter featured news of his collection and of his rarest find. When the family left the estate, and before Niki left Europe permanently, he gave the collection to the museum in Znojmo, where it remains as part of the local natural history display.

Despite the political turmoil surging through Central Europe during and after the catastrophic First World War that raged in the west and the east, life remained peaceful on the estates. The Goldschmidt boys received all of their education at home, in a part of the castle set aside for their schoolwork. Niki remembers three or four rooms fitted out with all the necessary tools for their studies, including regular school benches. Three tutors lived in the family home and taught sciences, mathematics, literature, Greek, Latin, geography, a full classical curriculum. 'We had to read parts of the *Odyssey* and the *Iliad* in Greek, and in Latin we did Ovid and Virgil. We had to study it well because on our exams later we had to translate passages from those works. The tutors were always there. They lived in the castle, and they would have their dinner with the family and then retire to their rooms.'

Languages were important; while German was the day-to-day language of the home, the boys also learned French and English, but there were no classes in Czech, the language of the villagers. That was left for the boys to pick up on their own.

Twice a year the students were required to go to Vienna to the Schottengymnasium for the general academic examinations. The 'Schotten' referred to the Scottish Benedictine monks who ran this particular school and who were renowned in the region for the quality of the tuition they offered to their students. Decades later Niki and his wife were visiting Vienna and stayed in a small hotel called the Benedicthaus. When they were shown upstairs to their room Niki had a surprise; it was the same building where he had taken his exams, decades before! 'I saw all the rooms neatly in a row and I remembered, those were the monks' cells! When we had our exams we would have to go into those little rooms, one at a time, to answer the questions put to us by the priest.'[4]

The first time that Niki experienced this ritual was in 1918, the year of the great flu epidemic, and on reaching Vienna he was laid low with that terrible illness. Fortunately he could stay with his uncle, and when he finally recovered, after some weeks, the monks set a special exam time for him. From that shaky beginning he made the trip each spring for eight years and met all the requirements as dictated by the authorities.

For the final exam in the last year the students could choose their own subject for the written portion and of course Niki chose his favourite, butterflies, but with an important addition which started with a family story.

When I was about twelve years old I was playing with one of the family dogs, a pointer, out in the courtyard, and suddenly it turned on me and bit me badly. Right away the carriage was called and I was driven to the hospital in Znojmo, where there was a famous surgeon, Doctor Stumme. He attended to me, and I remember lying on the operating table and looking out the window at the beautiful view of the viaduct carrying the train to Vienna. In any event, my wounds required twenty-four stitches to my face, it was very serious, but to this day all that remains is one tiny scar. Professor Stumme was also a great naturalist who wrote an excellent book about the plants and trees of the region. And so years later, when I wrote my exam I used material from his book, especially about the particular trees where the butterfly larvae live.

Whether his career path was set in the cradle or not, Niki remembers that there was always music in his home. While his parents, as he says, were 'totally' non-musical, there was a piano, and four of the boys (all except Arthur, the oldest, and Erich, the youngest) took piano lessons from the village priest, who came to their home weekly for their lessons. The design of the house meant that the salons and dining room were on one side, in one wing, and the music room on the other. Young Niki was free to 'bang away,' as he now describes it, without disturbing the household. The lessons were unorthodox. There were no scales, or tedious exercises. As soon as the boys could read and recognize a bass and treble clef, they began to play real pieces in arrangements for piano four hands with their teacher taking the bass and the pupil the treble. These sessions, playing duets, were perhaps not the ideal way to develop refined piano technique, but they did promote excellent sight-reading skills, and a broad knowledge of the musical literature. Niki remains convinced that it is the right way to start children with lessons. 'They must love the music first,' he says, 'before they get into all those scales.'

As they progressed, the brothers played a tremendously varied repertoire together; in that era before radio and television, before manufactured entertainment, they spent many happy hours learning all kinds of music. The nearby city of Brno boasted a notable lending library, a private business, containing a large section devoted to the world's great musical literature all transcribed for piano four hands. Symphonies, opera, chamber music, they were all available. Every month or so the boys ordered a new selection from the catalogue, often not sure of what to expect when it arrived. Schubert's *Trout Quintet*, a Bruckner symphony, whatever was on the list that looked appealing or was recommended by their teacher, they tried them all. Their best advice came not from their piano teacher but from one of their academic tutors. He was the nephew of Wilhelm Kienzl, the composer of a very popular opera of the day, *Der Evangelimann,* and as often as possible he played piano with Niki and his brothers. The boys went eagerly to the local post office to pick up the parcels of music, at least one of which was especially impressive. 'I remember one that was so huge we could hardly lift it; they had sent us the four-hand version of Wagner's *Götterdammerung*. You can imagine how long it took us to play it!'

The sound of music on a bigger scale appealed to the brothers, and on occasion the organ in their parish church provided an opportunity to extend their range. 'Because my mother was a devout Catholic we went every Sunday by carriage to our parish church, in the next village of Běhařovice. My father was the patron, of course, so the family sat in a special raised alcove. We all had to be still and pay attention. But sometimes, after the service, my brothers and I would be allowed to play the organ. We would always choose dramatic music, like Bruckner for instance, that would make a great sound. We had a marvellous time.' And then, in a more reflective tone Niki adds, 'I visited that church and its cemetery just three years ago with my nephew, who lives in the Czech Republic. We walked around and saw all the family graves there.'[5]

As he grew into his teens, music began to assume a larger importance to Niki, and to intrude into his academic life. Although he was a good student and eventually passed all of his courses, for a time it was touch and go. On one of the regular trips to Vienna he was almost late for his exams, owing to a performance of *Götterdammerung*, his first 'live' experience of the opera, after his acquaintance with it at the piano.

Vienna was enchanting for the teenager, with its great cultural institutions and the artistic legacy that accompanied them. It was a magical city, with an allure that endowed Niki with a musical discernment that has served him well throughout his long career.

Among all the history was an association in his mother's family that connected directly to Vienna's musical past. Whenever he was in the city Niki stayed with an uncle, his mother's brother-in-law, who lived just next to the Opera in a four-story building at Opernring 6. It was the former residence of Margarete von Goldschmidt's Uncle Adalbert, born in 1848 and coincidentally the youngest of six sons. He refused to follow the traditional family employment in banking, electing instead to become a composer, a distinctly uncertain profession even in that cultured city. He seems to have been an affable fellow, known as 'Berti' among his friends, a group of artists and performers who lived a carefree, Bohemian life, largely it seems on Berti's money. He was a great friend and indeed a benefactor of Hugo Wolf,[6] not only lending the more famous composer scores and books but also providing tickets for concerts and cash when Hugo's earnings dropped and his bills mounted. Adalbert admired his friend's music and no doubt wished that his own efforts would be received with equal enthusiasm, but in fact he achieved only limited success. He wrote songs, operas, and oratorios; the most frequently performed was entitled *Die sieben Todsünden*, in which there is a representation of Liszt as liberating mankind from the powers of darkness.[7] Liszt may not have performed any such transcendent act in real life, but he did transcribe two of Adalbert's songs for piano,[8] and Wolf, who during the 1880s wrote music criticism for the Wiener Salonblatt, singled out his friend's song *Sommertag* for special attention. In an 1887 review of a concert by Rosa Papier presented at the Bösendorfersaal he described the program as a 'mixed bag,' including works by Anton Rubinstein, Goldmark, and a setting of a Robert Burns poem by Ignaz Brull. 'Of all the novelties,' says Wolf, '*Sommertag* came off by far the best ... a charming song' with a 'fragrant character.'[9] (Given his relationship with Berti, the comments may not have been entirely impartial, although Wolf was known to be uncompromising in his musical views.)

Adalbert's wife, singer Paula Kunz, was her husband's most avid supporter, devoting her entire performance career after her marriage to his songs, primarily at the Sunday afternoon musicales given in their fourth-floor apartment in the residence at Opernring 6, 'where all the greatest artists of the day used to appear.'[10]

Liszt attended at least one of these soirées to play the piano and discuss the music of Wagner, a favourite topic among the musicians and artists of the day. At the time Niki's mother was a young child and years later she recalled being taken along to her uncle's home to hear his great friend perform. Niki still laughs, and sighs with regret, when he tells the story. 'My God, I said to her, you heard Franz Listz? Tell me, how was it? What was he like? And she gave me that priceless answer. "I can't tell you. The only thing I remember was that I wore a blue dress."'

Later the stories surrounding great-uncle Adalbert took on a less humorous note. When young Niki told his parents that he wished to study at the Vienna State Academy with a view to making his career in music, his parents were dismayed. Adalbert, who died in 1906, had spent all of his money, leaving his widow nearly destitute, living in a small room in Vienna, supported in part by a monthly stipend from Niki's parents. It was not an auspicious example of what the musical life might offer their fifth son.

But before the academy, Niki had to complete his early training. Having learned as much as possible in his lessons at the castle, he began weekly lessons at the conservatory in Znojmo, a city of about twenty thousand people and a twenty-six-kilometre bus ride from his home. Under the direction of Czech composer and pianist Albert Peck, it was an institution with a good reputation. Mr Peck took the young Niki in hand, giving him structured piano instruction, including the dreaded scales.

During this period, and in the best romantic tradition, the young Nicholas tried his hand at composing. At the time he was smitten by the youngest daughter of Baron Ferstel, son of the famous Viennese architect and close friend of the Goldschmidt family. Niki decided to write a song cycle for the object of his affections and chose five poems by the famous poet Nikolaus von Lenau. Entitled the *Schilflieder*, they were very melancholy, Goldschmidt recalls, but suitable to his purpose. He set them to music and performed them himself, in what was likely the first lieder recital he ever gave. Mr Peck heard them and urged the young musician to orchestrate them, which he did, and Mr Peck conducted them in one of his regular symphony concerts at the theatre in Znojmo with a professional singer as soloist. No reviews remain, so we do not know whether the conductor's confidence in the songs was justified. We do know that it was the first and last attempt by Niki Goldschmidt to be a composer. He did not follow in Uncle Adalbert's footsteps.

In 1927 Nicholas Goldschmidt entered the State Academy of Music and the Performing Arts of Vienna, one of the most prestigious institutions for music training in Europe. He received a valuable, indeed essential scholarship, essential because support of Uncle Adalbert's widow had become the least of the strains on the family finances. Following the First World War, the Czech people were determined to assert themselves and establish their own homeland. The new state of Czechoslovakia was formed, uniting a number of territories of Central Europe including Bohemia, Moravia, and Slovakia. Tomas Masaryk was its first president, and during the 1920s and early 1930s his government instituted an extensive program of land reform that included the break-up of the large estates and redistribution of the agricultural land to peasants and workers. The owners of the estates received very little compensation, the equivalent of pennies on the hectare, and lost the return on those lands that was their primary source of income.

Niki's family was no exception, and although his father supported the reform measures, feeling that they were just and appropriate for the post-war age, they left him in no position to finance years of study for his son. Therefore, to pass the entrance examination and gain a scholarship was fundamental to Niki's plans. And it wasn't easy. Another student of the time described it this way: 'You had to be above average to be accepted at the Academy. Of two hundred and twenty that tried to get in, maybe eighteen would be accepted.'[11]

It was a full program of study, in the same classical tradition as Niki's basic academic education, with a core curriculum consisting of piano, counterpoint, harmony, composition, music history, choral conducting, and fencing. The latter was required just in case he decided to go on the stage as an opera singer, but Niki soon dropped the fencing course, convinced that his talents did not lie in that direction. In fact, his goal was to become a conductor. But he did add voice studies to the list, which led eventually to many engagements on the stage, not as a singing-actor, but as a singer of lieder.

In the formal atmosphere of the academy, of course, it was not just a matter of signing up for voice lessons. An audition was mandatory, before a jury of five professors. Niki remembers it still. 'I can see them sitting there, very formal. My selection was "Neugierige" from *Die Winterreise* by Schubert. I sang and they didn't say a word until I came to the one word "Ja," sung forte, and then they said "thank you." That was all they wanted to hear, that one forte. They just wanted to know if I had a voice.'

And so began the in-depth study of the vocal literature where Niki developed the understanding and the principles of singing that have stayed with him for his entire life. His singing teacher, Corneil de Kuyper, told him that he did not need instruction in how to sing 'piano,' because, he said, 'you have a natural voice for that, what you are doing is right.' But the professor did instruct him in the importance of enunciation, about moulding the word. This was the lesson that Niki recalled when he heard Ann-Marie MacDonald in Whitehorse all those years later. Pivotal to his teacher's approach was the insistence that there are three equally important components to singing lieder – melody, poetry, and piano. The piano is integral, not secondary, not 'just' accompaniment, according to the teacher, a belief that Niki put into practice in his later career when he gave lieder recitals in which he 'accompanied' himself at the piano.

But that was to be saved for the future. Voice students were not allowed to take any engagement outside of the school until they completed their six years of training, no matter how much they might have needed the money.

The academy was a lively place, engaging the interest and energies of the young Goldschmidt. He recalls that he was 'a good student for the things I liked to study,' and he also remembers being surrounded by 'terrific' talent and brilliant teachers. His principal teacher was Joseph Marx, composer and critic for the *Wiener Journal* who was generally considered to be at the conservative end of the range, musically speaking. New sounds in music had recently emerged in Vienna and were spreading across Europe, sounds arising out of the work of Schoenberg and his disciples Webern and Berg, provoking powerful arguments and rivalries between the various factions. There were those who vigorously championed the unfamiliar twelve-tone system, while others remained firmly committed to more traditional forms. In Vienna the division was reflected at the academy. Walter Taussig, in the year 2000 celebrating fifty years as a conductor and coach at the Metropolitan Opera in New York, was a student contemporary of Niki's. Taussig laughs when he remembers the arguments over styles. 'Goldschmidt studied with the competition. That's how we spoke about it, 'the competition,' because some teachers wanted nothing to do with the new twelve-tone composers, and others were very interested that we examine these new ways,' he says, and quickly adds, 'But they were always friendly arguments.'[12]

The counterpoint classes were rigorous, with only eight students, each of whom was expected to bring a newly composed piece every week for review – fugues, preludes, all kinds of exercises. Niki remembers two or three very good students in his class, including Paul

Ulanowsky, who became the accompanist of Lotte Lehmann. Years later, when that great singer gave her first annual recital at New York's Town Hall, Niki was conscripted by Ulanowsky to turn pages for him.

Joseph Marx knew Richard Strauss and liked to tell his students a story about that great composer to focus their minds on the critical matter of orchestration. Niki has never forgotten that lesson:

> A student wanted Strauss to look over something he had written and give comment especially on the orchestration. He was very insistent, so finally Strauss obliged. He read over the score and told him, 'If you want to learn to orchestrate don't try to do it like Richard Strauss. You must learn your craft and you can do it yourself without any teacher. But you must apply yourself. Here is the secret; you must study, in depth, rigorously, three scores. A string quartet by Haydn, the Prelude to Wagner's *Lohengrin*, and the entire score of *Carmen*. They will teach you all you will ever need to know about orchestration.'

Whether the anonymous (and perhaps apocryphal) student took the advice we will never know, but the heart of the lesson certainly stayed with Marx and with his student, the young Goldschmidt. Although the latter never aspired to become a composer or orchestrater, the in-depth knowledge gained from his teacher in Vienna provided a solid foundation for all his subsequent endeavours, on the podium, teaching, and behind the scenes programming musical events.

Niki considers Marx the first of three men who have affected his life profoundly, the other two being his uncle, the Belgian foreign minister Paul Hymans, and the great conductor Bruno Walter. Given Niki's life-long love of song and singing, it is understandable that Professor Marx made such a strong impression on him. In the larger musical world, Marx is still remembered as a skilled composer of songs that are often included in contemporary programs. 'Just a few years ago I went to a recital given by Leontyne Price in Roy Thomson Hall here in Toronto. She included a group of songs by Joseph Marx and afterwards I went to see her and was able to suggest another of his songs, quite a glamorous, elegant one that neither she nor her accompanist had heard of, and they liked it. His songs are quite lovely, influenced by Hugo Wolf; no doubt it is through those songs that he will be remembered.'

But in his Vienna days images of a place called Toronto and world-famous American sopranos were not part of Niki's world, not even of his subconscious musings. He has always lived in the moment, and as a student he was fully engaged with the tasks at hand, as he has been throughout his long career.

> I sometimes carried Professor Marx's food parcels for him, after class, and we would have long talks about music and art. It was very important to him that his students understand the connection between music and the times in which it was created. Baroque music and baroque Vienna were all part of the same social context, the period. He really did make all those connections for us.
>
> I was very touched when I graduated and one of my relatives told me that Professor Marx had commented about the fugue I wrote for my final exam, 'I never expected Goldschmidt to have so much composing talent!' It was a lovely compliment, but you know my fugue was all based on *Die Meistersinger*.[13]

While Niki was attending to the work as set out by Professor Marx, in the rival class with composer Franz Schmidt (who was greatly interested in exploring the avant garde) was the young man who went on to become perhaps the most famous student of the school in the twentieth century, conductor Herbert von Karajan. Niki remembers that there were mixed feelings about him: 'He was very conceited; however, we all liked him because he was shining with talent. At the end-of-term concert he conducted the overture to *William Tell* and the percussion player missed a cue. Karajan exploded on the podium. He was so furious. We all felt sorry for Karajan, but the audience went wild because they sensed even then how gifted he was, and they could see it in that concert, right at the start of his career that of course developed very fast.'

During their school years, Niki and Karajan on occasion played piano four hands together at casual get-togethers the students held, sometimes in Niki's own apartment. In the early 1960s Karajan conducted a concert in Toronto and the two former schoolmates met for a talk in the maestro's dressing room. Karajan wanted to talk about what had happened to one girl or another whom they had known at school. Niki didn't even remember their names, so that line of conversation went nowhere, but the meeting was cordial. Their one professional collaboration occurred in 1959 when Niki engaged Karajan for the opening concert of the second Vancouver International Festival.

But in the Vienna of the 1920s it was the exciting and rich atmosphere that surrounded them every day that enhanced their musical studies. Classes in music history were illustrated not only by musical examples, but also by the city's great historical architectural and artistic works. And in the ferment of new sounds and images, Schoenberg and his musical colleagues were discussed in the context of trends like the Bauhaus and its relationship with art and evolving technology.

And of course, there were concerts, extraordinary evenings that enhanced the students' knowledge of the music. In fact, much of their real learning took place in those grand opera houses and concert halls. Niki remembers his introduction to *Lucia di Lammermoor* when Toscanini came with La Scala from Milan to perform at the Vienna State Opera. 'We stood in the fourth gallery and saw and heard *Lucia* for the first time,' he recalls. 'It was unforgettable. Every tone was immensely dramatic even if it was just oom pah pah.'

A particular love for choral music was growing within the young Goldschmidt during those years. Singing in the chorus at the academy, he learned in detail a body of great choral literature, and live performances heightened his understanding and his delight in this repertoire, including Schoenberg's colossal oratorio *Gurrelieder*.

But the pivotal event that occurred just before Niki entered the academy and set the tone for all the years to come was the 1927 centenary of Beethoven's death, celebrated in Vienna with a tremendous festival of his music.

The inaugural affair was a political not a musical one, a prestigious gathering of European leaders, one of a long series of meetings that formed part of the reconstruction efforts in the unstable period between the great wars. In this case it was the foreign ministers of Central European countries who attended the meetings chaired by M. Eduard Herriot, French foreign minister and, appropriately for the occasion, a biographer of Beethoven. This august body opened the celebrations to the sounds of Beethoven's great *Ode to Joy*, selected for its theme of brotherhood, which was meant to exemplify the purpose of the gathering.

The festival featured new delights every day. Niki marvelled at a performance of the great *Missa Solemnis* with Elizabeth Schumann, and a memorable evening of piano trios with violinist Bronislaw Huberman, cellist Pablo Casals, and pianist Ignaz Friedman. (Like so much of Niki's experience in Europe in those years, this concert had its sequel nearly thirty years later when Niki was involved with the summer school at the University of British Columbia in Vancouver. There he met and presented music by composer Barbara Pentland, a resident of that west coast city and the wife of John Huberman, son of the great violinist from Vienna.)

As at any good festival, there were performances of works that were heard infrequently and were unfamiliar to the majority of the audience, including, for example, *The Ruins of Athens*, and the overture and ballet music *The Creatures of Prometheus*. Niki took it all in, going from event to event experiencing the variety and excellence of this amazing celebration.

The Beethoven centenary stands out in Niki's memory as a singular event, but he recalls other outstanding years at the Wiener Festwochen (Vienna Festival) and the Salzburg Festival. He was present to hear Lotte Lehmann singing Leonora in Beethoven's *Fidelio* for the very first time. Niki remembers her as being 'divine' in the role, both vocally and dramatically, finding the essential element of the character and bringing it to life on the stage

The richness of the opportunities was stunning. One week's concert list featured, Monday evening, Richard Strauss at the Vienna State Opera conducting Wagner's *Tristan and Isolde*; Tuesday, Toscanini with the Vienna Philharmonic in concert; Wednesday, Bruno Walter and chorus and orchestra with the *Missa Solemnis*; Thursday, Otto Klemperer and an all-Beethoven program; and finally, on Friday, another concert with the legendary Wilhelm Furtwängler! Although he did not perhaps realize it at the time, Niki learned an important lesson from those years in Vienna that was not part of any curriculum at the academy but was central to his later challenges. They offered a stellar example of how to make an exciting and memorable festival.

In that atmosphere, Niki's musical education in Vienna took place both inside the academy and out. In his six years of study he learned the fundamentals through a rigorous series of classes with exacting standards and high expectations. And the opportunities offered by the city made those standards very real. It didn't take a special festival to tempt the students away from their books. On any given night, Niki and his young colleagues could find their way to one of Vienna's many performance spaces, purchase the cheapest tickets, and stand in the galleries high above the elite below, to hear the best, titans of their age, and three-quarters of a century later still recalled with reverence.

To get places in the standing room, at the railing where you could see and hear best, we would line up, and when the doors opened we would almost throw our tickets at the usher and race up the four floors to the gallery. I perfected the art of getting in even if the performance was sold out. All the tickets were the same colour, so if there was an artist or conductor I just had to hear, and no tickets were available, I would buy one for the next night. Then, when I went in I would push the ticket at the usher and be long gone up the stairs in the crowd before he discovered that the ticket was for the wrong night.[14]

(On some occasions a group of students were engaged by an artist's representative to be part of the claque at the opera house. The fee was one schilling to applaud loudly for the aspiring star.)

The memories of those concert-going years in Vienna tumble out of Niki still, as though he can hear every note, see every gesture.

I vividly recall Richard Strauss conducting. He was director of the Opera together with Frans Schalk. Strauss was a first-class conductor, but not a show-off. Of course the orchestra respected him because he was such an important and gifted man, conductor, and composer, and so they played divinely for him. It was not always like that – there were others who could not get the same result. But Strauss brought out the emotion of the music through his personality, not really through his beat. Now, Clemens Krauss was there at the same time, and there were many who thought that he conducted the Strauss operas better than Strauss himself. In fact there is one story that was famous in Vienna at the time. Strauss was conducting *Rosenkavalier,* which as you know is very long. In the second act he turned to Arnold Rosé, the concertmaster, and asked, 'How long is this dreck going to go on?'[15]

One of those Strauss evenings was the Viennese premiere of *Arabella* with Lotte Lehmann in the title role. Immediately before the curtain rose an announcement was made that Miss Lehmann would sing as announced, but would take no bows, since her mother had died just a few hours before.

Niki remembers other nights when things didn't go smoothly. He heard the Vienna Philharmonic under the legendary Felix Weingartner become hopelssly confused and lost in the Scherzo of Beethoven's *Eroica* symphony, forcing the players to stop and start again, a rare occurrence in any concert hall, and unheard of by that orchestra. On another night Furtwängler forgot a recitative in the first act of Mozart's *Marriage of Figaro,* but the muscians did not, and ignored his down beat until after two attempts the great conductor realized his error and got things quickly back in order. Then there was the time when Victor de Sabata was the guest conductor for *Othello*; he gave his down beat, the orchestra responded, but the stage crew were evidently not paying attention. The curtain did not move and the opera could not go on. Again, the down beat, again nothing from the stage! It took three tries from the pit and some loud muttering from the audience before the great Verdi master-piece was properly begun. As most professional musicians do, Niki loves to recall those moments of near disaster in the famous opera house. They remind him, perhaps, of the excitement and the humanity of it all, the risks and the thrill when it all does come together. And of course in Vienna most often the performances were splendid; Niki, watching from his place at the rail in the top gallery, took in every detail. 'I remember the great Victor de Sabata came and conducted a tremendously exciting performance of Dvořák's *New World Symphony*. When he came to the last movement he interpreted it like a boxing match, with his hand move-ments mimicking that punching action. It was incredibly effective.'[16]

Today's students hear re-engineered recordings and wonder what it really must have been like to sit in the hall and experience those con-certs live. Despite the passing of a century, the repertoire and the artists from that time provide the foundation of Western concert literature and the standard for its performance, even as we enter the new millen-nium.

But in 1933, as he ended his time at the academy, the tall, angular young man with the bushy eyebrows was not thinking about the great his-torical significance of what he had experienced. Niki Goldschmidt needed to figure out how he could use his new skills and knowledge to make a living. As his wife pointed out many years later, just the matter of setting out to support himself was a challenge for the young man. Nothing in their youth had prepared the Goldschmidt boys for such an eventuality.[17]

Of course it was not only the Goldschmidt wealth that had disap-peared. Europe was tossed by economic and social turbulence that in a few short years would hurl it once again into the chaos of war. Not an auspicious time to launch a career, but the enthusiasm and optimism that have carried Nicholas Goldschmidt through many rough times were there from the beginning. Undaunted and unafraid as he has always been, and supported with love and pride, if not with money, by his family, he stepped out as a professional musician, looking for the opportunities and the engagements he was sure would follow.

2

Upbeat and Down in an Old World

Exciting anticipation, edgy anxiety, fear of rejection, confidence that fame and fortune are one call away; these are the unsettling emotions of young performers starting their careers. Place and time make no difference. New York in the year 2000 or Vienna in the 1930s, the view of someone outside wanting to get in is always the same. The mythical notion of the 'overnight success' is in truth the story of talent, training, and hard work, years of it, refining a craft, learning how it all really works. So it was in Europe as Nicholas Goldschmidt completed his studies and prepared to begin his career as a conductor. It was not an auspicious time to look for work, any work. No one was making any extra effort for young hopefuls in the theatre; the average working person just hoped to keep bread on the table and avoid social and financial turmoil, at least as far as that was possible.

The very date, 1933, is synonymous with worldwide depression, and political instability.

In Niki's family there was one man who understood the gravity of the situation better than anyone. This was his Uncle Paul, Paul Hymans, foreign minister of Belgium and a man who had been at the centre of European efforts to create peace since the end of the First World War. He signed the Treaty of Versailles on behalf of his country and subsequently chaired the meeting of world leaders in Paris in 1919 that framed the Covenant of the new League of Nations.[1] Later, at the first assembly of the League held in Geneva in 1920, he was elected its president. It was a daunting challenge, fraught with procedural wrangles, complex and diverse interests, and a crowded agenda. One historian reported that 'Hymans performed his task admirably';[2] another describes him as 'a wise and gentle diplomat,' and 'an ardent internationalist.'[3]

To Niki, this imposing figure, whose life unfolded on the potent stage of world politics, was a hero and a lifelong mentor. His house in Brussels was a second home to his nephew, who listened intently to lively discussions about critical world issues and understood that a phone call could interrupt the most glittering dinner party, summoning his uncle to attend a critical negotiation.

Niki recalls one evening when he was dining with his uncle and aunt, just the three of them at the table, and the telephone rang.

'Answer that, please, Niki. I am not at home,' his uncle said. Niki answered as instructed, and asked who was calling. 'C'est la majesté la Reine.' It was Her Majesty Queen Elizabeth of Belgium, calling to say that she wished Ambassador Hymans to write a speech for her. Niki laughs as he describes how quickly he summoned his uncle, and how immediately the latter responded!

From time to time Niki went to hear his speeches in parliament, models of fine oratorical skills. 'My uncle always told me that he worked hard on his speeches, refining, reworking them until they were just right. His rule was that before you can start a speech you must know where it will end.'[4]

Niki took the lesson to heart and became well known for his own engaging and convincing speeches.

Uncle Paul not only gave his nephew a sense of focus and attention to detail, he also left him with an abiding interest in politics and in the world scene. Throughout his adult life Niki has never failed to read the paper every day, to follow the political news closely. He may show no interest or understanding of the day-to-day trivia and gossip that fill the 'style sections' of the contemporary news media, but he can discuss in detail the latest political machinations, whether they be local, national, or international.

Paul Hymans was married to Niki's father's sister, Thérèse, known in the family as Aunt Kra, a cultured and musically well-connected personage who could persuade artists of the stature of Paderewski to come and play at a benefit for her favourite charity.[5] But it was the uncle who dominated, made the decisions, offered the advice. And it was to the family's country home that Niki went for his annual summer visit after leaving the academy.

This was a beautiful place, a gracious chateau in Facqueval in a valley of a tributary of the Meuse River, near the south Belgian city of Huy. Niki returned there every summer until the Second World War; it was a place where he could enjoy the company of the many relatives who came and went. It was not unusual to have upwards of twenty people for dinner, and around the great table the conversation was wide-ranging, intelligent, informed; politics, of course, and the arts were favourite topics. Niki, with his gregarious nature, enjoyed the company, and after his graduation he was particularly grateful for the opportunity to spend time in this beautiful and serene rural atmosphere surrounded by family members, as he once had back home in the Czech countryside. However, he was under no illusions that he could enjoy this agreeable and leisurely life indefinitely; he was well aware that it was time to find work, just as soon as he could.

In August of that summer, 1933, when an opportunity for employment presented itself, he was obliged to move quickly. He received a letter from his mother, in which she discreetly enclosed a clipping from a Prague newspaper announcing that in Teplice-Šanov, a city in northwestern Bohemia, then part of Czechoslovakia, the local theatre required the services of an assistant coach. Niki knew of the town, largely because it was famous in artistic circles for its Goethe Steig, the path where Goethe and Beethoven had their only meeting, while each was out walking.

'It is reputed that Beethoven took off his hat first, to acknowledge the great writer,' says Niki, recalling the story.

But to the young aspiring conductor it was more important that the city offered the possibility of work. When his written application was accepted he set out at once by train to audition for his first professional engagement. The director of opera for the theatre that year was Rudolf Bing, who had left Germany as the Nazis began their political ascent, and had taken the position at Teplice out of necessity, for the income.[6] He was shortly to be recruited for an audacious new opera venture at Glyndebourne in England, later was granted the title of 'Sir Rudolf' and most importantly became the general manager of New York's Metropolitan Opera. It was this august figure who auditioned the applicant, requiring him to sight-read a work of Haydn. Niki was undaunted by that demand. His early years sitting at the piano with his brothers and his teachers reading through the world's great musical literature had given him a facility for sight-reading that now served him well. The audition did not take long, and the job was his.

So in the autumn of 1933 Niki achieved his first position, and recalls that in a world where titles were very important, his was the lowest in the ranking. But it was a job. 'It paid so little that my aunt in Belgium had to supplement my income (shades of Uncle Adalbert), and let me tell you how we lived. After work we went to the coffeehouse for our supper and mine consisted of black bread, an egg, and a glass of milk. For the black bread I ordered some butter, and my colleagues said, "Can you afford butter?" Of course it was only because my aunt was helping that I could do it. I still remember it very clearly.'

The matter of the butter made such an impression that it was echoed many years later in a conversation with a famous singer, talking about opportunities in the country that would become Niki's long-time home.

But for the time being the excitement was the job, low pay and black bread notwithstanding. As in most theatres, Niki's first action was to check the board backstage to see what his assignment would be. His name was down as pianist for a ballet rehearsal of *The Merry Widow*, followed by rehearsal of the chorus for an opera, then coaching singers for upcoming roles, playing the piano and instructing them in interpretation of the parts. Every day was busy, and routine. No starring opportunities here!

And then came his conducting debut. 'The first time I ever conducted sitting in the pit, I took over a performance of *Blossom Time*. I conducted it without rehearsal, because it was standard practice that after ten performances the first conductor handed the show over to the junior, without rehearsal. I felt then that this was as important as if I had been asked to conduct a performance of *Tristan and Isolde*.'

The conducting debut of any young assistant was always marked with enthusiasm by the other employees, the wardrobe staff, the stagehands, the technical staff, and the other coaches who came around to wish their colleague all the best for the big debut. And with a successful performance to his credit, having made no stumbles, Niki was established in the theatre as a regular assistant.

So followed a busy winter season, which he still credits as an invaluable learning experience, doing everything, playing the piano at rehearsals, coaching singers, working with the chorus and orchestra, learning how to deal with stagehands and all the technical business; the job description was as broad as the management required, with no rules or contracts to limit what any one person would be required to do. As he says, 'It is the kind of environment that just doesn't exist today, where we learned so much repertoire and expanded our knowledge through working at every job.'

The entire region was full of municipal theatres that provided this rich training ground. Every city, even as small as twenty thousand people, had its theatre, presenting a season of opera, dance, operetta, and drama. It was usually possible for the performers to find another engagement within a short train ride if the current situation was not suitable.

When Niki's first winter season came to an end he looked around for summer employment. His winter wages did not provide a cushion for savings to carry him through the summer months, so off-season employment was essential. Almost at once he found plenty of summer arts activity in the spa towns of northwestern Bohemia, Karlovy Vary, Mariánské Lázné, and Františkovy Lázné, or, to use their German names more familiar in the West, Carlsbad, Marienbad, and Francesbad.

Niki was engaged for the theatre in Francesbad, a city with a resident population of about thirty thousand people. That number was multiplied several times over in the summer as visitors came to enjoy the pleasant atmosphere, take the waters, and attend the theatre. Again Niki's job took in everything, conducting operettas, coaching singers, and even expanded to appearing on stage, but only once; in Francesbad he made his first and last outing as an actor. It originated with the politics of the time.

Benito Mussolini, the Fascist dictator of Italy with grand ambitions to extend his country's sphere of influence, had written a play, appropriately enough based on the life of Napoleon. In Francesbad, part of the Sudetenland, there was considerable sympathy for Mussolini's political views, and his name on the program almost guaranteed a large audience, the kind of opportunity that rarely fails to influence the choices of any impresario! So, politics aside, it was a prudent selection for the summer theatre bill. The play in question required a large cast that taxed the resources of the summer theatre. Everyone, including the young conductor, was recruited to take part. Niki's role was to run onto the stage and announce, with great excitement, that Napoleon had landed in France from the island of Elba.

As Niki tells it, 'I was supposed to rush in, but not having a great acting technique I was running too fast and couldn't stop in the right place; I crossed the whole stage, passing by the people to whom I was to tell the news, stopped right at the opposite edge and announced loudly from the wings, "Napoleon has landed." That was the end of my acting career.'

While Niki is still amused by the recollections of that unfortunate experience, he acknowledges that again it was all part of the learning process, another chance to understand every aspect of what goes on in a theatre to make it work.

Since appointments in the theatres were commonly for a finite period of time, the young conductors were always looking ahead for the next engagement, and instead of applying to various theatres directly were obliged to go back to Vienna to audition. Despite the political changes and democratization of Czechoslovakia since the First World War, theatrically speaking Vienna still controlled the region. Many agents arranged these auditions, to which the theatre directors came to hear singers. Niki recalls one agent who had a special connection to the young musicians from the academy, often engaging them to play for his auditions, actually paying them to do so, an extraordinary windfall.

The aspiring conductors were evaluated on their ability to accompany the singers at the piano, with no advance notice about what would be sung. Once again, agility and accuracy in sight-reading were a definite advantage. Niki recalls one of those auditions: 'It was there I found out how cruel those theatre directors were. The agent brought in the singer, and the voice from the seats called out, "What are you going to sing?" "I want to sing the prologue from *Pagliacci*." I started to play and the singer began, was two bars into the music when the voice came from the director, "Thank you, next," and the singer was dismissed. It was a tough life.'

A position offered did not mean an income secured. The vicissitudes of life in the regional theatres often resembled the ups and downs of a complicated opera plot. The municipal theatres were rented out to impresarios who received a modest subsidy from the city and from the state, and then were left on their own to make money or lose it, depending on how skilled they were. The government took no further responsibility for the operation of the theatre.

Twice Niki found himself working for impresarios who went broke, once just three days after the season had commenced! It was too late to look for alternative positions, since all the other theatres had filled their rosters for the season. Being an enterprising lot, and feeling deeply the need to eat, the artists, musicians, dancers, actors, singers, and conductors took the only action possible; they assumed responsibility for the theatre as a co-operative. Apart from their artistic and technical responsibilities, they did the promotion, sold the tickets, managed the finances, and shared whatever profit they made at the box office.

Again, Niki depended on his aunt, who regularly sent him the equivalent of about $20.00 per month. When Niki was working in a theatre where the impresario actually made money and paid salaries, Niki took home about 450 Krowns ($10.00) per month. Like his colleagues, he lived modestly in rooms in private houses where rent included breakfast. It was a mobile lifestyle with no roots or ties to any one place.

Through the 1930s he moved around, working his way up from coach to assistant conductor and chorus master, to conductor, all in the German theatres in the region of Czechoslovakia north of his ancestral home. His last major appointment was as conductor in the theatre in Troppau (in Czech called Opava), a small industrial city near the border with Poland. There he conducted his first *Parsifal,* a full dress rehearsal with no preparation, having been assigned the task the night before. It was a nerve-racking experience, since performers and conductors are often measured in the theatre by the ability to produce at a moment's notice, and the dress rehearsal is considered to be almost as important as a public performance. Niki met the challenge, one that was repeated when he subsequently conducted *Tosca* without rehearsal.

Years later, describing those days to a group of young people, Niki observed that they reflected the 'daring of youth' but also the spirit of adventure that has been characteristic of his career.[7]

But it wasn't all ad hoc. Old playbills show that he prepared and conducted performances of a full repertoire of operas, and of course the popular operettas of the day by composers such as Lehar and Kalman and Lortzing. From *Ault-Wien* by one Josef Lanner, to that popular standby *Cavalleria Rusticana,* Niki's assignments challenged his versatility. He was choral director for a production of *Aida,* and in March of 1936 he conducted a full performance of *Andrea Chenier,* followed by Puccini's *Madama Butterfly,* then a relatively recent addition to the repertoire.

Many of the performers who shared those productions became longtime friends, including bass-baritone Erich Kunz, later a famous Papageno at the Vienna State Opera who also sang at Salzburg, the Metropolitan, all the major houses. Very early in his career Kunz went to Troppau to appear in *Der Evangelimann* by Wilhelm Kienzl, who was celebrating his seventieth birthday. Niki enjoyed that particular assignment, not only because of the work and the very fine cast, but also because the composer was the uncle of the music tutor with whom he had learned so much music through four-hand arrangements.

Irene Jessner, soprano, appeared at the theatre in Troppau; she later emigrated to the United States and in 1952 was recruited by the University of Toronto, where she became a distinguished teacher of many of the singers with whom Niki would work. And it was in Troppau that Niki first met Herman Geiger-Torel, who was the resident stage director for the operas. Just a dozen years later the two would be working closely together in Toronto to build a new opera school and company.

Meanwhile, as the 1930s passed and the engagements became more regular and at a more responsible level, Niki began to make a little money over and above his daily needs. His parents were very proud of him and his accomplishments and his father was happy to encourage his son's one indulgence, travel. Niki promised his father that he wouldn't smoke and wouldn't hunt, and in return Robert Goldschmidt aided his son's passion to see new places, although his resources at that time limited those travels to Europe.

Niki saved his money for one special trip that he remembers to this day with satisfaction. He wanted to take his mother to Rome. She was an extremely devout Catholic, with a faith so profound that Niki believes that if marriage had not been an option she certainly could have been a nun.

So off they went, mother and son, to Rome, with his first savings. They stayed with his mother's sister-in-law, who lived in the Italian capital, and spent their days touring the city, seeing all the marvellous sights. His mother, of course, was eager to see St Peter's and the Vatican and if possible to attend an audience with Pope Pius XI. Good fortune intervened on their behalf in the person of a bishop, formerly Count Huyn, who in the early days was the parish priest in the church where Robert Goldschmidt was patron. Having risen through the church hierarchy and now appointed to the Vatican, he gladly opened the door for his former parishioners to be present at one of the pope's special audiences. It was a great thrill for Margarete Goldschmidt, and Niki still beams proudly when recalling his mother's pleasure.

During these European years Niki often travelled to visit one or another relative, part of a large extended family on his father's side. In Basel, Switzerland, through one of these family connections, he first met the great pianist Rudolf Serkin. In the late 1920s the remarkable Busch family, violinist Adolf, conductor Fritz, and cellist Hermann, had protested the alarming anti-Semitism in Germany where they were then living. [8] They relocated to Switzerland and Serkin followed; he later married Irene, the daughter of Adolf Busch. Niki and Serkin met from time to time, there and in Vienna. Many years later, writing to Niki about the latter's Bach piano competition, Serkin referred to the pleasant times they had had together.[9]

They were good years for Niki, building a career, travelling around Europe meeting artists and spending pleasant days with his large family, and of course going to the theatre and the concert hall as often as possible. He heard Lotte Lehmann in many recitals, memorable concerts that he credits with teaching him the essentials of interpretation of lieder. And of course, Lehmann became for him, as she is for many, the definitive Marschallin in *Der Rosenkavalier.*

All the opportunities of those years and all the travel continued to be played out against a political background that was increasingly tense and troubling. Through his Uncle Paul, Niki was constantly made aware of how each new crisis was leading to one inevitable conclusion, a second great war. In 1934 Chancellor Dollfuss of Austria was assassinated by the Nazis; in 1935 Italy invaded Ethiopia (Abyssinia) and in 1936 occupied the capital, Addis Ababa. The League of Nations was powerless to stop the turmoil. Fascism was on the rise, Germany under Hitler was on a tear repudiating old agreements, making new unholy alliances, and in Spain there was civil war.

In the music world many artists found it impossible to continue to work in the increasingly hostile, politicized atmosphere of Germany, Italy, and Austria. Toscanini himself was finished with all three.[10]

Of the Ethiopian crisis, Uncle Paul said, 'This is only the beginning,' and in 1937 he told his nephew that it was time to leave Europe. There was no future there to make a career.

Niki took his uncle's advice seriously and began, in the summer of 1937, to sort out his affairs; he visited the old home, where he gathered up his things, saw his butterfly collection installed in the museum, and said goodbye to his family. Niki speaks now of that time in a matter-of-fact tone, but the changes that were to happen in his life from that time forward were almost unimaginable. The estates, of course, had long since gone from the family's ownership. The house in which Niki had grown up eventually became a forestry school, the second chateau on the estate a home for handicapped people. His brothers had dispersed. Leo, the third oldest, had been killed in an auto accident in 1927; Ernst, the fourth brother, was now an art historian living in Belgium; the rest eventually joined the Czech army in exile in England.

One touching family story had its beginning in that pre-war time, and with its sequel was told to Niki in a letter written in 1948 by the maid, Mathilde, who had looked after him as a child. Written from Vienna, and bearing the censor's stamp, it is a deeply affecting account that captures the feeling of life in the grand house in which Niki grew up, and the profound sense of loss at a world shattered by war. She recounts how before the war Niki's mother had made the servant a gift of her beautiful silk wedding dress. She tells the tale in the context of the life that they all had once lived on the estates contrasted with post-war Europe. In despair she wrote to Niki:

> A few days ago I gave my sister Marie the little package you were so kind to send me ... The pleasure was enormous because the times are awful. For my sister, she is very courageous. She is terribly hungry and was practically frozen but never complained ... I like to write to you because you and your poor brother Leo, you two were my favourite boys. I took care of you for two years and now because of what is happening I am thinking of you, about everything in the past, in that wonderful time which will never come again.
>
> Now you were a terrible screamer, a screaming baby. Once you started this noise it took two hours, and you could almost hear you to the other castle. You would go absolutely crazy and we had to let you scream until you finished. Nothing would help, only the song about Archduke Johann. I loved that song and we always loved to sing it because you would stop screaming when you heard it.
>
> I am still thinking about it because if all had thought of their profession as early as you did perhaps we would not have had this terrible war. It would have been better if many had sung this song and made music instead of the terrible military marches all over.

Mathilde then recounts a series of events, the telling of which still moves Niki to tears:

> I am sending you out of gratitude a little piece of material from the collar of your lovely mother's wedding dress. Keep it well and safe, and honour it. Mrs Goldschmidt gave it to Marie with one suggestion. She said that if ever something happens and she is in need she could sell the dress. But we could not separate ourselves from that dress. It was well preserved in a drawer.
>
> And then came the most awful hour for Marie, and I also could not help. I cannot forget those hours as, on one cold Sunday, we had no wood and were terribly hungry. We spread the bride dress over the bed to keep Marie warm. We could have sold it very easily. We sat several hours, and Marie told us about the happy bride and about all you brothers and how wonderful time was in the castle Takovic. I know that within herself she was terribly sad ... Her voice was very soft and it was already dark and we were almost frozen stiff so we couldn't move our hands.

And then something unbelievable took me, in my inner self, and I told Marie that we must fold up the dress again, that I did not want to take it away ... I was incredibly heavy in my heart and mind. I spent a sleepless night, until falling asleep about 4:30 in the morning, and then I had a dream. In it I went to a cloister and walked in a great dark church. Many people were there, as if they were waiting for something special to happen. And then, behind the altar from a long cloister came two officials carrying candles and between them walked the tiny Holy Teresias of the Jesus Child (St Theresa), and she carried the bride dress of your mother. And when she saw me she called with a loud and joyous voice, 'That's Mathilde.' But it was the voice of your mother.

There was a moving sequel to the dream, as Mathilde explained:

I got up and told Marie about the dream and we knew that this dress could not be sold. We were very happy in spite of the terrible times we were going through. I searched to find a place where we could donate the dress, and heard about a church in Schruns where the altar of the church had burned down and they could not replace the altar cloths and the priest's vestments. So we sent the dress to a convent in the Tyrol and the sisters embellished every piece of the cloth from the dress with gold thread so that it could be used on the altar. I added to it a linen shirt that had belonged to your mother's sister.

And now the two sisters are together on the altar at Schruns. How happy they would be with this result. I want you to know that the only condition I made was that they pray for your family in that church.

And finally, the old nursemaid has a last piece of advice for her former charge:

Now you have heard this unbelievable story; as long as we are living it will give us pleasure. The dress serves God. There are sometimes unbelievable happenings in this world, which you cannot explain immediately, but I know that in your deepest feelings you will understand. Your mother was devout. She prayed a great deal for her children. Never forget that. I hope that you will be happy with this tiny little piece of cloth from a happy bride, wife, and mother.

This letter comes from my heart, and I hope that you understand it. With it I send my greetings, wish you all the best ...[11]

The letter was an amazing testament written by a Czech peasant woman. And understandably Niki treasures it as a tangible connection to his childhood, and to his family. Years later, in the 1990s, Niki and his wife, Shelagh, visited the little church in the town of Schruns in the Voralberg province of Austria, just over the border from Switzerland. They heard the mass that is said once a year for the Goldschmidt family in remembrance of the gift of the dress and the beautiful silk altar cloth that is its legacy.

The letter captures the horrible aftermath of the Second World War, and the drastic upheaval it brought to people's lives. However, Niki knew nothing of the dress in 1937 as he packed up his belongings and said his good-byes, following the direction of his Uncle Paul. The latter, sure of the disaster that was coming, declared that the United States was the best place for his nephew, offering maximum opportunity to a young conductor/musician. From Czechoslovakia, Niki returned to Belgium, where Uncle Paul provided him with letters of introduction and a bank guarantee that the young man would be looked after should he require financial assistance in America.

Among the few belongings that Niki took with him are two treasures that he has carried on his person every day for over sixty years. The first is an exquisite miniature of his mother as a child; the second is a Belgian gold coin. On the fluted edge of the coin is a tiny slot that allows it to be pried open. Inside is a photograph of his Aunt Thérèse, Uncle Paul's beloved wife and Niki's patroness in those first years in the theatre. His uncle had worn the coin on his watch chain throughout his long career, keeping it close to him at the critical moment when he brought down his gavel to open the first session of the League of Nations. Niki wears these keepsakes on a chain, touching reminders of the life that he left behind in late 1937.

Niki Goldschmidt sailed from Le Havre on the steamship *Normandie*, 'modestly housed,' as he says, 'in an inside cabin many levels below deck.' Loving travel as he did, he was jumping with excitement about his first crossing of the Atlantic, but disappointed that his quarters would certainly diminish the pleasure and limit his experience of the voyage. At once his proactive nature revealed itself as he took matters in hand and sought out the purser to see if he could make an arrangement that would be mutually satisfactory and solve his accommodation problem. How would the purser like to have some entertainment? A recital or two perhaps? Some Czech folk songs, some Schubert, all self-accompanied, no need to have a pianist.

At first the purser demurred; there was no money to pay for such an event. Niki assured him that no money need change hands. 'But can you find me a better cabin?' he asked. The purser was happy to oblige, and the deal was made. Niki made his shipboard debut, and enjoyed a pleasant second-class outside cabin for the rest of the voyage.

Hugo Wolf wrote, in 1885, that 'lieder recitals are slowly becoming epidemic,'[12] but went on to qualify that he was primarily unhappy about the trivial repertoire selected by unthinking artists, noting that they could choose from among '600 songs by Schubert.'[13] One can assume that he would have approved of the entrepreneurial and musical choices of his old friend's descendant.

In 1937 many artists were crossing the Atlantic from Europe to the USA, some for limited engagements, many more to escape the Nazi onslaught. The passenger list on that crossing of the *Normandie* included conductors Pierre Monteux (whom Niki would meet later in California), Erich Leinsdorf, and Maurice Abravanel, long-time conductor of the Salt Lake City, Utah, Symphony Orchestra. Niki discovered that Helene Thimig, the actor and second wife of the great director Max Reinhardt, was on board; with his customary boldness, he sent a note of introduction to Ms Thimig, who graciously replied with an invitation to tea in the first-class lounge. They reminisced about her husband's famous theatre in Vienna where Niki, while still a student, had seen Reinhardt's famous production of *Hamlet* in modern dress, and had also been enthralled with the Vienna premiere of the *Threepenny Opera* of Kurt Weill.

Despite the rough seas on that crossing, Niki remembers it as being a wonderful time. He was young, full of hope, travelling to a new continent and new adventures. On 8 November 1937 the ship docked in New York. With his spirits high, and his pockets full of letters of introduction, the only tangible connection he had to that old and troubled world, Niki descended the gangplank, passed through the United States of America's immigration queue with no difficulty, and set out to discover what thrills and surprises this new country and this great city had to offer him.

3

New World Overtures

New York in 1937 was crackling with energy, seven million people looking to a brighter future. While Europe was on a downhill slide, each day more depressing and anxiety-filled than the last, the United States seemed to be swinging around, putting the gloom and despair behind, at last finding its way out of the Great Depression. True, breadlines, homelessness, and bitter strikes remained, and the isolationism of the post–First World War period rested deep in the country's psyche, but there was a new air of optimism. Within the arts community a growing number of gifted artists – musicians, writers, painters, actors, and directors – were arriving from the beleaguered European continent bringing with them formidable creative talents.

In 1937 NBC created a new symphony orchestra especially for Arturo Toscanini (already at home in New York), while a relative unknown from Leeds, John Barbirolli, assumed the podium of the New York Philharmonic. The year before, Rudolf Serkin had made his debut with that orchestra, and in the year Niki disembarked in this new world, Arthur Rubinstein was beginning his long association with impresario Sol Hurok.[1] But it wasn't all European romanticism. Among the artists who arrived in America in the 1930s was a pack of composers including Hindemith, Korngold, Milhaud, and Schoenberg.

At the same time America was beginning to listen to its own voices. Aaron Copland told an interviewer in 1964, 'The thing I remember best about the Thirties was the sudden *need* for our music ... somehow in the Thirties music became more democratic in the United States. I suppose because of ... the recording of serious music for the first time; the radio helped a great deal, to make a mass public aware of serious music that had never been true before in the world's history.'[2]

Copland's remarks, while addressed specifically to the matter of contemporary composition, spoke to the exhilarating atmosphere, an auspicious moment for a twenty-nine-year-old conductor to arrive in New York. Niki had no room for regrets, for feeling that he had left behind all that was worthwhile in the music world. Here was a continent of opportunities spread out before him, and he was ready for discovery, armed with the training and experience he brought from Europe together with his indefatigable sense of optimism and openness to fresh challenges.

His first stop was the Wellington Hotel, near Carnegie Hall. The famous cellist Emmanuel Feuerman, a friend of Niki's cousin in Switzerland, had suggested it. 'Just tell the manager I sent you,' he said, in a gesture characteristic of all touring musicians. Niki took his advice, and for $60.00 booked a room for a month.

More particular to the times and to his European background was the package of letters of introduction that Niki brought with him, hoping to open doors to engagements in the New World. Those letters were the 'networking' tools of that period, providing introductions for hopefuls in all sorts of situations and professions. There was no expectation that every contact would bring immediate and positive results; in Niki's case, only one turned out to provide that critical first step in a series of contacts that led to eventual employment.

In the language of the Old World Niki speaks of 'depositing' this letter, the all-important correspondence addressed to Nicholas Murray Butler, the eminent president of Columbia University. The specific connection that actually allowed Niki to get in the door was Butler's other role as president of the Carnegie Endowment for International Peace, of which Niki's Uncle Paul was also a prominent member.

Niki dutifully delivered his letter for an appointment, thinking that he would probably have to wait a very long time. But the next day he received a telephone call from Dr Butler's secretary at Columbia summoning the young immigrant to an audience. On the day and at the time specified he nervously presented himself at the university, where he was handed over from one intimidating receptionist to another in a progress that brought him ever closer to the great man himself. Finally, the president's secretary ushered him into the presence of Dr Butler, who rose from behind an enormous desk and came forward to shake his hand.

As Niki recalls it, the conversation was polite, and brief:

'I am pleased to meet you, Mr Goldschmidt. How are your uncle and Madame Hymans?'

I replied, 'They are very well, and I am very grateful to be able to present myself to you.' And then he said, 'I am happy to assist you. I will telephone to the head of the music department and ask them to meet you; they will take it from there. It was nice of you to come, I wish you all the best, you will not see me again.' That was it; five minutes in all, to set the course for the next several years!

And it paid off. Shortly after his encounter with the president, Niki received a call from Douglas Moore, at that time head of the Applied Music Division at Columbia and later chair of the Music Department (from 1940 to 1962).[3] Their first meeting over lunch was the event from which much of Niki's career in the United States flowed. Moore, a graduate of Yale and a Guggenheim Fellow who had been at Columbia since 1926, was a respected figure in the musical life of the United States, in part because of his academic connections, but also because he was a successful composer. It was that side of Moore's musical life that formed the basis for Niki's continuing connection with him; Niki presented Moore's works on several occasions in the United States and later in Canada. But at their first meeting early in the New Year of 1938 that was all in an unimagined future. Moore asked the new arrival to come and perform a short lieder recital for the faculty at Columbia, and at the same time recommended Niki to Leighton Rollins, a wealthy amateur theatre producer who ran a summer theatre school, at that time located on Long Island in East Hampton. Rollins hired Niki at once for the coming summer to oversee the music program, which included choral singing for all the actors as well as the production of musical theatre works. Moore entered the picture again that summer when Niki conducted his operetta, *The Headless Horseman*, based on Washington Irving's amusing tale about Ichabod Crane in the *Legend of Sleepy Hollow*. The Rollins School production was Niki's opera debut in the United States, and Niki enjoyed it enough to repeat the work a few years later at Stanford University in his debut at that west coast institution.

As part of that first summer's activity, Rollins, a pacifist like many of that generation, wrote a set of poems inspired by Goya's series of drawings 'The Disasters of War' and asked Niki to provide music to accompany them. Niki agreed, taking a folk song as the base from which he developed a set of musical sketches illustrating the pictures. They were included on the program of one of the several summer concerts, this one attended by a number of prominent pacifists including Nicholas Murray Butler. Niki insists that these little pieces in no way represent any aspiration on his part to take up composing; the sketches were 'incidental music' and not significant to his larger musical career.

Niki's connection with Rollins continued off and on over many years, in the off-season between other obligations. That 1938 summer employment was one such brief interlude. Not long after his arrival in New York, Niki had decided that he should look at all the possibilities in this huge new country. Consistent with his passion for travelling he set out on his own personal version of the 'grand tour,' not the capitals of Europe, but instead the sweeping diversity of the United States. The obvious means of getting around at that time was the train. For $90.00 he purchased a basic round-the-continent coach-class ticket and with suitcase in hand he embarked from Grand Central Station, heading south. His first stop, however, was far from typical of this trip. In Washington, DC, he enjoyed a fine lunch with the Belgian ambassador, again courtesy of Uncle Paul's letters of introduction. For Niki it was a pleasant, and unusually comfortable, break from his spartan travelling style.

Niki's six-week North American odyssey continued into the deep south to New Orleans, a city like no other he had ever seen and one to which he would return several years later; then it was west to Santa Fe, for a brief stopover allowing him a look at the exotic New Mexico landscape, especially the area around Taos well known for its pueblos and for its lively arts settlement. With its strong Native American presence and its Spanish heritage, it was a completely new experience for this young European.

Leaving New Mexico, the train was held up for twenty-four hours by a flash flood washing over the track. Niki was quick to take advantage of the situation. He may have been new to the country, but he understood very well how things worked. Because they were not moving, and the terms of his coach ticket specified that its conditions applied 'while in transit,' Niki persuaded the conductor to give him a sleeping berth for the duration of the delay, for just one dollar! It was the kind of bargain Niki has always enjoyed.

Finally they crossed through the mountains and on to the west coast, where Niki broke his journey briefly in Los Angeles. He looked up Eugene Zador, a composer whose songs he had sung in recital back in Vienna. Zador introduced him to many of the artists working in the movie colony, affording him the opportunity to tour the studios and see famous actors of the day on the set, even Bing Crosby doing scenes from his next hit. One introduction led him to Erich Wolfgang Korngold, the famous Viennese composer of concert music and opera who was earning his living writing film scores. Niki was invited to one of his recording sessions, and remembers it as being 'terrific,' with an orchestra of eighty or ninety players, all very skilled and with a wonderful rich sound. They were playing a soundtrack with many waltzes, and at a break Niki had a look at the score, where he discovered the waltzes all written in 6/4 time. When Niki questioned the composer about this odd practice, 6/4 instead of 3/4, Korngold told him that in Hollywood the copyists were paid by the bar, and since everyone was very dollar conscious this was his way of cutting costs!

Although Niki enjoyed this first visit to Los Angeles, he knew that the city already sprawling over the southern Californian landscape was not the place he would settle. So he set off again, north to San Francisco, a city that he immediately embraced with its grand views and its cosmopolitan style. On the strength of a letter of recommendation from Douglas Moore and Daniel Gregory Mason from Columbia, he met the directors of the San Francisco Conservatory. This famous school began life as the Ada Clement Piano School in 1917, and was incorporated as the San Francisco Conservatory of Music in 1923 with its founders, Ada Clement and Lillian Hodghead, as co-directors. These two formidable women led the school until 1925, returned in 1931 after Ernest Bloch's tenure as head, and remained until 1951.[4] When Niki presented himself for an interview they asked specifically what he could do. Apart from his general musical credentials he offered to present his signature performance, a self-accompanied lieder recital. The ladies agreed, and arrangements were made for the event to take place almost immediately. It was impressive enough to gain the confident new immigrant from Europe an offer of a position at the conservatory commencing in September of 1938.

Now that his future was settled, at least for the time being, the intrepid traveller was able to relax and continue his voyage of discovery, north through California to Seattle, and then east again, across the vast North American plains, and into Winnipeg, his first look at the country he would later call home. Then it was over the border again, south to Detroit and once more into Canada, this time to Toronto, and then back to New York. He had covered more than ten thousand miles in six weeks, had seen deserts and mountains and plains and the contrasts of the Gulf and Pacific coasts, visited the centre of the exciting new movie industry, made a host of personal contacts, and landed a job. Now he could enjoy New York, and his summer employment with Rollins, before returning to the west coast and his first major engagement in North America.

Niki speaks about that train trip around North America with great fondness. Although in the intervening years he has revisited every region of the continent, most of them several times over, he still remembers with real pleasure and appreciation the spectacular beauty of the landscape, the variety of towns and cities, and the people he met in 1938. He mentions the discomfort of ten thousand miles by coach only in passing, to convey the flavour of the journey, not to complain or to make a story out of hardship.

September arrived and he was back on the west coast ready to get on with the duties of his first permanent job in North America. In order to introduce himself to the musical world of San Francisco, Niki turned to the repertoire and the presentation with which he was most familiar, the lieder recital. He prepared a series of three Friday evening concerts, accompanying himself, as he always did. On the first program he included a selection of songs by Schubert, Schumann, and Hugo Wolf, together with some Czech folk songs. It was a musical place where he could feel comfortable for this important public debut. And it did turn out to be important for the professional enlargement of his opportunities in San Francisco. Aside from introducing him to the concert-going audience, the recital also brought him to the attention of the respected art and music critic of the *San Francisco Chronicle*, Alfred Frankenstein, who liked what he heard.

'Impeccable taste was the keynote of the evening,' he wrote. 'It was the kind of vocal concert that makes you feel and understand that the song literature is a thing of infinite musical and poetic riches.' Niki's insistence on the equal balance between poetry and music came in for special mention. 'Goldschmidt sings simply, without pretense or histrionics but with the utmost concern for the finest shadings of the phrase, both in text and tune.'

He also commented on the matter of the singer as accompanist, a performance practice that is sometimes questioned and often denigrated by other musicians. Frankenstein saw it in its own context, writing, 'He is one to whom a song is obviously not an excuse for vocalism, but a complete expressive entity, and therefore he plays his own accompaniments. But as he plays them they cease to be accompaniments, and weave themselves into the total fabric. His voice may not cause sleepless night among the high salaried baritones, but there is not one of them who could not learn a vast amount from his method.'[5]

From that initial concert a collaboration developed between the two men, Frankenstein and Goldschmidt, resulting in a further series of six recitals, sung and played by Niki with commentary by the famous critic. The programs included major works from the lieder repertoire, including *Die Winterreise* of Schubert and Schumann's *Dichterliebe*. It was an opportunity for the capacity audiences to hear repertoire not often performed in the Bay city, made more meaningful through the insights of Frankenstein, who had a singular understanding of every composer and indeed every individual song.

Niki continued to perform both roles, singer and pianist, over many years in a number of cities, and in radio broadcasts. Commenting from the perspective of the late twentieth century about Goldschmidt's concerts, musicians and others frequently focus their remarks on this dual role; it does not sit well with some, with others it is an anachronism. In conversation it often takes precedence over discussion about the music. This is not the case in reviews from concerts given within a few years of the San Francisco cycle. In New York and in Montreal, for example, self-accompaniment is included in critical comments, but is not singled out as the most remarkable event of the evening. It may be that the issue of self-accompaniment was not so disturbing to musical sensibilities before mid-century as it seems to have become later, a point relevant to Frankenstein's own awareness of changing attitudes: 'In a broad sense you can never be right. There is no such thing as lasting critical evaluation. Works of art last ... but critical insights are limited by period, and works of art are not. This does not mean that criticism is of no value; it merely means that its value does not transcend the moment.'[6]

Niki's recitals, and his work at the San Francisco Conservatory, led to other contacts which greatly enriched his life in that city. For example, in early 1940 he performed a recital at the Century Club that once again included a wide range of repertoire. Frankenstein's review in the *Chronicle* was glowing, complimenting Goldschmidt on everything from his sensitive piano playing to his tasteful singing. Frankenstein especially liked the inclusion of a pair of songs by one of Niki's new friends: 'He resigned the piano to Albert Elkus for two delightful lyric songs of Elkus' own, which helped to show that ... one does not always have to blush and crawl when a singer gets to the American end of his recital.'[7]

Elkus responded to the sensitive treatment Niki had given his music by inviting him to the University of California at Berkeley to hear Ernest

Bloch's graduate school lectures on *The Well-Tempered Clavier* of Bach. Niki has never forgotten the experience. 'He had a blackboard, but no other material. He went through each section, explaining the music and meaning of Bach through the notes, which he wrote out from memory. Everyone was completely absorbed, it was truly inspiring!'

Another significant musical connection resulted from a letter of introduction provided by Niki's Uncle Paul, this one to Herbert Hoover. During the First World War the former president had been head of the Committee for Relief of Belgium when that small country was in dire need of food supplies, so it is highly likely that Niki's uncle and the prominent American had more than a passing acquaintance. Acting according to protocol, Niki sent the letter to the Hoover residence, and shortly after he was visited at the conservatory by a friend of Mrs Hoover's, apparently sent to check out this new arrival. Having made an acceptable impression, Niki was invited to dinner at the Hoover home in the hills overlooking Stanford University. Niki found the former president stiff, and not a little dull, but his wife friendly and outgoing, interested in all the musical developments in the community. She was acquainted with Warren Allen, then head of music at Stanford, and shortly after that first dinner meetings were arranged which resulted in Niki being taken on staff at the university with the mandate to bring opera to the campus. He welcomed this additional responsibility, happily travelling out of the city, meeting new colleagues and students, and planning how he could infuse this wealthy western campus with excitement for opera.

His major production at Stanford was of Douglas Moore's *Headless Horseman*. Since opera did not have a history at the university, when it came time to assemble the large chorus called for in the score Niki immediately ran into resistance. He looked around, took stock of what resources were available, and with his uncanny sense of where to find the main chance, decided that the fraternities offered the most likely source for recruits, especially the always scarce tenors and baritones. But the 'jocks' in the fraternity houses were scornful; singing opera was for sissies and they were definitely not interested. Niki was astonished by their attitude; it was far from his own experience as a student, but characteristically he refused to be defeated. Exercising all of his persuasive powers, he talked up the project, convincing a sufficient number that if they would just give it a try they would undoubtedly enjoy it!

Horseman was the first of three American operas conducted by Niki during his San Francisco years. Aaron Copland's *Second Hurricane* was next. Written for and premiered in 1937 by the Henry Street Settlement in New York, with a libretto by dance critic and poet Edwin Denby, it is intended for presentation by a high school cast. It is a story about students recruited to help with flood relief who are themselves stranded by the storm. The theme is co-operation and the real feeling of freedom that it can bring. Copland was clear about his intent: 'This opera was for American youngsters to relate to in their everyday lives and language. Settings, costumes and orchestrations had to be elastic – stretching to accommodate the circumstances and simple enough for young people to put together themselves.'[8]

Virgil Thomson described it as 'a very beautiful work, a very rich work, touching, exciting, gay, and a real music-pleasure.'[9]

Niki produced the opera in early 1941 under the auspices of the San Francisco Conservatory. Its students, together with a high school chorus assembled by the local school board, joined forces with the conservatory orchestra augmented by a small core of professionals. Almost at once, before the first rehearsal, Niki found himself in a predicament about money. He did not have enough in the budget to pay for the bassoon player that he needed. In the first try at what has become a long career seeking and finding funds to realize favourite projects, Niki needed to make a personal appeal to a donor. He went to see Mrs Sigmund Stern, a generous supporter of music and opera in the Bay area, to ask for $40.00, the union fee required for the bassoonist. He has not always arrived on the doorstep of a donor at such an auspicious moment to put his case. That day Mrs Stern had just returned from making a substantial donation to the University of California. Niki laughs as he remembers what he calls her 'unforgettable' answer to his request for assistance.

'Mr Goldschmidt, I just gave $350,000 to the university. I don't know if I can help you!'

It was an absolutely true reply, and a good-humoured one; Niki left with a cheque for $40.00, and the production went ahead.

Presented in a local school auditorium, it was well received by everyone. Alexander Fried, writing in the *San Francisco Examiner*, spoke of Niki's 'spirited conducting' and said, 'In a difficult score, Goldschmidt and his ... chorus and ... orchestra accomplished wonders.'[10] The critic especially liked the musical bridge between scenes that represented the hurricane, apparently unaware that the rush of sound, blasts and blares, squeaks and wails, was the improvised part of the score created on the spot by the young players.

Altogether, this west coast premiere was a success, and once more Niki found a new contact that lasted for years. Composers are frequently attracted to performances of new works by their colleagues, and in this case the audience included Darius Milhaud, who was pleased enough with the opera to speak to Niki after the performance. They warmed to each other at once, speaking in French, and Milhaud invited Niki to visit at Mills College, where he was artist in residence. The two met often and spoke about the difficulties of presenting contemporary music, always a very risky proposition. 'New music has no box office,' the two agreed. Milhaud was impressed that Niki had taken the chance and gathered all the forces necessary to stage a work as large and complex as the Copland.

As they talked Niki brought up the subject of a recital he was planning. Would Milhaud coach him in his cycle of songs, *Le Catalogue des Fleurs*? Niki's idea was to combine that cycle with Poulenc's *Les Bestières*. Milhaud, excited by the idea for what was then a novel program idea, agreed at once to assist. Again Niki played piano for himself, and the concert, given at the conservatory, attracted Pierre Monteux, who came with Milhaud. Once more Niki seized the moment as they chatted after the performance, explaining to the famous conductor that he was organizing a series of concerts at the Veterans' Auditorium, and asking if the Maestro would consider making introductory remarks at these concerts to help familiarize the audience with what would be new repertoire for many concert-goers. Monteux agreed, appearing at several of the evenings. Niki recalls that the audience was small, but the musical importance great, since much of the music was being heard for the first time on the west coast.

Niki's San Francisco life revolved around his work, and as many concerts and performances that he could find time to attend. He recalls his favourite, Lotte Lehmann at the San Francisco Opera in a controversial production of *Der Rosenkavalier* performed in modern dress. Lehmann refused to appear as the Marschallin in the costume as designed, demanding the traditional one from Vienna that in her view embodied the very spirit of the work. She prevailed, and appeared on stage, the only character costumed from another era. Some opera-goers rationalized the anomaly, seeing it as symbolic of the Marschallin as a figure from the past, beauty and love having passed to a new generation. To Niki it was nothing more than an amusing theatrical contretemps.

Meanwhile the news of growing turmoil in Europe continued to reach Niki, even as he rushed about the Bay area seeing to all his musical undertakings. Occasionally the politics of the time came right to his doorstep. Not long before war did finally break out in Europe, the San Francisco Conservatory hosted a non-musical event by a famous and controversial musical figure. Paul Robeson, invited by the two directors, who were known to be left-leaning in their politics, came to the Conservatory to give a lecture on Russia and European affairs. Niki recalls that the audience numbered about one hundred, including faculty and distinguished members of the area's music community, and although there was some controversy within the institution about the appropriateness of the event, most listened respectfully to what Robeson had to say. Speaking as he always did, from the perspective of an African American who had suffered the injustices of poverty and discrimination, Robeson presented his point of view about what was happening in Russia. Robeson was a captivating speaker, and although Niki might have preferred a recital, his interest in politics meant that he listened carefully to Robeson's highly personal account of one important element in the turbulent European scene.[11]

Despite the growing tension in Europe, or perhaps because of it, Niki made a trip back to Belgium in the summer of 1939. It was not a well-timed visit, perhaps even ill-advised; it was clear that war was inevitable and sooner rather than later. As the summer passed Niki recognized the urgency to make immediate arrangements for his return to the United States. But how to accomplish that was a major problem. Every available ship leaving Europe was booked solid, carrying peoples of all nationalities desperate to flee before all-out war was declared. England looked like the best bet, and again with the help of his uncle, and with no time for proper goodbyes to his family, Niki quit Brussels for London. But he found prospects for passage to North America almost non-existent, and he was becoming increasingly discouraged when a friend advised him that a ship was leaving shortly for New York from Göteberg in Sweden. Making his way to Hull, on England's east coast, the intrepid traveller obtained a ticket to Sweden, arriving just in time to obtain a place on the SS *Küngsholme.* Within days he was at sea, on a ship displaying large Swedish flags painted on its sides, announcing to any prospective attackers that this was a neutral ship.

It was a harrowing crossing of the Atlantic; just a day or two out the passengers listened sombrely to the crackling wireless as Prime Minister Chamberlain made his famous broadcast, declaring that Britain was at war with Germany. The distress among the people assembled in the lounge was unmistakable; Niki has never forgotten it, the stillness of deep emotion and then a comment that jarred and rattled like a jack-hammer. One of the passengers, a prominent United States senator, shrugged and announced that it didn't have anything to do with him. 'Who cares about another war in Europe? I just want to get home to my ranch,' he said. It was a shocking sentiment to Niki, who cared profoundly about what was happening in Europe.[12]

But the United States was not to remain in peaceful isolation. The year 1941 is an infamous one in U.S. history, but at that time, for Niki and the musical community of San Francisco, it was noteworthy only as the 150th anniversary of the death of Mozart, an opportunity to revive some of the great composer's works, particularly less familiar pieces that had not been heard for years.

Apart from the inclusion of chamber music and vocal works on concert programs, Niki planned a Mozart evening in December at the Museum of the Legion of Honour; the second half of the program featured Mozart's youthful chamber opera, *Bastien and Bastienne.* Playing the charming little shepherdess was Lois Moran, who had forsaken her Broadway career when she married Colonel Young, the president of Pan American Airways. With Niki's usual ear for talent and his uncanny ability to persuade artists to appear in unusual productions, he convinced Ms Moran to take on the role of Bastienne. Once again he suffered the usual headaches of preparing a production with primarily student forces, but all the elements gradually came together until the night of the dress rehearsal. It began well, when suddenly there was a commotion and the caretaker rushed in, announcing that they must stop at once. 'Pearl Harbor has been attacked by the Japanese,' he cried. It was 7 December 1941. San Francisco was in disarray. Radios blared news of the disaster, repeating in dire tones rumours of a Japanese armada positioned just off the coast ready to attack the city. People were being urged to turn off their lights, to prepare for the worst.

At the rehearsal the shocking news caused turmoil. The first violinist dropped her violin, collapsing on the floor of the pit. Later she told Niki that her husband was in the navy, stationed in Pearl Harbor. It was a horrifying evening, and the end of rehearsing the light little eighteenth-century opera. It looked like the end of performances of any kind in San Francisco for a very long time.

However, as events became clearer, and San Francisco realized that invasion was not imminent, daily life began to settle down, and in fact the opera was presented a few nights later, this time as a benefit for the USO with which Ms Moran was associated as president.

Another benefit for the USO came later in the season with a production, again produced and conducted by Niki, of Douglas Moore's *The Devil and Daniel Webster*. Described by the composer as a folk opera, and based on a story by Stephen Vincent Benet, it is set in New Hampshire in the 1840s and involves an enchanted fiddle, a Faustian pact with the devil, and a villain named Mr Scratch. As usual, Niki had an eye for a work with dramatic popular appeal, written by an American and possible to produce with limited resources.

Douglas Moore came from New York for this west coast premiere and at breakfast the next morning he offered Niki a position at Columbia University beginning in the 1942 school year. Niki's University Appointment Card shows that he was an Associate in the Music Department from 1942 to 1944.

On 29 June 1942 he sent a telegram to his Uncle Alfred in Basel telling him of his appointment to Columbia, asking him to give his Aunt Thérèse Hymans the good news, and informing him that he would be leaving for New York in August.

Niki was delighted to be going to the big city, but he left San Francisco with some regret. In retrospect he places the San Francisco Conservatory of that period at the level of a good 'community' school, rather than a first-level professional training institution. He smiles when he acknowledges that he probably never produced a really prominent voice from the ranks of his students, but at the same time emphasizes that they all learned a good deal about lieder, about choral singing, diction, and performance, and best of all, they appeared to enjoy doing it.

Niki likes San Francisco very much and returned often in subsequent years, to visit friends and make contacts for new projects he was planning. On these visits he took every opportunity to attend whatever offering might be interesting, and often these trips had their share of typical Goldschmidt adventure, and humour. Once he was on his way to a master class given by Lotte Lehmann in Santa Barbara and as is his custom, being a non-driver, he took the public transit to get there. He asked the bus driver to let him out at the stop from which he could walk to the music school. Unfortunately the driver forgot, and looking in his mirror, seeing the tall thin stranger still sitting in his place sometime after they had passed the correct stop, he was full of apologies. As Niki tells it:

He stopped at once and directed me to cross over the road and wait for the bus coming back. I was standing there on the corner, very upset because it was getting late, when along came a car with a lady driving. She stopped and asked if I was the man going to the music school. I told her I was and she said, 'Get in and I'll take you. My husband called me and said he had forgotten to let you off his bus and asked me to come and pick you up.' Now wasn't that a charming thing to do?

On another visit to Santa Barbara, he went with his old friend Leighton Rollins to hear Leopold Stokowski conduct at a summer evening outdoor concert. Again, things did not unfold quite as they should have:

There was a place for the audience, and the orchestra shell, and an open space behind that. Overlooking the whole place was a big grey building, very formidable, institutional. Well, when the orchestra began to play faces appeared at the small windows all along the side of the building, which was in fact a prison. And then all those prisoners started to yell and jeer and of course Stokowski looked up and was obviously annoyed. So he stopped the orchestra, and left the stage and he was gone for some time, but the orchestra and the audience just stayed, waiting. Finally he returned, picked up the baton and began again. And this time, the prisoners at the window listened quietly, and there were lots of them. We learned later that he had gone over to the prison and asked the warden if he could address the prisoners, which he did, and gave them a good lecture on the music and how to enjoy it. I think it is a wonderful thing.

That is the kind of story with all the elements that Niki enjoys, music taking place in the community, reaching beyond the concert hall, and above all someone taking affirmative action to overcome an obstacle!

Spring of 1942 saw the end of Niki's tenure in San Francisco. He finished the last of his coaching at the conservatory and set out on a west coast recital tour that took him to Seattle and to Victoria, British Columbia.

Canadian composer John Beckwith, who would later work with Niki in Toronto, was a student in Victoria at the time. He recalls that as long-term engagements were few during the war years, many artists took to touring as a way of maintaining their careers. At Victoria's summer school for teachers there was a regular noon-hour series of concerts and it was there that Beckwith first heard Niki. 'I was hired to put up stands and move chairs and get the posters out so I heard all of the recitals. Along came this tall European, accompanying himself in a recital of lieder. I remember being quite impressed. It was a light voice, musical, and he did an interesting program. I especially remember the songs by Hugo Wolf that I had never heard before.'[13]

In late summer Niki was in New York ready for his new job. His primary duty as spelled out to him by Douglas Moore was to be musical director of Brander Matthews Hall, where he was to develop a new opera program. Opened in 1940, this small theatre on 117th Street, seating fewer than three hundred, was named for the distinguished essayist, critic, and scholar, and was built with the optimistic hope it would be an important centre for opera at Columbia University. But like many ventures of that time, the new program was disadvantaged almost from the beginning as people's energy and attention were directed toward the war effort.

At Columbia, the Composers' Forum included a concert series featuring contemporary music of many genres, especially chamber and vocal music. On the opera side, the students explored a variety of music by composers such as Vaughan Williams, Otto Leuning, and Ernest Bacon, whose *Tree on the Plains* was presented during Niki's tenure. By then he was accustomed to the difficulties of casting a production with limited student resources, and he was developing what is now recognized as almost a sixth sense when it comes to finding the voice he needs. In New York, as it has so often for him, serendipity presented him with the right circumstance. He needed a strong contralto voice, and was having no success in finding one through the usual channels. Then one Sunday while attending church he heard the woman next to him singing the hymns in a lovely rich contralto voice, just the voice he needed. Never shy about asking, even strangers, he spoke to the woman after the service, complimenting her on her singing and asking if she would like to participate in their student production at Columbia. Niki cannot remember now who she was or whether she ever sang on the stage again, but he does know that she did a creditable job for their production.

In the case of the baritone there was no intervention of fate that ensured success, just the presence of an outstanding young singer whom Niki recruited at once. He was Theodore Uppman, who later starred at the Metropolitan Opera over twenty-four seasons, and at Covent Garden in 1951 appeared as the first Billy Budd in the Britten opera of that name. Uppman and Niki remained friends over many years after that modest beginning in New York.

At Brander Matthews Hall it was not all contemporary music on stage. In December 1943 the production there by the Columbia Theater Associates was *Two Misers,* an operetta in two acts by André Grétry, a Belgian composer of the eighteenth century. Premiered at Fontainebleu in October 1770 on the occasion of the marriage of Marie Antoinette, the opera was updated and presented in a new English version for this New York production. Niki conducted what the *New York Times* described as a 'highly intelligent' performance of the 'opera comique in the style of Mozart.'[14]

At the same time, as has been his habit all his life, Niki looked beyond his own immediate work, attending other presentations to see what was happening, and to learn. One great opportunity that he describes as 'incredible' was to hear a lecture by Béla Bartók, who occupied the Chair of Ethnomusicology at the university.

Niki attended one session when Bartók spoke to the faculty; he says of the famous Hungarian: 'He was the most aristocratic-looking man you can imagine. He spoke in detail about his research into Hungarian and Romanian folk songs, about the songs that he had collected. It was very gripping. The entire faculty was there, opera director Herbert Graf, the dean, everyone, because they recognized that this was a tremendously important contribution that Bartók made to music, apart from his own composing.'[15]

Bartók's discourse added to the material that Niki used for his own lecture/recital given in Montreal in early 1944 on the subject of Czech folk songs. He was speaking to the 'People's Forum,' pointing out that folk songs represent a national determination to retain identity, and in the case of the Czechs 'they represent a national shrine to their ideals of freedom and humanity.'

He went on to discuss, and illustrate musically, the 'malleability' of the folk song and the many possible ways of interpreting it. Expanding on his theme he illustrated it with compositions by so-called serious composers and introduced works by a number of Czech composers not familiar to his audience.[16]

Back at Columbia, opportunities in the developing opera program were severely limited by the war, and as it dragged on into 1944 Niki thought often of his three brothers in the Allied forces fighting in Europe, and of his own need to be involved in some way in the war effort. His knowledge of several languages was a definite asset, a commodity in demand by the Office of War Information. So, for the first time since his graduation from the academy, Niki moved away from his chosen profession; he became producer in foreign languages of news broadcasts for the Office, a position that lasted a little more than a year, until the war ended. He was producing information programs in three languages: German, French, and Czech.

It was a high-energy place, with a constant stream of bulletins and news flashes being delivered by messengers rushing from desk to desk, and like the theatre from time to time it had its miscues. On one occasion the announcer on the Czech desk stubbornly shook his head at Niki's signal, refusing to break from his regular broadcast to read a special high-priority flash that had been placed on the desk in front of him. Niki cued him again, and again he ignored the direction. 'I can't,' he finally explained to the furious Goldschmidt, 'they've given me the French copy.'

Although war information and emergency bulletins had only a superficial similarity to the world of theatre, Niki actually met a man at the Information Office who had a link with both his past and his future. The famous Czech actor Jan Voskovec, who was known as one of the great comedians of the Czech theatre, was living in exile in New York. He held an important position in the Czech section of the Information Office while Niki was there. Years later the same actor played with Hal Holbrook in a production of *Who Has Seen the Milky Way?* at the Vancouver International Festival, when Niki was artistic director.

News never replaced music in Niki's life, in spite of the temporary job shift. In April of 1945 he gave a lieder recital at Town Hall that was rather more varied in repertoire than had been his custom at earlier concerts. Along with the usual Schubert and Wolf, he included Dvořák's *Turn Thou to Me* and songs by Douglas Moore, together with a set of Czech folk songs and a group of Old English airs. The critics were complimentary, noting that both the singing and accompaniment 'were matched and of high quality.'[17]

In 1945 the end of the war approached and the U.S. faced fresh challenges as it began planning for the reintegration of thousands of veterans into civilian life. Niki's news job was coming to an end, and he began looking around New York for post-war opportunities.

A chance meeting solved his dilemma, at least for the immediate future. Walking on the street one day, just in front of Steinway Hall he met Walter Herbert, whom he had known in San Francisco as the man in charge of music for the Works Progress Administration or WPA, President Roosevelt's employment scheme during the depression. In 1945 Herbert was going to head up the New Orleans Opera, and he invited Niki to come as Assistant Conductor and Coach for the 1945/6 season.

Niki remembered the Louisiana city from his brief stopover there during his round-the-country rail trek, and it seemed to him like a fascinating place to spend a year.

The New Orleans Opera is one of the longest continuously operating companies in North America, having staged André Grétry's *Sylvain* in May of 1776![18] Plans for the season that Niki was about to join called for six operas including *Carmen, Tannhäuser,* and Mozart's *Abduction from the Seraglio,* starring Canadian tenor Leopold Simoneau in the role of Belmonte.

Simoneau says, 'It was my first encounter with Nicholas Goldschmidt, and the beginning of a friendship and collaboration that have lasted ... more than half a century.'[19] It was nearly fifty years later that Niki was asked to speak about the dazzling career of the famous tenor at an elegant ceremony in Ottawa's National Arts Centre when Simoneau received one of Canada's highest honours, the Governor-General's Performing Arts Award.

In 1946 Niki knew little about Canada except what he had seen during brief recital engagements, but as is his style he asked many questions, one in particular that took Simoneau by surprise. 'He asked me one day: "Is butter easily available in Canada?"'[20] Niki had still not forgotten the circumstances of his earliest working days in Czechoslovakia, fifteen years and thousands of miles in the past.

New Orleans was a different world, a colourful place to work, at least for one season. From October 1945 through April of 1946 Niki was kept busy, coaching singers in the season's repertoire and giving seminars and lectures on lieder. In his free time he rode the streetcar seeing the sights and even had one memorable dinner at the famous Antoine's. He recalls that on one of his early excursions he took his place on the streetcar, toward the rear, and the conductor admonished him. 'You can't sit there,' he said. 'Back there is for Negroes.' Niki was shocked. Despite all of the class distinctions in the Europe of his upbringing, he was not prepared for the blatant racism of the south at that time. He didn't understand it, and could not relate to it. He was not bothered with race, it was music that mattered. 'Often it was my job to meet visiting singers, and I would have to go along to the train station because that is where they would arrive. The African American porters would sit on the luggage carts waiting for the trains. And spontaneously they would begin singing their spirituals, the music of the region. It was beautiful, delightful. I have never forgotten it.'

Niki did not see New Orleans as a permanent home. Despite its charm and its French feel, the heat and humidity did not suit his more northern sensibility, and the career possibilities for the future were not encouraging. So at the end of his contract he headed once more for New York, thinking that perhaps he might open his own studio there, based on the number of singers he had met in New Orleans who indicated that they would welcome such a move.

But again luck, or the musical gods, intervened, this time thrusting Niki into an entirely new milieu, a place where he would build his career and make musical history for more than half a century.

Once more he walked over to 57th Street, this time to visit the dark, musty office of Henry Levinger, associate editor of the *Musical Courier,* whom Niki had known in Vienna. The two old friends chatted, with Niki laying out his plans for a coaching studio. But his sense of adventure, his drive to create something new, moved him to add, 'If you hear of anything, particularly any new opportunities where I can perhaps build something, keep me in mind.' Niki then got up, and went down the hall for a visit with another old friend, the agent Thea Dispeker. He had only just sat down when the telephone rang. It was Levinger, for Niki, urging him to come back to his office right away. Levinger had just received a call from Arnold Walter, head of the Senior School at the Toronto Conservatory of Music, looking for a music director for their new Opera School beginning in October 1946.

Niki says now, 'In that one minute on that visit with Henry Levinger, whom I had not seen in twenty years, my whole life changed.'

He was setting out on a great adventure, this time without the blessing and encouragement of his parents and his beloved Uncle Paul, who had exercised such an influence on his early adult life. Sadly, all three had died during the war. Although his extended family remained in Europe, the individuals who had been most influential in his development were gone. Niki was on his own. He speaks of the loss plainly, solemnly, but without dwelling on any details. He recalls each of these important figures in his life with great affection, and moves on to speak of other events as they have influenced his career and his long life.

His varied experiences of his eight years in the United States gave him a new self-confidence. He had learned how to get on in a new world. He had worked with professionals and amateurs, children and adults. Most important of all, he had gained an insight he would call on many times in the decades to come; he had discovered his own talent for shaping substantial ventures out of slim prospects. Niki Goldschmidt was ready to embrace all the challenges and the opportunities that Canada offered.

4

New Home, New Voices

Niki Goldschmidt arrived in Toronto on the last weekend of September 1946. After checking into the old Ford Hotel, a down-at-heel establishment long since demolished, he went out to look around the city. It wasn't an encouraging or uplifting sight. Toronto presented a dreary scene for the young man from Vienna, a very different place from the cosmopolitan centres to which he was accustomed. He couldn't buy a bottle of beer in a restaurant, Ontario's Sunday 'blue laws' kept the cinemas shut tight, there was no Sunday newspaper to browse through, and there was scarcely anyone on the street. It was quiet and deadly dull.

In fact, post-war Toronto was a relentlessly conservative city, without the stylish vitality of San Francisco, the colour of New Orleans, or the aggressive energy of New York. To Canadians at that time the only sophisticated city in the country was Montreal, and Toronto residents looking for a good time on the weekend went over the border to Buffalo!

But Toronto, although serious and gray, was a city of promise, with solid financial institutions and a growing industrial base at its doorstep, looking to the future, ready to take advantage of the expected post-war boom.

In the arts, Toronto had a creditable foundation on which to build. Since the first half of the nineteenth century, touring companies and individual artists had visited the city regularly, playing in one of the many downtown theatres. Musically, the city had a long and distinguished performance tradition. In the area of choral music, always dear to Niki's heart, a number of choral societies were formed in the mid-nineteenth century, presenting the great oratorios and cantatas for appreciative audiences. In 1894 Augustus Stephan Vogt established the Mendelssohn Choir of Toronto (now the Toronto Mendelssohn Choir)[1], an ensemble of nearly one hundred voices, which would be a major participant years later in Niki's important choral festivals.

On the very same day that Niki was to take up his new position, 1 October 1946, the Women's Musical Club of Toronto, founded in 1898, opened its forty-ninth season, after a wartime hiatus. The club's programs over the years had featured the best of Canadian musical artists as well as an astonishing list of international stars including Marian Anderson, Dame Myra Hess, and Nathan Milstein, and from Niki's past, violinist Bronislav Huberman, who appeared in the 1935 season.[2]

The Toronto Symphony Orchestra, descended from the Toronto Conservatory Symphony formed as early as 1906, in spite of continuing financial woes and some stops and starts had survived the depression as a going concern. In 1946, under the direction of Sir Ernest Mac-Millan, the orchestra was presenting a regular subscription series in the 2800-seat Massey Hall, (each concert repeated to accommodate the demand), a regular pops series that was broadcast nationally,[3] as well as children's concerts and an educational program aimed at older students.[4] Throughout its history the Toronto Symphony's repertoire was similar to that of most orchestras of the day, featuring the major works of the eighteenth and nineteenth centuries. The twentieth century was occasionally represented; for example, when Stravinsky appeared in 1937 as guest conductor, he included on his program both *Firebird* and *Petrushka,* pieces with which the orchestra and its audience were already familiar. The guest artist list over the decades included famous names like Fritz Kreisler, Mischa Elman, Sergei Rachmaninoff; among the singers who graced the stage at Massey Hall were Alma Gluck and Leo Slezak, whom Niki had heard twenty years earlier in Vienna.

The Toronto Conservatory of Music (which in 1947 was renamed the Royal Conservatory of Music of Toronto and in 1991 became simply the Royal Conservatory of Music or RCOM) was incorporated in 1886 and almost immediately began offering a full range of instruction together with an extensive set of examinations that gave it a significant presence across the country. Augustus Vogt, of Mendelssohn Choir fame, became principal in 1913, and during his tenure Healey Willan, Canada's pre-eminent composer of that time, was appointed vice-principal. Also during this period the total number of students rose to 7500.[5] Sir Ernest MacMillan, a major figure in Canada's musical development, followed Vogt in 1926. MacMillan understood the limitations of the conservatory as primarily a collection of independent teachers working under its administrative umbrella, a system that left an inconsistent level of teaching, both in terms of content and standards. MacMillan made great efforts to improve the entire concept of the conservatory, and is credited with developing there a 'first-rate choir, a symphony orchestra, and an opera company.'[6]

So, in almost every aspect of its musical life, Toronto was accustomed to quality programming, provided by the best Canadian and international touring artists, together with resident ensembles steadily improving in performance standards and breadth of repertoire. Opera was the exception. Since the early nineteenth century, various touring companies had appeared in Toronto, often starring famous singers of the day in major roles. Toronto opera fans heard Emma Albani, Feodor Chaliapin, and Adelina Patti. They saw the full Metropolitan Opera Company in 1899, as well as the much less refined San Carlo Opera Company, which toured to the city regularly during the first half of the twentieth century. But all of this was sporadic, and uneven in quality.

The Conservatory Opera Company inaugurated by Ernest MacMillan in 1928 offered real promise for advancement. Over two seasons the company managed several productions, most notably Humperdinck's *Hansel and Gretel, The Sorcerer,* a Gilbert and Sullivan favourite, and Purcell's *Dido and Aeneas.* All signs pointed to Toronto's readiness to support an opera company. Imagine, for example, a hotel opening featuring an opera performance as part of the celebration! It actually happened, in Toronto in the infamous year of 1929 as part of the festivities surrounding the opening of the CPR's magnificent Royal York Hotel. Ernest MacMillan conducted, in the hotel's own concert hall, a production of *Hugh the Drover,* by Ralph Vaughan Williams.[7] But circumstances again militated against artistic initiative. The great crash of 1929 and the ensuing economic depression put an end to efforts to establish this most expensive of art forms as a permanent ingredient of the city's cultural scene.

When Niki arrived, cheerful and full of anticipation, in 1946, it was impossible to know what to expect in the future, but the immediate plans certainly seemed to have promise. In 1944 Dr Arnold Walter had joined the staff of the Toronto Conservatory. He was another European expatriate, like Niki born in Moravia, educated first in law at the University of Prague and later in Berlin where he pursued studies in music.[8] Again the familiar and dreadful political circumstances of Europe, and Germany in particular, during the 1930s disrupted a career in the making, and after several moves he settled in Toronto in the late 1930s. In

1944 he joined the Toronto Conservatory and in 1945 was selected to head up the new Senior School, dedicated to the training of excellent students who had the promise of pursuing a career in music. One year later, supported by Edward Johnson, the Canadian tenor who was also general manager of the Metropolitan Opera and chairman of the board of the conservatory, Walter was given the mandate to create an Opera School at the conservatory (with the agreement of the University of Toronto, under whose aegis the conservatory operated).

Ettore Mazzoleni, principal of the conservatory at that time, later wrote about the purpose of the opera program: 'The aims were simple – to look for the best young talent in the country, to offer it the finest possible training in every aspect of opera, and then to give it an opportunity to prove itself to the public.'[9]

With that mandate in hand, Walter made his first two important appointments. Niki was engaged officially as conductor of the Opera School. His duties as spelled out in a letter were 'to train and to conduct Soloists, Chorus and Orchestra: and to give lectures and classes in conducting and accompanying.'[10] The salary for all this was to be $4200 per annum.

On the same day, 26 September 1946, that the letter confirming Niki's appointment was sent, Dr Walter wrote to Niki in another letter that he had contacted the Department of Immigration asking permission for Niki to enter Canada. He explained that he was not sure whether the department's answer would arrive before the coming weekend. The department responded with dispatch, allowing Niki to enter the country in time for the new term. But there was a price attached to this bureaucratic activity; just over a week later, on 7 October 1946, a letter was sent to Dr Walter from the Department of Mines and Resources, Immigration Branch, saying, 'This Department incurred an expenditure of $1.12 in forwarding telegrams authorizing the entry to Canada from the United states of Mr. Nicholas Goldschmidt, and I would be pleased if you would arrange to remit that amount to this office at your early convenience.'[11] Dr Walter replied on 11 October thanking the official for his help in expediting Niki's entry and assuring him that payment of the $1.12 was forthcoming.[12] So, Canada had acquired a new 'resource,' this time a musical one, for the bargain price of one dollar and twelve cents!

The second major appointment to the new Opera School was Austrian-born Felix Brentano, student of Max Reinhardt, stage director of the New Opera Company in New York, and a well-known Broadway director. Unlike Niki, he did not take up residence in Toronto, but continued his career in New York. After an exchange of correspondence with Dr Walter through the summer of 1946 his appointment was confirmed, beginning on 1 November, until May. He was to come to Toronto for bi-weekly sessions of four days each and in April he was committed for four full weeks. His salary was $3500 for the season.[13]

Everything was ready, then, for the launch of this exciting new initiative when Niki arrived at the conservatory building at 135 College Street, at the corner of University Avenue. After his first dismal weekend wandering around the city he was immediately energized by the atmosphere in his new place of employment. 'It was so exciting,' he says. 'I felt it at once. There was a feeling of anticipation, of optimism. The students were hurrying along the corridors in that old building, eager to get to a class or a lesson, wanting to do things. They wanted to make things happen just as I did.'

He set to work at once. John Beckwith, later a prominent Canadian composer who had first encountered Niki when he went to Victoria to present a recital, was employed as a rehearsal pianist playing for the conservatory's classes. He recalls how hard everyone worked and how progress was made very quickly: 'We went from nothing to something in a very short time. Here were people who had worked in opera houses in Europe and could pass on that tradition and their knowledge.'[14]

George Crum, who went on to be the long-time conductor and musical director of the National Ballet of Canada, also joined the staff in that first year, hired to coach, and play for auditions and rehearsals. He has recollections similar to Beckwith's. The lack of any ongoing opera company in Toronto meant that few if any musicians knew the opera repertoire. Crum had a basic knowledge of eight or nine operas, acquired by playing for a singer friend, so when he joined the conservatory he was learning as well as assisting. He remembers that Dr Walter was rather stiff, formal, but efficient and always supportive. Niki, whose studio was next to Crum's on the second floor, seemed to be in perpetual motion, always busy, never wasting a minute. He made time, though, to help the young aspiring conductor and coach.

He taught me that when working with singers the piano is no longer a piano, it must be the whole orchestra, it has to mimic the other instruments, to sound like them, to feel like them. It needs a combination of touch and imagination. When I first heard him I thought that he was just faking it, leaving things out because they were too difficult, but then I realized that to be too precise was too unoperatic, too unfree. It is a question of helping the singers, of creating the effect. That understanding has stayed with me.[15]

Many of Niki's colleagues of that time make similar comments. They share the view that in terms of technique he may not have been the very best pianist in the profession, or have had the finest voice, or the most precise conducting style, but they all agree that he knew the repertoire intimately and understood the essence of the music in a way that always resulted in remarkable performances.

And he wasn't afraid to take chances, to fully embrace every opportunity. On 16 December 1946, only a few weeks into the program, he and Brentano demonstrated their confidence in their new venture by offering a public performance of operatic excerpts, given at Hart House Theatre on the campus of the University of Toronto. Among the performers were Andrew MacMillan, Louise Roy, and Mary Morrison. The program included selections from *Otello, La Bohème, La Traviata,* and *Der Rosenkavalier,* the last scene of act 3 of Gounod's *Faust,* and the Prisoners' Chorus from Beethoven's *Fidelio.*

Niki remembers that there was a comparatively large number of good male singers at the conservatory. Most of them were recently discharged servicemen, which gave Brentano the brilliant idea to have them wear their uniforms for the *Fidelio* chorus. The result was memorable. Over forty years later, Helmut Kallmann, an editor of the *Encyclopedia of Music in Canada,* wrote to Niki on the occasion of his eightienth birthday, 'I do remember the Prisoners' Chorus from *Fidelio* in that very first Opera School performance, and I remember many other wonderful things you have conducted or organized.'[16]

Saturday Night magazine, in an article about the program, said it was 'pleasing,' and made much of the future promise of the school, saying that 'time may prove it significant for all Canada.'[17]

It had been an exhilarating beginning, so exciting for Niki that on 23 December when he was back in the Barbizon Plaza Hotel in New York he wrote an enthusiastic letter to Arnold Walter. 'I want you to know that I am rejoicing with you about our recent success.' He went on to say that working with Dr Walter was a privilege and that his job at the conservatory has 'under your guidance become for the first time a profession.'[18]

To Niki, that evening in Hart House was the point from which 'opera became a permanent fixture' in Toronto. Now they were really into building a school and what ultimately became an opera company. The already hectic pace accelerated as they moved into the New Year. Walter replied to Niki's ebullient letter on 2 January, noting that he was looking forward to seeing him back at the conservatory the following Monday, and asking him to 'please think about our Broadcast,'[19] as the Canadian Broadcasting Corporation had tentatively offered five broadcasts for the coming season. Since the national broadcaster was moving to become a major catalyst for the development of opera in Canada, this was a vote of confidence for Walter and his colleagues. In the 1947/8 season the CBC broadcast three of the conservatory productions, and by 1948 formed its own company to produce opera for 'CBC Wednesday Night,' a distinguished radio series that presented the best of drama and music. Niki served as conductor and member of the decision-making committee that was chaired by Charles Jennings with Harry Boyle, administrator, Terence Gibbs, producer, Geoffrey Waddington, music advisor, and Arnold Walter.[20]

Amid all this planning for the future the daily work went on, learning new repertoire, putting together new programs. Niki and his singers were working continuously. On the evenings of 28 and 29 April 1947 they gave their first full production, Smetana's *The Bartered Bride*, sung in English and performed at Eaton Auditorium. This 1200-seat hall, located on the seventh floor of Eaton's art deco College Street department store, was a favourite of Toronto audiences, and added weight to the growing reputation of the Opera School. The family of Oskar Morawetz, then a promising young composer in Toronto and a Czech expatriate, arranged for authentic Czech national costumes to be made available for the production of this quintessentially Czech composition. Financially the production came in just under budget, a result appreciated by the often-beleaguered Arnold Walter. 'The total cost of our production amounted to $5,208, a very close shave since I had only $5,308 in the kitty,' he wrote.[21] And in another letter he expressed his ongoing frustration: 'Unfortunately I cannot do all that I know ought to be done for lack of funds and lack of general understanding. There [are] a few people ... doing wonderful work and helping me at every turn of the road ... the University, of course regards the Opera as an illegitimate child with which they are not quite reconciled yet.'[22]

Choral music was more familiar than opera in Toronto, and on 27 March 1947 Niki conducted what the printed program called an 'Hour of Sacred Music' at the Conservatory Concert Hall, at 5 o'clock in the afternoon.

The program featured just two works, *Stabat Mater* of Pergolesi, and Bach's Cantata no. 140, *Sleepers, Wake!* It was the first in what became a regular part of the school's schedule, a continuing round of choral concerts, most often given in one of the city's many churches.

During the summer that bridged from the first season to the second, planning continued almost non-stop, and Niki, typically, was a whirlwind of activity. In the spring and summer of 1947 there was a constant exchange of letters and urgent cables between him and Dr Walter: Niki in May writing from New York urging Dr Walter to hire a particular choreographer to teach dance and movement at the school[23] (Walter was unable to find the necessary fee); Niki in June writing from a Pan Am 'Clipper,' elated at flying twenty-five thousand feet in the air and landing at Gander, Newfoundland;[24] Niki later the same month from Belgium urgently seeking permission to purchase an important selection of scores and parts from the sale of a private library;[25] Niki in August from Lenox, Massachusetts, excited about a possible future summer school at the conservatory, and laying out plans for a paid chamber chorus touring in Ontario that could 'offer the communities a concert for $600.'[26] Dr Walter assiduously answered each letter, approving initiatives where he could, cautioning restraint in other cases because of budget limitations.

Niki's residence at Lenox during that summer marked a renewal of the collaboration with Leighton Rollins that had in effect launched his North American career. Rollins had relocated his Theatre School from Long Island to a rambling white frame house just across the road from the famous Tanglewood Music Center in the Berkshire Mountains. As director of music, Niki had a large class of students, including a group from Toronto, among them Kate Reid, who later had a distinguished career as an actor in theatre and film. A feature that summer in which all the students took part was a production of Shakespeare's *Midsummer Night's Dream* for which Niki took the unusual step of adapting the music of Purcell's *Fairy Queen*. This innovation engaged the attention of Leonard Bernstein and Aaron Copland, whom Niki had met at their lectures in association with the Tanglewood music-training program. Bernstein and Copland agreed that the music was more in keeping with the spirit of the text than the more familiar Mendelssohn score. Niki relished the discussion of how music serves the theatre best, and treasured especially meeting Bernstein, with whom he would have a long acquaintance.

The summer wound up with a working visit to New York, primarily to purchase scores, and then it was back to Toronto where the momentum continued into the new season, a ground-breaking year with events that have echoed in Niki's life and career for over half a century.

. After another term of coaching and classes, the first production that season was Humperdinck's *Hansel and Gretel* given at Eaton Auditorium in December. That production remains in Niki's memory because it was the launch of what has grown to be a hugely important component of Toronto's cultural life, a vigorous opera scene. He also remembers fondly the small boy sitting right behind him; there was no pit, so the boy had an excellent view of Niki's conducting. Apparently fascinated by Niki's baton going up and down with such vigour, at one break in the music he asked his father in a very loud voice, 'When will the man make his yo-yo go again?' To Niki it was a charming comment, funny and childlike, qualities that he has always enjoyed.

Just two months later, on 6 February 1948, Niki and his colleagues were back at the same location with a production of Gluck's *Orpheus and Eurydice*. George Bernard Shaw said about this work, 'Listen to Orfeo, and you hear that perfect union of the poem and the music.'[27] Given Niki's passion for works that skilfully marry drama and music, it is no surprise that *Orpheus* is one of his favourites, included in many of his programs over the ensuing years.

The 1948 production featured Louise Roy as Orpheus, Mary Morrison as Eurydice, and Beth Corrigan as Amor. (Kate Reid was one of the Furies.) Sponsored by the Women's Musical Club as part of its season, the production was a great success. Helmut Kallmann, reviewing the production for the university paper, noted the difficulty in the simplicity of the work and pronounced the result 'excellent.' He praised Goldschmidt for inspiring the forces with his enthusiasm, saying, 'the overall impression was one of unity between performance and the spirit of the music.'[28]

Vincent Tovell, long-time friend of Niki's, recalls that performance and Niki's emergence on the scene at that time: 'I remember earlier watching him rehearse the Prisoners' Chorus, and excerpts, and they were remarkable, but I especially recall the *Orfeo*. There he was with those long arms and his hair flying, animating the music with life and grace. Niki was definitely becoming a force in Toronto.'[29]

Orpheus marked the Toronto stage debut of Niki's former colleague from Opava, Herman Geiger-Torel, who at Niki's urging joined the faculty at the Opera School, initially for one term. While Brentano directed the Gluck (and annoyed Niki by his now well-known and unsuccessful demand that he cut the famous recitative before the 'Che Faro' aria), Geiger-Torel was choreographer and went on to direct Pergolesi's *La serva padrona,* which Niki conducted at the Art Gallery in April. Although Brentano staged *Rosalinda* (an adaptation of Strauss's *Die Fledermaus* arranged by Erich Wolfgang Korngold) in May 1948, his association with Niki and Dr Walter never really jelled, and his contract was terminated. He was replaced by Geiger-Torel, whose contribution to opera in Toronto and the Canadian Opera Company in particular has been well documented, most recently by Ezra Schabas and Carl Morey in *Opera Viva,* their engaging fiftieth anniversary history of that company.

Geiger-Torel's full duties commenced in the following season, 1948/9. Meanwhile Niki and the others were busy with *Rosalinda,* which ran for two weeks at the Royal Alexandra Theatre and starred Jeanne Merrill, who had sung the title role under Brentano's direction on Broadway. Another import was the ballet director Herbert Bliss, who had worked with Balanchine and re-created the latter's choreography for the Toronto production. The remainder of the cast was Canadian, including Andrew MacMillan, who played leading roles in all the productions of that season. (Arnold Walter wrote to MacMillan, later in June asking for the return of the shoes he had worn in the production. Apparently the singer had mistakenly thought he could purchase them for a modest sum.)[30] And among a list of familiar names in the program are Victor Feldbrill, concert master (Feldbrill has had a long career as a conductor, in Canada and abroad), and George Crum, assistant conductor to Niki, while Irving Gutman, who went on to become a major force in Canadian opera, especially in western Canada, was the assistant stage manager.

That production was a mixed success. Arnold Walter catalogued the list of problems in a letter to Brentano in June. 'The Trade Fair [which had been expected to stimulate ticket sales] amounted to exactly nothing,' wrote Walter. 'The elections weren't any good either. It was late in the year, the weather was hot and the press was lousy. They all said it was lovely, of course, but they said it in such a way that the uninitiated audience has the impression they were talking about a school-show on the collegiate level. Speaking of Merrill – she did not cut much ice in the City. She has little voice appeal and no sex appeal whatever. Certainly she was useful in steadying the Show, but she was no special Box Office attraction.'[31]

He summed up this list of problems with the disappointing box office numbers. Just 50 per cent of the tickets were sold, for total revenue of

$25,000, resulting in a shortfall that he was able to cover only by economizing in other areas and convincing the university 'to unfreeze some unused accounts I had.'[32]

Walter goes on, in the same letter, to discuss ambitious plans for the future, exhibiting after all the bad news the kind of confidence that Niki felt throughout that busy season.

And it had been a memorable one. Niki had conducted on three CBC opera broadcasts, including *La serva padrona*, which was carried on CBC Radio International. And on 28 April he had conducted the first broadcast in Canada of Mozart's *Mass in C Minor*, which was also his first performance with the great Canadian soprano Lois Marshall, with whom he was to have a long association. In Niki's opinion, of all the singers he has known she came nearest to perfection in both the beauty of her voice and her artistry: 'That first collaboration with her was unbelievable, she sang so beautifully. And from then on I was able to say on many occasions about performances I heard, "Not as good as Lois Marshall." It was a privilege to make music with her.'

The 1947/8 season, as far as Niki was concerned, left the best for the last. On 26 June 1948 he married Shelagh Fraser at Deer Park United Church in North Toronto. They met when Shelagh attended that first choral concert at the conservatory under Niki's direction. She smiles when recalling the program: '*Sleepers, Wake* really was appropriate. It made that audience, and Toronto, sit up and take notice that here was somebody, Niki, who was really going to stir things up, make exciting things happen.'[33] And Shelagh knew her city well. Her father, Alexander Fraser, a native of Inverness-shire in Scotland, arrived in Toronto in 1886 at age twenty-six; he had been recommended by Sir Charles Tupper to join the editorial staff of the *Mail* (later the *Mail and Empire*) and served as that paper's city editor until 1896. He was a prolific writer, a historian, and a fervent Scot, and was celebrated as a Gaelic scholar. At his urging, the Archives of Ontario was established in 1903 and he became the first provincial archivist. In 1916 he was appointed aide-de-camp to the lieutenant-governor of Ontario, a position he held until his death twenty years later.

In 1900 he purchased a large comfortable house on the brow of the hill overlooking the city that at that time scarcely reached to what is now considered mid-(down)town. He named the house 'Kineras' after his home in Scotland, and the name is still displayed on the front of the house, which has remained Shelagh and Niki's home for over fifty years.

As a young woman Shelagh was an avid concert-goer, frequently at the conservatory. This beautiful and gracious member of the audience soon captured Niki's attention and affection. Their relationship flourished as Shelagh attended rehearsals and performances of the operas and choral music, and they began to have dinners together, and attend other social and concert events. Just over a year after their first meeting, Shelagh accepted the proposal of marriage from the eager European. In typical fashion, plans for their wedding were decided quickly and were made to fit in with Niki's busy summer plans. The ceremony itself was held in the morning, with Charles Jennings as best man, and Shelagh's sister Helen Ignatieff and an older brother also attending. The wedding luncheon for the dozen or so guests was held overlooking Shelagh's beloved garden at Kineras and then the newlyweds hurried off on the first of what has become hundreds of trips together.

'I didn't have a passport,' Shelagh remembers, 'and we were due to sail very shortly to Europe, so the minister at my church where we married, and a lawyer he knew, were very kind and looked after all the details so I could get a passport within a few days. In fact they sent it on to me en route so I had it before we embarked at Halifax.'[34]

With Shelagh driving, they began what was a formidable automobile journey in 1948, travelling first to Lenox, Massachusetts, to visit with Leighton Rollins and his wife. (Niki never has learned to drive a car. His brother's death in a car accident, his own poor eyesight, and, as Shelagh puts it, his concentration on his work rather than what is going on around him all made it a wise choice to refrain from ever getting a driver's licence.)

Soon they were on the road again after Lenox, stopping in Boston, where Niki wrote a friendly letter to Arnold Walter, part business, part pleasure. He commented on the 'wonderful time' in Lenox: 'glorious weather and the very nice company of Darius Milhaud,' another old friend to whom he could introduce his bride.[35] Then it was on to Nova Scotia, with its forests and rocky coastline, which Niki was seeing for the first time. But his 'first' was nothing in comparison to Shelagh's, headed to Europe to meet Niki's family.

They sailed on one of the so-called Drunken Duchesses, famous for their rolling progress across the North Atlantic. Arriving in Europe, the newlyweds travelled by train to Brussels and then on to the summer home of Niki's family. There, Shelagh was confronted by the relatives, all arriving for their vacations, and eager to meet Niki's wife.

It was daunting, there were so many people, forty-two of them, imagine! The older ones were all dressed in black and they were frightfully severe looking. They didn't speak English and I didn't speak French. It was all so strange to me I was quite overwhelmed. After all, at first I was a sort of curiosity from another world. But it was very beautiful there, and with lots of activity, tennis courts, a pool, wonderful walks through the forest where the wild boars rooted around for truffles, and children playing games and having fun. It was really extraordinary and marvellous. Everyone was very kind and I grew to love the family.[36]

The life there in Facqueval echoed Niki's boyhood experience: nannies and cooks and gardeners and chauffeurs, all the traditional help familiar to the great homes of Europe, catering to the comfort of the family members and their many guests.

The couple spent four weeks in Belgium before travelling on to Edinburgh to take in the exciting new festival there that was attracting international attention and helping to give Britain a much-needed boost in that dismal post-war period. Characteristically, Niki wanted to see what was new, what was happening, who were the young artists making a name for themselves, how other people were doing things. After just two years in Toronto he was not content to settle into a repetitive pattern, no matter how successful it might be.

Again he wrote to Walter, saying that he and Shelagh would be arriving in Montreal on 8 September on the *Empress of France*. His note, dashed off on an eight-by-five-inch sheet of blue airmail paper, covered all the diverse details about the upcoming year that were on his mind: music he wanted to purchase, casting for the operas, audition dates, the piano for his studio, rehearsal space requirements, Herman's address in South America, all bracketed by cordial greetings to Walter and his wife, and a question, 'Anything exciting about the spring production(s)?'[37] It was classic Niki! In the course of organizing his multitudinous projects he has made many such lists.

So the third year of the Opera School began, and in spite of the usual difficulties, arguments, and changing plans, the basics were in place to ensure the future of opera training and production in Toronto. There were ongoing disputes about the use of limited space by the opera students and students following other programs. Ettore Mazzoleni frequently sent around memos urging the opera staff to be sure their students vacated the Recital Hall at the appointed time to make way for other users, while Dr Walter's office continually exhorted them to return the printed parts and scores they had been using. The whole place crackled with energy. Former students recall that Geiger-Torel was bombastic, often exploding, shouting at the cast and crew. But they knew he was on their side and they worked hard, although John Beckwith says that Geiger-Torel made him so nervous it was hard to play the notes. Niki, in his classes, wanted energy, a release of inhibition. Looking over his glasses, he exhorted his students in his most theatrical style to engage with the music. The personalities of the two teachers made a powerful presence. It was no place for the faint-hearted!

Performances followed one after the other, on the stage, and on the CBC; in the next decade the original outstanding roster of singers was filled out with another list of performers who achieved major successes in Canada and abroad. Baritones Ernest Adams, Robert Goulet, Alexander Gray, and James Milligan, sopranos Marguerite Gignac, Barbara Franklin, and Joanne Ivey, and bass-baritone Jan Rubeš are only a few. In 1952 the *Montreal Star* reported that among the scholarship students at the Royal Conservatory Opera School for that year were Don Garrard from Vancouver, Bernard Turgeon from Edmonton, Patricia Rideout from Saint John, New Brunswick, and Jon Vickers from Prince Albert, Saskatchewan.[38] The average scholarship was $200.

Niki's association with many of these singers lasted on and off for several years. Jon Vickers was one. The great *Heldentenor* recalls, like many others, that while Niki was not always the most consistent conductor on the podium, his ability to inspire and his knowledge were tremendously effective:

> Quite early in my studies he gave me the confidence to do opera. He gave me roles in the operas, on stage and for the CBC, things like *School for Fathers*, and the Duke in *Rigoletto*, which was my first role on the opera stage. Actually it was not the role for me, probably I should not have done it, but nevertheless it was good for me to gain the experience on stage at that time in my development.
>
> Niki was also the first person to tell me that I would sing Wagner, and in fact that I would sing *Tristan*. Of course, I didn't believe him then. Niki always had faith in the people who worked with him, and never put people down. He was encouraging and so got the best.[39]

In the mid-1950s, in fact, Vickers sang his first Wagner, the first act of *Die Walküre* and the third act of *Parsifal* for the CBC, with Niki conducting.[40] That was significant not only for Vickers and the other singers but also for the opera-loving audience across the country, who had almost no opportunity to hear such music.

Carl Morey, who later became the dean of the Faculty of Music at the University of Toronto, was a young student in the 1950s, acting as a kind of apprentice to Niki, and mainly doing any job Niki called for. Morey loved opera, but at that time had never heard any Wagner in live performance. He was in the old CBC studio on College Street when the Wagner broadcast took place.

'I had only ever heard short excerpts before. Of course I couldn't judge what it was really like, but to hear a whole act in the studio – I was so knocked back it wouldn't have mattered what it sounded like.'[41]

Niki agrees. 'Jon was stunning. We had several serious coaching sessions just on the *Walküre*, and it was worth every minute. I will never forget that broadcast.'

Morey also remembers the *Rigoletto* to which Vickers refers as producing at least one evening that was extraordinary. Morey was working backstage doing technical chores when he became aware that what he was hearing from the stage was different from other nights at the opera.

'It was electrifying,' he says. 'The whole performance was amazing. Edward Johnson came rushing backstage after that first part and he, with all his experience, was as excited as I was!'[42]

Patricia Rideout, featured in opera and oratorio and known for her performances of contemporary music over a long career, remembers those early days at the conservatory as a solid foundation for the future. 'When I was first at the conservatory we did the opera coaching and rehearsals that were very intense, and eye-opening for us as we learned the roles. But we also had classes at night, singing a lot of choral music, like the Bach *B Minor Mass*. When Niki conducted it was almost as if he was overcome by the music, it was so special. He made us all feel as though we were privileged to be singing this music, and that sensibility is something I never felt with anyone else.'[43]

From rehearsal to stage, the collaboration of Niki and Geiger-Torel over the next several years took the singers through a full range of productions.

The Eaton Auditorium successes in the 1948/9 season, *The Marriage of Figaro* and *La Bohème,* inspired the first Opera Festival under the aegis of the Royal Conservatory Opera Company at the Royal Alexandra Theatre in February of 1950, with Verdi's *Rigoletto* joining *Figaro* and *Bohème* on the bill. Niki conducted all three.

The budget for that first festival was $29,000, a staggeringly low number even at that time for three fully staged productions taking place over two weeks with six evening and two matinée performances in each. In spite of the fact that once again Arnold Walter was able to report that the event had been a sell-out with no deficit, the university informed him that it wanted no more responsibility or risk for a production company. It was willing to co-operate with an independently incorporated company, allowing participation by students and staff and use of conservatory facilities. But the offer would stand for only forty-eight hours.

The story of the founding of the new professional opera company (which eventually developed into the Canadian Opera Company) has been well documented elsewhere.[44] Again it was built on that enthusiasm and that refusal to admit failure that have carried Niki through many tight spots. There was already in place the Opera and Concert Committee of the Royal Conservatory of Music, comprising a group of women who worked tirelessly raising money, selling tickets, doing all kinds of volunteer jobs, and enlisting their prominent husbands to extend support for opera in Toronto. Niki and Shelagh called a key group asking them to come to their home for an emergency meeting. Niki recalls:

> We said that we had to tell them the sad story that the opera might not continue. So they came, even giving up tickets to a Rudolf Serkin concert at Massey Hall. Mrs Lorimer Massie, Dr Pratt, Mrs J.D. Woods were among them. We told them we not only had to have a new organization but we had to have a $20,000 guarantee. So one said that she would see that the money was raised and another said she would get a board in place. And I went to Jack Godfrey [later Senator Godfrey] and he helped us get the incorporation in place to meet the deadline.

Godfrey pointed out that they needed a name for the legal work. Niki responded with the first name that came into his mind, 'The Opera Festival Association of Toronto,' and the deed was done. In two days they had a board, chaired by Lorimer Massie, had raised the necessary guarantees, and persuaded Ernest Rawley, manager of the Royal Alexandra Theatre, to be general manager.

> On Saturday morning, the chairman and members of the new board went to see Mazzoleni in his office to tell him they had met all the conditions. Shelagh and I and Herman waited in the next building, watching out the window, and as soon as they came out we ran down to them and they said, 'All in, we have the festival!' It is one of those wonderful stories you remember because it was such a major event in Canada. It was a first.

And it was a first. The Opera Festival Association eventually developed into the Canadian Opera Company, the earliest of the post-war professional companies established across Canada that put down roots in their communities and made opera an essential part of the artistic life of this country.

In the new company's first festival in 1951 Niki again conducted three operas, *Figaro, Madama Butterfly,* and Gounod's *Faust.* That spring a new letter of agreement was drawn up between the conservatory and the Festival Association in which the conservatory insisted that, in view of their obligations to the school, 'Messrs. Goldschmidt and Geiger-Torel will each be available and in full charge of their respective functions for two of the operas only.'[45]

The 1952 festival held a special thrill for Niki when he conducted Mozart's *The Magic Flute* with Lois Marshall as Queen of the Night, Mary Morrison as Pamina, and Andrew MacMillan as Papageno. George Crum was assistant conductor and Irving Gutman was stage manager.

The printed program that year reflected a new lighter mood in Toronto. Designed by Niki's niece Marion Goldschmidt, with a clever cartoon-style cover and line drawings of opera characters throughout, it featured advertisements that showed Torontonians could take their opera with some humour. 'You just know Papageno is wearing Dack's Shoes,' one declared.

Gradually appreciation for the Opera School was growing in the community, partly because of the extraordinary effort Niki made to reach out to different audiences. In December 1949, he and four singers sang for the Women's Press Club Christmas party and the next day popular writer Margaret Aitken wrote in the *Telegram* that it was 'beautiful beyond words,' and went on to praise the cultural contribution being made to Canada by Arnold Walter, Herman Geiger-Torel, and Nicholas Goldschmidt. 'In their company are Canada's finest singers who would otherwise never have had the opportunity to study and develop.'[46]

In 1956 Aitken recounted the impact of a concert given at the University of Toronto's Convocation Hall on behalf of the Hungarian Relief campaign. Niki conducted a program of excerpts amid what the writer called 'moments of high drama when Nicholas Goldschmidt ... explained the meaning of the words to a Mozart song the choir sang. "In these holy halls where no traitor can hide and where we do not know revenge."'[47]

Niki's connections in the city expanded as opera was expanding, and led to engagements of a different sort. In October 1952 he conducted a concert for the German Canadian Club, and in 1957 at Massey Hall he was on the podium for a concert with a special guest artist. The occasion was the eleventh general assembly of the International Union of Geodesy and Geophysics, meeting in Toronto. The Canadian organizing committee offered their guests a concert by the CBC Symphony Orchestra, conducted by Nicholas Goldschmidt and featuring the young Canadian pianist superstar Glenn Gould playing not one but two concertos, Bach's Concerto in F Minor on the first half, and Beethoven's Fourth, the Concerto in G Major, on the second! Niki rounded out the program with Weber's Overture to *Der Freischütz, Rossignol* by Stravinsky, and *Overture to a Fairy Tale* written by Oscar Morawetz, the young fellow-Czech also resident in Toronto.[48] It was a stellar program, as brilliant as any revelations the geophysicists might have considered in their daytime deliberations.

As success followed success the press became even more enthusiastic. *Saturday Night* noted the growing importance of the Opera School to Canada as a whole, pointing out that with students coming from across the country it was more than a Toronto program.[49] The *Telegram* was so impressed with the productions that it published an editorial asserting that 'The people of Toronto owe heartfelt thanks to all those responsible for the Opera Festival,' adding that 'the fledgling opera company has opened a door of beauty and enchantment' to artists and audiences.[50]

Eric McLean, distinguished critic for the *Montreal Star*, attended the 1950 festival and raved about the 'three hits.' 'To Toronto,' he said, 'goes the credit for the first properly organized Canadian opera company which has concentrated on preparing a uniformly good production, both visually and musically, rather than import its leaders at an expense which prohibits adequate attention to the thousand details which make an opera.' He described all the 'fine voices' and the 'fresh' production, especially in *Rigoletto*, and then expressed his biggest surprise: 'Musically it was not only up to a professional standard, but surpassed the majority of operatic productions I have seen anywhere. This was the responsibility of the Royal Conservatory's Nicholas Goldschmidt. The conservatory orchestra knew the score, and had been painstakingly drilled in rehearsal with soloists and chorus. It was as close to flawless as it would be possible to imagine.'[51]

At the same time, the *Globe and Mail* featured a long article by Thomas Archer praising the festival, and saying, 'Mr Goldschmidt is a conductor who thoroughly understands the nature of opera. He conducts tensely, but with commendable restraint and invariable control.'[52]

A National Film Board release entitled simply *Opera School* spread the reputation of the Opera School even further. What might now be called a 'docu-drama,' it employed real singers, Marguerite Gignac and Louise Roy, playing the roles of a young singer and her roommate, and follows the course of a developing student from her first tentative steps finding her way through the old building on College Street, through coaching sessions and rehearsals to her first major role. The film took first prize at the 1952 Canadian Film Awards, and was widely reported on in the press across Canada. Niki, on his way home from a visit to Salzburg in the summer of 1951, was delighted to find it on the program when he stopped again at the Edinburgh Festival. He was even more pleased at the reception given the film, and the school.

'The film was good to see,' reported the film critic of the *Scotsman.* 'It shows that Canadians are establishing what may well be a fresh and vigorous tradition in the theatrical arts.'[53]

The reach of the opera program also began to extend beyond the big city. Very early on, Niki and Herman began touring with their singers to the smaller cities and towns of Ontario. George Crum, who was frequently the pianist for these performances, says:

> We played in places like St Catharines, and Kingston, and London, usually in what were then movie palaces, almost always named either the Capitol, the Palace, or the Grand. I remember a performance in London of *La Bohème* where Herman played the role of the Innkeeper and Niki conducted. All of the singers in that second-act scene conspired together and none of them would take the bill from the innkeeper. You remember that Rodolfo and his friends have run up this big tab and the innkeeper presents it to them for payment. Well, Herman went round from one to the other, as the music went on, and finally just burst out laughing right on stage. But despite the joking, we gave good performances and had good audiences.[54]

Huntsville is a town in Ontario's Muskoka region, famous as a recreation area; in 1954 it was one stop on the conservatory's touring circuit. The local paper noted that the visit of Nicholas Goldschmidt and singers from the Opera School 'could be described as of a pioneer nature.' It was the first visit to that town of opera. It was the first time that the singers had played to kindergarten-aged children, and the first time that they had played a matinée, two performances, for over one thousand high school students. The program featured excerpts from *Rigoletto.* The teachers, using an outline of the story, had prepared the audiences. 'Comments of the children afterwards belied any suggestion that it might have been above them,' the newspaper said. It then went on to report that 'the evening audience gave long and sustained applause,' and added that the singers were Gilles Lamontagne in the title role, Patricia Snell as Gilda, and Jon Vickers as the Duke of Mantua.[55]

And apart from the touring there was the CBC, bringing opera with these Canadian voices to every region of the country, and proving that the audience was receptive and knowledgeable. From the first broadcasts, the corporation received hundreds of letters from grateful listeners in every region of the country. One listener, pointing out that he had heard opera all over the world, commented on an early broadcast of *La Bohème*, the first full opera in the broadcast series, featuring Mary Morrison, Jimmy Shields, and Edmund Hockridge: 'It outdid anything we could ever hear from New York.'[56]

It was most important that the CBC executives were pleased with the product, so Niki welcomed a letter from Harry Boyle written the day after that first *Bohème*. 'I thought "La Boheme" ... was a beautiful piece of work ... another milestone for Canada,' he wrote, and added the all-important assurance that 'the Director General of Programmes was "thrilled" and sent his "grateful" thanks to the conductor and all who collaborated to make this another CBC triumph.'[57]

The Koerner family members, who would later play a pivotal role with the Vancouver International Festival, were early supporters. Walter Koerner wrote to Kenneth Caple at the CBC to say how much he had appreciated the broadcast of *The Bartered Bride* and later Mrs Iby Koerner sent a telegram to Niki saying, 'I enjoyed the excellent Turandot and recital congratulations and good wishes ps telegraph operator says she enjoyed it too.'[58]

Many Canadians look back on those years as a golden period in Canadian broadcasting. Niki recalls perhaps his favourite performance from that time, Lois Marshall singing the part of Leonora in *Fidelio*: 'It was the best singing of that aria that I have ever heard, from anyone, anywhere. It was the best, because it had an incredible warmth, lyricism, total control, emotion, and intelligence. It was unforgettable.'

As the Opera School and the festival developed, Niki continued his whirlwind of activity, 'continually on the move, never wasting a minute,' as Carl Morey now describes it. Students knew that Niki was impatient with anyone who came unprepared, or wasted time, but was always willing to help anyone who really wanted to learn, to do their best.

Incredibly, in between teaching, rehearsing the festival productions, touring, conducting concerts, and giving his own recitals, Niki found time through the early 1950s, working with Geiger-Torel, to conduct a series of opera excerpts and small operas. They were performed at the Hart House Theatre at the University of Toronto with a repertoire that pushed the offerings available to Toronto audiences beyond the nineteenth-century canon. New to the Toronto audiences were operas and excerpts by Gian-Carlo Menotti, Ibert, Martinu, and Kurt Weill's *Down in the Valley*, featuring Don Garrard, Alex Gray, and Jon Vickers as Brock Weaver. Mario Bernardi, who became one of Canada's most eminent conductors, shared the piano duties with Niki for that particular program in May of 1953. (In a departure from the more standard programming for the main festival at the Royal Alexandra Theatre, Niki conducted Menotti's *The Consul* as part of the festivals in both 1953 and 1954.) Ernesto Barbini joined the Opera School in 1953 as coach and conductor, primarily of the Italian repertoire, bringing his own special knowledge and temperament to the scene. Niki confirms that this represented an important addition to the school in terms of what it was able to offer to the students in class and on stage.

Choral music concerts continued throughout these busy years as Niki constantly tried to present new and substantial repertoire, for the benefit of both the singers and their audiences. A 1957 concert was a good example. Performed at the Church of the Holy Trinity, which nestles almost hidden now behind Toronto's vast Eaton Centre, it featured what John Kraglund, critic for the *Globe and Mail*, reported to be the first public performance in Toronto of Haydn's *Lord Nelson Mass*. Niki had searched out the score in Vienna the previous summer, together with that of Mozart's *Litaniae de Beata Maria Virgine*.

George Crum says about Niki and his skill with a chorus: 'He had a special gift for getting a refined sound. He had a great ear and could pick up the least wandering from the pitch. His choir always had a beautiful sound.'[59]

Those years from 1946 to the late 1950s were filled with beautiful sounds made by singers who knew they were part of something special and never forgot the experience. Many of them joined the crowd that assembled over thirty years later at Toronto's St Lawrence Centre to celebrate Niki's eightieth birthday. The commemorative book from that occasion is thick with messages of affection; two stand out as testimonials to those foundation years.

Jan Rubeš, a fellow Czech, began his letter with a description of the gifts St Nicholas brings to children in his native country. He went on: 'I met another Nicholas in a far away land ... It was the 3rd of January, 1949. I sang for him ... and he gave me his first gift; arranged for me to replace a Canadian basso ... in a CBC radio production of La Traviata. I earned my first $75.00! Many, many more gifts followed. Well, dearest Nicki, to me – and I guess to music in Canada you are the real St. Nicholas. Thank you and Happy Birthday!'[60]

And from Lois Marshall, a brief but elegant tribute that sums it all up: 'Dearest Niki: You are a shining inspiration to me and I must believe to all the aspiring singers of my generation. We never forget the glorious musical opportunities and experiences we had at the beginning of our musical lives thanks to you.'[61]

It had indeed been a momentous time for Niki. He and his colleagues from central Europe were responsible for a giant leap forward in the development of opera in Toronto and across the country. Looking back over half a century at the artistic and social development of Toronto at that time, it is tempting to stress the negative, what a chore it must have been to get things going in such a conservative and unsophisticated place. But Niki never speaks of their accomplishments in those terms. The excitement of the challenge and the satisfaction of their successes animate his conversation about those times. He talks about the singers and performers with whom he worked and who would be part of his professional life for years, and the patrons, music lovers who would assist him to realize future dreams.

Although he left the school permanently in 1957 to pursue a daring new venture in the west, through the Opera School Niki had discovered a new country, which he adopted as his own. With Shelagh by his side he became very much a citizen of Toronto, his home and his base, from which he has embarked on a multitude of artistic ventures.

5

Vision and Vicissitudes

Niki is a restless man. He needs to be occupied, preferably with a creative challenge that makes something happen. Toronto was growing, the opera program was expanding, but he still had free time and it was Vancouver, on the west coast, that filled the vacuum. The year was 1950.

Mention Niki Goldschmidt and Vancouver together and typically you will hear, 'Oh yes, there was that big festival, with a bunch of famous conductors, Karajan, Bruno Walter, and Joan Sutherland making her debut in some Mozart opera. Nothing ever like it out there before.'

Well, there was a big festival, and, yes, those names were part of it. However, there was so much more. Launched in 1958, the Vancouver International Festival featured programming with a sweep and a variety that even today would cause a stir anywhere. But long before those exciting festival years, Niki was already a summertime resource in the fast-growing city by the sea.

The story of the founding of the Vancouver International Festival parallels in its essentials the story of the Opera Festival Association of Toronto and its emergence from the Opera School; there were many similar elements, a university with key people who wanted to expand their programs, talented students eager to learn, the connections to bring it all together, and Niki with his determination that it couldn't fail.

I had this long vacation time from my duties in Toronto and I said to Shelagh, you know, I would like go out west and do something there. And again, another one of those coincidences, as if it was meant to happen. Shelagh and I had visited friends in Vancouver and not long after that I received a letter from a wonderful woman out there, Dorothy Somerset, the head of Theatre at the University of British Columbia. Within a very short time I was asked to take on music at the UBC summer school.

That's the bare framework of a story rich in its musical particulars, and its relevance to the events that followed.

The University of British Columbia boasts the most scenic location in a city full of natural splendours. Occupying the tip of Vancouver's West Point Grey, it features grand views out over the Strait of Georgia and Burrard Inlet to the coastal mountains beyond, rainforest walks, and challenging climbs down the cliffs to secluded beaches. In that setting it always attracted summer students; as early as 1938 UBC established the Summer School of the Theatre under the expert direction of Dorothy Somerset, a highly professional theatre artist described by colleagues as 'welcoming, and encouraging, a person who gave the whole program a sense of camaraderie.'[1] Painting, sculpture, and photography followed, and by 1950 the enthusiastic president of the university, Dr Norman (Larry) Mackenzie, together with Dean Geoff Andrew, was anxious to make the campus a lively summertime centre for all the arts. That meant adding dance and music, through the university's Extension Department.[2] The facilities were limited; all they had was the old auditorium and the student centre, Brock Hall, pre-war buildings only marginally suited to performance, and a collection of army huts acquired after the war. But the will was there, and Niki was adaptable. Accordingly in February 1950 his notice of appointment as Guest Director of Opera Studies for the period 3 July to 12 August was signed, allowing for remuneration of $500 plus $200 for travel expenses.[3]

In the first year or two the program was small, but enrolment increased rapidly in numbers and in quality; summer music-making at UBC flourished with Niki's involvement for almost a decade.

Not unlike his earlier experience at Stanford, Niki found that students were reluctant to sign up for the new program and he needed additional voices, especially the always-in-demand tenors. One of the students told him about a promising candidate and Niki was more than willing to hike down the cliff if it meant finding that voice: 'He told me that the likely place to find him was down at the beach, just below the campus, where this tenor always went to swim. So I said "Let's go and see." And sure enough there he was, that young man, and I told him I heard that he was a singer, a tenor, and I asked him if he would come and sing with us. He said that he would be happy to. So he came along, and helped fill in that gap in the tenor ranks.'

Speaking in the year 2001, Niki recounts the follow-up to that story:

Just a few months ago Shelagh and I went to a concert, here in Toronto, a choral concert I believe, and as we were standing at the steps just before going in I felt a tap on my shoulder. I turned and a man was there and he said, 'I haven't seen you for a long time.' I looked at him and said, 'I'm sorry, but you'll have to help me. I don't remember who you are.'

'I'm the tenor from the beach,' he told me. 'I sang in the chorus at UBC.'

I was just amazed. He is a retired businessman and he wanted to know when I am doing another choral festival. When I told him that plans are in the works he said, 'I'll be there for sure.'[4]

That one man is typical of many whose lives were touched by the music of those idyllic summers.

In spite of the focus on opera in his official title, Niki recalls more: 'We did all kinds of music, choral works, lieder, opera scenes. It was wonderful, a beautiful setting, and students who wanted to participate. In two or three years it expanded and we were giving full opera performances.'

The independence to plan as he wanted allowed Niki to concentrate on his first musical love, lieder. He had never stopped giving his own recitals, in Toronto in concert and on the CBC, but in the daily sessions at UBC there was time to talk, to pass on to the singers his sense of the music and his long acquaintance with it. He was able to tell them about the great lieder singers he heard in Vienna: Lotte Lehmann, who of course he says was unsurpassed, and Helge Lindbergh and Gerhard Hüsch (who was also a famous Wolfram in *Tannhäuser* at Bayreuth). These were more than just tales of past glories; they were part of the teaching. In particular there was an important lesson from a concert he had heard given by Elizabeth Schumann, accompanied by Richard Strauss:

'It was a Richard Strauss evening. There is a famous song called *Ständchen* [Serenade; Niki sings the opening bars as he recreates the scene]. There comes a climax toward the end, and when Richard Strauss played it for her he doubled the bar with the high note at the climax, to give it more emphasis. I have never forgotten it. Ever since, when I have taught this song to students, I have told them to double it up, and when they say that it's not in the score I just tell them that I heard it from Richard Strauss himself playing for Elizabeth Schumann, so if it is good enough for them it is good enough for you too.'[5]

This was the kind of rare insight that made the UBC program exceptional.

The conditions were not always ideal, however. Niki's very first lieder recital at the university, given in one of the huts and attended by the elite of the university administration, had a decidedly comic aspect.

> There was the president, Larry Mackenzie, and Gordon Shrum [dean of Graduate Studies] and Geoff Andrew, who all came along to see what I would do, how I worked. They had never seen me give a recital before and didn't know what to expect. It was noon hour and it was very hot. And, there were thousands of mosquitoes, all buzzing around me. So as I sang and played, every two bars or so were punctuated by the sound of me slapping at those mosquitoes as they landed on my hands and arms.

Not an auspicious beginning, but the summer program flourished and by 1956 Aksel Schiotz, the great Danish tenor, Hans Busch, director of the Opera School at Indiana University and a frequent director in New York, and Mario Bernardi had all joined Niki on staff.

Dr. Bryan Gooch, pianist and scholar, was a young student right out of high school at the time, working for Niki doing whatever jobs were necessary. He describes the effect of the music program on the students: 'We all went to as much as possible, noon-hour concerts, and evening recitals at Brock Hall. We would spill out onto the terraces at intermission and talk about the music. One summer Aksel Schiotz sang the *Winterreisse,* and there was so much else, we heard a lot of music by the end of the summer.'[6]

The opera repertoire expanded; in 1955 Niki conducted the Vancouver premiere of Menotti's *The Consul,* featuring soprano Theresa Gray and baritone Don Garrard. Milla Andrew, who went on to study in Toronto and made a distinguished career in Britain and Europe, was also in that production. *Cosi Fan Tutte* followed in 1956, and the following summer the double bill of *The Medium* and *Gianni Schicchi.*

For the participants it was an opportunity to learn a new repertoire, and to be involved with all aspects of production. (Milla Andrew is listed, for example, in a singing role and assistant to the stage director.)

George Zukerman, bassoonist and impresario, is another in the long list of Canada's artists and arts managers who had their start under

Niki's tutelage. Zukerman describes himself as a 'brash youngster' in the 1950s in Vancouver, and his first association with Niki was as a member of the orchestra for the production of *Cosi*. With all its short-comings – an inexperienced pick-up orchestra, primitive stage condi-tions, and young singers – that production left happy memories. 'What an extraordinary love of Mozart he inculcated in all of us,' writes Zuker-man. 'What a joy it was to be a wind player in Niki's passionate Mozart.'[7]

And for a substantial part of the audience, particularly the summer students studying in other disciplines, Niki's concerts of sacred music (including Mozart's *Coronation Mass,* and the *Lord Nelson Mass* of Haydn), the operas, and the recitals opened up an entirely new musical landscape.

Writer Ernie Perrault later wrote about those years, 'Audiences packed the auditorium to listen to such difficult and unusual works as Menotti's 'The Consul' brilliantly performed and handsomely staged.'[8]

Niki, of course, was always looking to make his programs exciting, challenging for everyone. One summer he decided that it was time to do a concert version of excerpts from Mozart's *Magic Flute,* a plan that was greeted with considerable scepticism. Dr Lawren Harris, the famous painter and member of Canada's Group of Seven, was a friend of the Goldschmidts, and a supporter of the summer school. He warned against this latest scheme, as Niki remembers with a smile.

> I did a concert performance of the *Magic Flute*, with full orchestra, and of course it had quite a high budget. Lawren Harris told me, 'No one will come!' But I was determined. So I went out and found the singers and we did it and it was lovely, and we turned away I think about one hundred peo-ple, there was such a crowd. Even Lawren Harris didn't have a ticket! The next morning Dr Shrum came to me and said 'Congratulations.' I thanked him. And then he said, 'It was wonderful, we had a full house!' Nothing about the music, only about the tickets, that meant revenue!

The *Vancouver Sun* termed it a 'good production,' and assured the public that 'opera enthusiasts who sat through the hot weather in the UBC auditorium to hear Nicholas Goldschmidt and his summer stu-dents were well repaid.'[9]

Bryan Gooch sums up the experience of those summers:

> Niki was very demanding, but in the right way. I remember playing for the final rehearsal for the *Coronation Mass*. It was in one of those old huts and we were all crowded in, the chorus and Niki, and I was playing away on an

old upright piano. Suddenly I could feel Niki's eyes on me, and I didn't want to look up. Finally I did and saw those eyebrows going up and down. I asked him if there was a problem. 'Bryan,' he said. 'There is a great difference between sentiment and sentimentality, and you are too young to be in love.' I had just been emoting, too much rubato and it was really schmalz! When I reminded Niki of this the next year he said, 'Oh I never said such a thing.' But I told him, 'You did and you were right.'

It was an example of his candour, of his intuition about what is right, and insisting on it. Niki could be impatient, but at the end he always said thank you. I never heard anyone complain that they didn't feel valued. He had an enthusiasm that came from deep inside him, that you could see in his eyes. It was an invaluable experience for a young aspiring musician.[10]

For Niki and Shelagh UBC meant new friends, many of whom became long-term 'old friends.'

In the first summers, they stayed in a residence on campus, where one of those long-term and long-distance friendships began. As Shelagh tells it:

> After the evening rehearsals we would go back to the residence with some of the students and I would make tea or hot chocolate and perhaps some sandwiches, and they could all relax. And one night we heard some music coming from down the hall. When we went to investigate we found there were six students from Ethiopia; as it turned out some were nephews of then-emperor Haillie Sellassie. One, Tafara Deguefree, became a dear friend and we visited him in Addis Ababa several years later. And in fact, he was sitting in our living room in Toronto in 1974 when the news came of the revolution in Ethiopia.[11]

Niki's musical presence extended beyond the campus into the city, where he made connections and put down musical roots that would bloom before the decade ended into a great international musical celebration. As early as 1950 he was heard on CBC Vancouver conducting Menotti again, this time *Old Maid and a Thief* in a broadcast originating from the Mayfair Room in the Hotel Vancouver. He demonstrated, as Norman Newton reported in his radio review, 'great respect for the music and the same humility before the unity of the idea (the fusion of words and music) that Goldschmidt has always shown.' And Newton added that 'Goldschmidt is a better conductor than anyone we have out here at the moment.'[12]

Also in 1950 Niki conducted his first of several summer symphony concerts at the Malkin Bowl under the giant cedars and firs in Vancouver's spectacular Stanley Park. Sponsored by the BC Electric Company, the concert series was a favourite with Vancouver audiences, and after his debut Niki was re-engaged for the following 1 July in a letter from the manager that praised his 1950 appearance as a 'great success.'[13]

There were lieder recitals on the CBC, and a full radio presentation of Douglas Moore's *The Devil and Daniel Webster,* in June of 1953, starring Ernest Adams, Milla Andrew, Don Garrard, and Harry Mossfield.

Niki also conducted the Vancouver Symphony on more than one occasion. In 1951 he opened the orchestra's season on a Sunday afternoon in the old pre-renovation Orpheum Theatre, joined by Lois Marshall, who had recently graduated from the conservatory in Toronto and was yet to make her New York debut. The Vancouver program included the famous first-act aria from *Fidelio,* which the *Vancouver Sun* reported was sung with 'resonant tones and dramatic power' and met with 'sustained applause.' The reviewer remarked that 'Mr. Goldschmidt gave proof of his knowledge ... the epic sweep of Brahms' C Minor Symphony was a crowning triumph.'[14]

The appreciation for Niki's work in Vancouver was leading him beyond the confines of the summer courses.

> One evening Geoff Andrew took me down to Stanley Park, and we were sitting on the grass watching a performance of a musical, and he said to me, 'What do you think of this?' and I answered, 'You may not know it but this equals anything that one can see in the Vienna woods in the summer. Do you know how terrific this place is? As a matter of fact, it is so beautiful, with the campus and this park and everything. There should be a festival here.' And he thought that was a very good idea.

It was a new thought for a city so young, one that in less than seventy years had grown out of the forest and the ashes of a devastating 1886 fire that had destroyed every structure in the pioneering community.

But youth is bold, so discussions exploring the possibilities of a festival continued, centred at UBC. In 1956, under the direction of Dr John Friesen, the Department of University Extension published a brochure advertising its plans for a 'Summer Festival of the Arts' featuring outdoor sculpture exhibitions, a children's play, a new staging of Shakespeare's *A Midsummer Night's Dream,* chamber music, and Niki's full program of lieder recitals, choral music, and opera, with the emphasis on Mozart in honour of the two-hundredth anniversary of the composer's birth. But the problem was the same as in Toronto. UBC did not have the desire to get into the festival business.

So, in 1954, Niki produced his first-ever comprehensive plan for a major civic festival; it is a blueprint (modified to suit different communities) that has served him and Canada well for half a century.

This first iteration contained all the details for an ambitious festival to be situated at UBC celebrating the 'Mozart' year in 1956, and designed to 'pool as many resources of the community and the university as possible.' The plan unequivocally puts forward the philosophy and the vision realized in the Vancouver International Festival (VIF) only a few years later. Niki believed, and told his colleagues, that any festival in Vancouver had to headline international stars in order to attract the attention of the public and press. At the same time demonstrable depth and quality were essential. He suggested securing the 'services of a Tyrone Guthrie, a world-famous string quartet, together with the Vancouver Symphony and a University and community chorus ... famous musicologists and historians of art,' together with special exhibits and activities related to Mozart's time.

He went on to lay out a sample program incorporating all of those elements, and featuring performances by Vancouver's famous Theatre Under the Stars, a film festival, two concerts of music by Canadian composers, plays, opera, and symphony concerts. With his usual flair he added, 'One could perhaps even make use of the Swimming Pool and engage for daily afternoon performances an outstanding water ballet.'

The plan is remarkably complete, with a full roster of master classes, excursions, and youth activities, a projected budget, and a structure that would mark it as the 'start of an annual Vancouver or British Columbia summer festival of music and drama – let us say on the scale of Edinburgh or Salzburg.' The festival was to have its own incorporated organization with a committee for which Niki laid out his prescription for a perfect board, 'comprising the best brains, the most enthusiastic supporters, the most learned minds and the finest talent to be found in British Columbia and Canada.'[15]

The projected budget showed expenses at $107,200; revenues from carefully calculated ticket and program revenues were estimated at $64,000, leaving a deficit of $43,200. The use of the term 'deficit' was understood differently in the 1950s than it is today. Current budgeting practice shows all expected revenues, including donations, sponsorships, and grants on the revenue side. A 'deficit' is declared only when expenditures exceed that total revenue. But in the 1950s any dis-

crepancy between income earned at the door and expenditures consti-
tuted a deficit, an undesirable state of affairs. Public support for the
arts at that time was viewed as an afterthought, a kind of 'handout' to
cover failure, rather than as a legitimate participation by the public in
the cultural and artistic life of the nation's communities. This way of
interpreting accounts was very different from Europe, and it had considerable relevance some years later at the Vancouver International
Festival.

Although the 1956 Mozart Festival was never realized in its complete
form, twenty-two thousand people did attend the cultural events at UBC
that summer, and the momentum began building toward a major
festival for the city. Important philanthropists like the Koerner family,
Mary Roaf, president of the influential Community Arts Council of Vancouver, Kenneth Caple, regional director of the CBC, and Dal Grauer,
president of the BC Electric Company and a key figure, joined the
discussions.

With a determination usually associated today only with Olympic bids,
the committee members promoted the festival theme wherever and
whenever they could. To show his commitment, Dal Grauer made a
foundation pledge of $25,000, and by 1956 the Vancouver Festival Soci-
ety was a reality, with Niki as Artistic and Managing Director. Niki told
the board that 'the only way to start was to get the biggest, most important international figure to open it.' And he delivered on his own
advice. The first Vancouver International Festival premiered on Saturday, 19 July 1958 at the Orpheum Theatre with a concert featuring the
Vancouver Symphony and Maureen Forrester, all conducted by world-
renowned Bruno Walter! It had taken two trips to California and all
Niki's negotiation skills to attract such a brilliant headliner.

Aided by an introduction from a member of the festival's board, he
visited Walter in Beverly Hills, meetings that Niki calls 'the most exciting
in my life.'

It is impossible to overstate Niki's veneration of Bruno Walter. He
speaks about him with an extraordinary intensity. Their conversations
were like a series of life lessons that are recognizable in the way Niki has
lived out his musical career. 'I saw him in Vienna many times, of course,
and I fell in love with *Orpheus and Eurydice* when I heard him conduct it
at Salzburg in the late twenties. It was magical. And I said to myself then
that someday I wanted to meet that man!'

He had to wait nearly three decades, and until Walter had turned
eighty, for the opportunity.

Bruno Walter had an escalator arrangement on the stairs in his house, and I will never forget how awestruck and excited I was as I watched him coming slowly down to meet me.

He invited me in to his study and we sat down to talk. Those conversations at his home and later when he came to Vancouver are among the most treasured possessions of my life that I will never lose and never forget.

Their talks ranged over Walter's experiences as a conductor, capturing that direct connection to late nineteenth- and early twentieth-century music-making in Europe that was fast slipping away. They were endowed with the lessons of a full life in music.

Niki was especially impressed by one story that captured Walter's philosophy toward adversity.

Bruno Walter told me that when he was an assistant to Gustav Mahler himself, at the Vienna State Opera, it was during the time when Vienna expressed without hesitation very strong anti-Semitism. Mahler and Walter were both Jewish, and Mahler helped his assistant to do some conducting on his own. Every time Walter conducted he got the worst reviews possible from the critics who were not friendly to Jews. He was already twenty-six or twenty-seven years old and became absolutely desperate. One day he went to Mahler to tell him that he couldn't stand it any longer, all this terrible criticism, and, that he thought he should give up. And Mahler turned to him and said 'Don't you dare. Show them through deeds what you can do and you will succeed.' Bruno Walter told me that he never forgot those ten seconds, that they made him realize that he had talent and that critics could never destroy him if he worked hard.

Walter's great attachment to the music of Bruckner led to a more philosophical discussion:

Bruno Walter said, 'I will tell you about Bruckner. You know there was a time in Munich, I was about forty-three or forty-four, and I was terribly ill and had developed serious pneumonia. In fact I thought that I was going to die. But after a very long period I recovered. And you know, when I got well again I understood Bruckner.' It was incredible to hear a man of that kind say that to me, 'I understood Bruckner.' Bruckner had this enormous religious feeling, dedicating much of his music to God, and Bruno Walter discovered his own belief in that music. I am a believer too; it doesn't matter what you believe in, but it is the believing that is sustaining.

The subject of the young conductors of the day elicited another lesson in real musicianship. Again, Niki recalls vividly what he now calls one of the most profound statements he has ever heard. 'I had said to him that there were some very good new conductors coming up and he said to me, "Yes, there are some great talents but there is one problem. Some of them take all the time to memorize the scores, and that leaves them no time to memorize the music."'

Niki continues, 'That is not easy to understand. It is not a thought that you can explain to anyone. I think it takes a real professional musician to comprehend what he meant and only if he really wants to understand it. But it is one hundred per cent true. If you have to concentrate all the time on memorizing the score you are not reading between the lines to hear the music.'

And thinking about great music led to Walter's comments about Mozart and the problem with performers and conductors who fail to understand his depth and complexity, with less than satisfactory results. Niki had the opportunity to hear first hand what Walter meant.

> He invited me to sit in at a coaching session he was giving to Van Cliburn, on a Mozart concerto. Who could refuse such an opportunity? So I sat down in the corner, and Van Cliburn began to play. Bruno Walter interrupted him, and said, 'Why are you so nervous? Relax. You know, when you play Mozart it is all there. You don't need to do anything, but trust the music and listen to it. It's all there.' So Van Cliburn started again and I must tell you that it was totally different after that one sentence. He had been over-playing the music; too much emotion, everything forte, and I had thought that he certainly needed coaching. But Bruno Walter didn't tell him how to play, or correct specific bars. He just referred to the music but gave him the overall concept, the sense that he needed to respect the music. It was all he needed.

On that first visit to California, Niki spoke about his plans for the festival in Vancouver, and expressed the hope that Walter might consider participating, adding that he would not press for an answer, but would come back again, which he did, two months later. 'The second time I was more comfortable, and he asked me to give him more detailed plans for the festival. "Who will sing?" he asked. And I told him that for Brahms's *Alto Rhapsody* I was planning to have Maureen Forrester. "Oh, that's wonderful, we did Mahler's Second together," he exclaimed right away. And then he said, "When is it?" And I gave him the dates and he said, "I'll come!"'

From that moment the festival was on. 'He came twice to Vancouver. I learned from him. Just watching him was worth six years of academy studies, because he was very firm but not a dictator. He knew what he wanted and he knew how to convey that to the orchestra. His eyes were benevolent. They expressed the score and the orchestra adored him.'[16]

And so the Vancouver International Festival was born, an astounding four-week extravaganza that left even the sceptics breathless. The dedication ceremony at 3:00 p.m. on 19 July in the Orpheum Theatre was a glittering affair featuring George London and the Vancouver Bach Choir and Vancouver conductor John Avison. Platform guests included the mayor, members of the board, and Sir Ernest MacMillan. But Niki was not among them, nor was his name mentioned in the special program! John Kraglund, visiting critic from Toronto's *Globe and Mail,* commented on the omission, saying, 'It was as though someone dedicated the Stratford Festival without mentioning Tyrone Guthrie.'

Kraglund went on to give Bruno Walter a rave review for his opening concert. He remarked on the presence of royalty in the person of Princess Margaret, and Chairman Brooke Claxton and board members of the Canada Council, the federal agency recently established to support the arts.[17]

It was a dazzling launch, followed by a series of events featuring artists and works that have become legendary in musical circles. There was a line-up of extraordinary recitals: Glenn Gould playing Bach's *Goldberg Variations,* Maureen Forrester and Lois Marshall each with her own program, Aksel Schiotz singing Schubert's great song cycle *Die Schöne Müllerin,* duo pianists Vronsky and Babin, Leopold Simoneau and Pierrette Alarie in a joint recital. Every evening offered another special offering: Lois Marshall and Glenn Gould with the CBC Vancouver Chamber Orchestra in an all-Bach program, Glenn Gould and the Vancouver Symphony playing Beethoven, and the Verdi *Requiem* conducted by William Steinberg with a quartet of singers that seems like an artistic director's fantasy, but was wonderfully real: Lois Marshall, Maureen Forrester, Jon Vickers and George London.

The board wanted something 'in the popular vein,' and with Niki's customary refusal to compromise on quality he went for the best: the Oscar Peterson Trio, the Jack Teagarden sextet, and André Previn in concert.

The centrepiece of the festival, and the production for which it remains most famous, was Mozart's *Don Giovanni,* conducted by Niki and directed by Gunther Rennert, the famous intendant of the Stuttgart Opera, with a cast that made the production an international sensation.

With one memorable exception it was all-Canadian. The great George London sang the title role, Leopold Simoneau was Don Ottavio, Jan Rubeš was Leporello, and the import was Joan Sutherland, making her North American debut in the role of Donna Anna.

The story of how Niki came to engage the young Ms Sutherland differs from account to account. In her autobiography, the great soprano says that Niki had 'seen and heard me at Glyndebourne and engaged me.'[18] Niki insists that he actually held an audition at London's Wigmore Hall, where he heard her and hired her at once. But the circumstances of her hiring are unimportant; what counted was the result. Leopold Simoneau calls it 'a particular occasion when he showed his exceptional artistic flair.'[19] Bruno Walter came to the dress rehearsal and pronounced Ms Sutherland 'the best Donna Anna I have ever heard.'

The reviews were ecstatic – as Joan Sutherland wrote, 'enough to turn one's head!' John Kraglund, writing in the *Globe and Mail,* commented on the first-class performances, especially Joan Sutherland, while the *Vancouver Sun* praised the entire opera, adding a story about conductor William Steinberg, who 'made the sacrifice' of catching a 6:30 a.m. flight in order to attend the opening and confirmed that it was 'certainly worth it.'[20]

Don Giovanni was given six sold-out performances over two weeks. In between were the concerts already mentioned, and, incredibly for a city where the majority of the population in the summer could usually be found at the beach or in a sailboat, there was much more!

An eclectic festival on the Edinburgh model, the VIF also featured dance; in 1958 it was the National Dancers of Ceylon. The great French mime artist Marcel Marceau gave ten performances in the Georgia Auditorium, a creaky old venue where audience and performer gasped for air in the summer heat. In the same venue the festival presented another unusual event for Canada at that time, the premiere of a Canadian theatre piece commissioned by the festival. Lister Sinclair's *The World of the Wonderful Dark,* a play with music, based on West Coast Native themes, starred Toronto actor Barry Morse. It met with a mixed response, but did demonstrate a commitment on Niki's part to making the festival more than a succession of imported turns!

One of Niki's first projects involving contemporary Canadian composers took place at that 1958 Vancouver festival. A competition, to which composers were invited to submit scores, it unfortunately did not attract the number of expected entries. Despite the disappointing

response, the jury members, conductor Geoffrey Waddington and composers Claude Champagne and Aaron Copland, meeting in Niki's house
in Toronto, chose Paul McIntyre's cantata *Judith* as the winner of the
$1000 prize. The work was given a major performance on 10 August at a
concert conducted by William Steinberg (on a program that also featured guest artists Szymon Goldberg and William Primrose). The principals for the cantata were actor Leo Ciceri as narrator and Lois Marshall
in the title role. John Beckwith, writing in *Canadian Music Journal*, was
not entirely complimentary about the piece as a whole, finding it lacking in musical focus. Nevertheless, he reported that 'Mr. Steinberg gave
a good clear reading; the chorus and Leo Ciceri and Lois Marshall
seemed alive to their task. The performers indeed elicited a few cheers
from the festival audience, nice to hear after a new Canadian work.'[21] In
subsequent years the festival dropped the competition idea, but directly
commissioned composers to write for specific concerts.

Apart from cantatas, opera, chamber music, recitals, theatre, and the
rest, crowds were filling the Vogue Theatre three times a day to see more
than seventy screenings of feature films, documentaries, children's and
experimental films carefully selected from over three hundred entries
and representing twenty-eight different countries. The film section met
the high standards set for the festival as a whole, opening with the
Cannes award-winner from Russia, *The Cranes Are Flying*, and continuing
with Kurosawa's *Throne of Blood*, based on the Macbeth story, to name
only two of what remains an amazing list for its time or any time. The
film festival was a substantial component of the VIF through Niki's tenure into the 1960s, and nothing like it was seen in Vancouver again until
the early 1980s when the present festival began screenings.

During that month in the summer of 1958 the sun shone every day on
Vancouver, the evenings were warm, and people were out on the streets,
going from venue to venue, and from party to party. Board members
and friends of the festival arranged more than thirty receptions and dinners, entertaining visiting artists and supporters.

Bruno Walter later wrote to his friend Walter Stresemann about his
Vancouver experience, 'The music-making there filled me with happi-
ness as did the magnificent landscape.'[22] The entire affair was declared
a huge success, and before the curtain came down on the final performance of the dancers from Ceylon, Niki was on the phone making plans
for the next summer.

By this time he had resigned his position in Toronto, where the continuing reorganization of the conservatory and the Faculty of Music and

their relationship to the opera festival left him uncertain about his role there in the future. Vancouver offered the opportunity to make things happen, and he took it, not wasting a day looking back, never second-guessing himself.

And Vancouver wasn't looking back either, rushing the brand-new Vancouver Civic Auditorium to completion in time for the 1959 festival. Designed in the concrete and glass hard-edged style of the day, it threatened to upstage even the most stunning line-up of artists. After the opening concert, in fact, the *Vancouver Sun* raved about the 'Style Show at Festival,' assigning the featured artist two lines in paragraph four of a quarter-page devoted to flags, foyers, and fashion.[23] But the headliner could not be ignored, for it was none other than Herbert von Karajan, conducting an all-Beethoven program.

It was a tremendous coup on Niki's part to have persuaded his old schoolmate to come to Vancouver, and again connections were everything. At first Karajan was difficult to pin down. Would he come or not? Niki could not get an answer. Then another of those lucky coincidences came his way. Gunther Rennert, after directing *Don Giovanni* the previous summer, was in Salzburg with Karajan and advised the maestro to accept the Vancouver invitation, on the basis that the scenery was too beautiful to be missed!

Working with his old friend made Niki's job as artistic director more exciting than perhaps he might have wished. On the all-important opening night, Karajan failed to show up until just moments before curtain time. Niki was frantic, pacing back and forth when the maestro arrived, with his assistant behind taking his cloak and handing him his baton. When Niki confronted him, Karajan was unruffled. 'Why are you so upset?' he said. 'I still have a minute. One of the patrons loaned me his plane and I flew up to see Alaska!'[24]

A second confrontation with Karajan occurred at rehearsal for the next concert on which violinist Betty-Jean Hagen was slated to play the Beethoven Violin Concerto. A winner of several prestigious international prizes, she was already a veteran of appearances with many of the world's great orchestras. But Karajan was dismissive of this young Canadian, completely ignoring her at the rehearsal, turning away, making no effort to discuss the music or accommodate himself to her.

Niki was not pleased:

It was incredibly rude. Later at a garden party he said to me, 'How can you dare to put someone on the stage with me like this girl?' Just because she wasn't an Oistrakh or a Francescatti, someone he knew. And I told him, 'She may not be good enough for you, but you are very good for her. And that is the whole idea. I brought you here because I am a great admirer of yours and because it is important for us, for our artists to hear you and work with you and others like you.'

For the violinist it was a difficult experience, but she turned it to her own advantage. She told Niki that she was just going to ignore the ego beside her and play as she felt she could and should. To Niki that was the right thing to do. 'Something clicked, and it turned into a wonderful performance. So although I felt a little regret that I had him there, I was proud of the way it turned out.'

Karajan also caused some grief with the local Musicians' Union. Niki had carefully established good working arrangements with all the unions by meeting each group in turn, laying out for them the festival plans, before any public announcement. In fact, only a small number of the festival board members had the information before the unions. It worked well, until word got out about Karajan's fee. 'The Musicians' Union called me down, to put me on the carpet, because I was paying Karajan $10,000 for the two concerts. That was a lot of money and an unheard-of fee in Vancouver at that time. But I told them, "Maybe we don't do the same for our own people, but look what Mr Karajan and Bruno Walter have done for your orchestra. I can't even tell you what it is worth. And if I had the opportunity to do it again, I would."'

The union officials were so angry that they threatened to block Karajan's appearance. Niki, ever impatient with negative thinking, ignored them. 'It was a narrow, provincial attitude,' he says, disdainfully.

The disputes about imports spilled over into the theatrical community, where there were complaints about the appearances of Eva Le Gallienne and Viveca Lindfors in John Reich's production of Schiller's *Mary Stuart*. The issue here wasn't money; it was the matter of importing actors when Canadians were available. Ms Le Gallienne's stunning success on Broadway in the same play held no sway with the opponents to her appearance in Vancouver; the argument was part of a new national awareness by Canadians, emerging from the influence of Great Britain and Empire, only to find themselves overwhelmed by American cultural output.

Niki detests the term 'nationalism,' viewing it as inward-looking and limiting, while on the other hand 'patriotism' he sees as expansive, involving a sense of devotion to one's country and a desire to have it participate fully in world affairs, including cultural ones. His philosophy has always been to put the best of Canadian artists on the stage with the best from elsewhere. The result of combining that artistic goal with an astute sense of what will sell is productions like *Mary Stuart,* starring the two leading ladies of the stage at that time together with Canadians Bruno Gerussi, Ivor Harries, Robert Christie, and Lloyd Bochner.

In fact, the controversy in 1959 was short-lived. The detractors had their opinions, but others felt differently. As one member of the orchestra explained it, 'The festival brought an international standard of musical excellence to Vancouver that was non-existent before, and contributed a great deal to the future developments. For me, the experience of working with the great conductors of that era, such as Bruno Walter, von Karajan, and William Steinberg, was the highlight, that was an opportunity that was unimaginable for young Canadian orchestral players!'[25]

The festival's continuing ties with the university were also beneficial to all parties, according to a report prepared by John Friesen, director of University Extension. UBC students took part in the Bruckner Mass and in the opera chorus, and former students were involved in the crew and cast of *Mary Stuart.* The university hosted several festival events, and noon-hour recitals, lectures, and public discussions with the leading guest artists such as pianist Rudolf Firkusny and the dancers of the Ballet Espagnol were open to the students. Most welcome was the $2500 given by the festival for scholarships to the Summer School of the Arts.[26]

The offerings for 1959 included recitals, dance companies from Spain and Japan, a dozen large concerts (including Niki conducting the festival orchestra and chorus in Vivaldi's *Gloria* and the Bruckner *Mass in F Minor*), comedienne Anna Russell, the Montreal Bach Choir, the Hungarian Quartet premiering Harry Somers's String Quartet no. 3, and a full film schedule with sixty screenings – the quintessential Goldschmidt festival.

And Niki appeared everywhere, or so it seemed. Even with his own work, he found time to be out and about, hunched in a seat listening to an orchestral rehearsal, or backstage at the opera wishing everyone well, or circulating among the patrons at intermission, lighting up the lobbies with his enthusiasm, with his own delight in it all. 'Isn't it marvellous?' he would ask. 'You love it, yes?'

The opera in 1959 was Niki's old favourite, Gluck's *Orpheus and Eurydice.* In casting the title role he came across a picture in an opera magazine of European contralto Kerstin Meyer. Niki called Karajan in Berlin to inquire about the singer. Karajan told him. 'It's not a beautiful voice, but what a stage presence! If you can get her, engage her right away.' And he did. She sang the title role, opposite Mary Costa as Eurydice and Marguerite Gignac as Amor, in a production given a stunningly contemporary look in the design of Donald Oenslager. Again, it was memorable and Niki never regretted Karajan's advice on Ms Meyer. 'It was not a perfect voice, but on stage she was simply incredible. It was unforgettable.'

John Kraglund called Kerstin Meyer's singing 'truly moving' and the whole production one 'of which the VIF or any festival should be proud.'[27]

Howard Taubman of the *New York Times* called it a major-league production that 'justified the Vancouver festival calling itself International.'[28] And so was the final symphony concert, an all-Mozart program with Maria Stader, soprano, and conducted by Bruno Walter.

Niki remembers every detail of that event, especially one revealing moment. 'They were rehearsing the so-called Linz symphony and at one point Bruno Walter stopped the orchestra. There was a passage he wasn't happy with and the orchestra was struggling. Then he leaned over to Jack Kessler, the concertmaster, and said, "I think the bowing isn't right here. It must be all up-bow." And then he turned to the orchestra and said, "Here I am, eighty-two years old, and I have just learned how this passage should be played!" Isn't that an incredible lesson? I loved that man!'

The 1959 concert-goers were treated to Herbert von Karajan at the first concert and Bruno Walter at the last. In between, they dressed up for the queen, who came to town and officially gave the Civic Centre her own name. It became the Queen Elizabeth Theatre at a gala concert on 15 July at which Niki shared the stage with Sir Ernest MacMillan, and soloists Betty-Jean Hagen and Lois Marshall. Altogether it was another exciting summer for the audience, the board members, and the artists and staff of the VIF.

It was also an expensive one, with production costs at about half a million dollars, a substantial, and some would have said scary, sum for that time. As plans for the third festival were rolled out, *Maclean's* magazine gave a preview of the kinds of arguments and confusions that were to come. Calling it 'Vancouver's bold but shaky International festival,' Ray Gardner referred to losses in the first two years on the order of $150,000 to $200,000. These figures were not analysed in the article, but subsequent financial reports show that the calculations were made exclusive of grants and donations. The first festival did indeed have a net shortfall, of just over $90,000, less than 20 per cent of the total budget. In its second year the festival netted a small profit.[29] After praising the upcoming program, Gardner wondered if Vancouver would support the festival, saying that it 'must pack 'em in or pack it up.' Niki evidently took strong exception to this suggestion, with a typical quote. 'Nonsense! This is not a do-or-die year. Not at all. This is the year we *do*!'[30]

And what they did! It was another exciting line-up, with special events that had an impact on Niki's life, both musical and personal, far beyond Vancouver. The 1960 souvenir program opens with a photograph and message from Canada's governor-general of the day, His Excellency Major-General Georges P. Vanier. His greeting is brief, but elegant, reading in part, 'May this Festival leave both performers and spectators more complete human beings, filled with harmony and heightened sensibilities.' Niki treasures those words, and the handsome portrait of this distinguished soldier and diplomat whose bearing and career were so similar to those of Niki's beloved Uncle Paul.

As to the program itself, the overall mix was familiar, but the individual events were startling, even for an audience becoming accustomed to summertime delights. Kerstin Meyer was back, in recital, in concert with the festival symphony orchestra conducted by William Steinberg, and in an inventive collaboration with Glenn Gould featuring an all-Schoenberg concert. Violinist Jaime Laredo was a new face, as were the dancers of Jerome Robbins's company and Jean Erdman in her modern dance recital. Two days were devoted to the music of Canadian composers, while Hal Holbrook in his Mark Twain monologues and the Kingston Trio filled out the lighter side.

And then came the centrepieces, stunning then and still meaningful in terms of Canada's artistic history:

Noah's Flood, by Benjamin Britten. First performance in North America.

Madama Butterfly by Puccini, starring Teresa Stratas, with Louis Quilico, Richard Verreau, and Patricia Rideout.

The Peking Opera in its first North American appearance.

The New York Philharmonic Orchestra, conducted by Leonard Bernstein.

Noah's Flood, descended from the medieval Chester miracle plays, was premiered in 1958 at Britten's own festival in Aldeburgh, where Niki first heard it. Sir Kenneth Clark said of this work, 'To sit in Orford Church, Suffolk, where I had spent so many hours of my childhood dutifully waiting for some spark of divine fire, and then receive it at last in the performance of *Noye's Fludde*, was an overwhelming experience.'[31]

Niki says simply, 'I love that work.' With the devout Noah, his feckless wife and her gossips, animals, and birds, and the solemn voice of God, all joined together by Britten's touching music, it is a delightful mix of spirituality and poetry and humour. For Niki, it satisfies not only his high musical standards but also the ever-pressing practical considerations. With limited professional resources required, and the opportunity for large numbers of children (and the audience) to participate, it is perfect when programing to meet local community interest.

The Vancouver production was the first of several Niki has done directed by Joy Coghill, whom he first met at UBC and who has been his friend and colleague over the ensuing decades. Joy, a lively, curly-haired actor whose energy matches Niki's, calls that first *Noah* 'a great awakening.' Delighted by all of the great artists and the variety of offerings of those early festivals that had expanded the artistic life of Vancouver in unimaginable ways, she welcomed being a part of the action. With Myra Benson, Joy was running the children's theatre school called Holiday Theatre, which allowed her to prepare the children for *Noah's Flood* for several months.

'They gradually were trained to be real animals,' she says, 'not just a lot of kids jumping around. Because we were this little production on the edge of the big festival, being rehearsed in the basement of Christ Church Cathedral, no one really bothered us. In fact no one really paid much attention to how many tickets were being sold, and of course in the church you can't quite count the seats accurately so at the opening we had this huge crowd turn up, a lot of indignant families with the festival administrator, Peter Bennett, standing on the steps having to turn people away. It was a mess, but it was a terrific success too.'[32]

Conducted by John Avison, the production featured William Reimer in the title role, Milla Andrew as Mrs Noah, with Vancouver actor John Emerson as the voice of God. Almost unnoticed in the small role as the wife of Sem was the twenty-year-old Vancouver soprano Heather Thomson, another Canadian whose talent Niki recognized early and who went on to have a successful international career.

Niki speaks of his collaborations with Joy Coghill in glowing terms, using terms like 'enchanting' and 'such an imp!' 'She has a marvellous way with the children. She knows how to keep their attention, almost childlike herself, but she is very demanding. She always treats them like professionals, and they love it.'

The show was a winner with everyone. Jack Richards in the *Vancouver Sun* described it as 'touching' and said that it had a simple beauty that left the 'adults more excited than the kids.'[33]

While the children's tale was enchanting audiences at the cathedral, there was enchantment of another kind up the street at the Queen Elizabeth Theatre where Teresa Stratas was making her debut in *Madama Butterfly*. Fresh from winning the Metropolitan Opera Auditions, she was just twenty-two years old and the critics raved. English critic Humphrey Burton, in a CBC review, praised everything about the production, except the acoustics of the hall, and said that Stratas was 'the undoubted star of the evening ... an artist of intelligence, a name to remember.'[34] The production, too, was one to remember, given a traditional treatment authentic in every detail. Niki had met the gardeners at the famous Japanese gardens at UBC, and they advised him on all matters of design and protocol; how the shoes must be turned when left at the door, what the bridge should look like. The wigs and costumes, each one wrapped in its own perfectly folded packet to avoid creasing, came from Japan, and Shelagh drove to Seattle to find an authentic rickshaw! The *Vancouver Province* was so impressed that it carried an editorial in praise of the opera, calling the staging and costumes 'first rate' and congratulating 'Nicholas Goldschmidt and all those responsible' for the festival.[35]

Patricia Rideout, who was the much-applauded Suzuki in that production, remembers it fondly.

> I remember opening night I was backstage with George Brough, the backstage coach. There was a little hole in the curtain for George to look through, to know the exact moment to give Teresa her cue to enter over the bridge ... The stage was beautiful, and the village maidens entered, all dressed in these exquisite identical kimonos. Well, as soon as the lovely ladies started across the bridge the audience went into wild applause and everything stopped! George was beside himself, not knowing when to give the cue. But you know, it was all right.[36]

The critics didn't mind. Humphrey Burton said that Niki conducted with 'care and affection' and said it was 'refreshing to find the Artistic Director of a Festival doing something actively artistic.'[37]

The third showcase event in 1960 was more than an artistic coup. It was a political and logistical triumph, given the environment of the time. The Peking Opera, or, to use its proper name, The Chinese Classical Theatre, already had a tremendous reputation in Europe when Niki began his efforts, as early as 1957, to engage the company for the VIF. It was a complicated business. First, since the United States had no commerce with Communist China, it was impossible to book the company as part of a larger North American tour. Niki not surprisingly saw that as a plus. 'What a windfall for us,' he told a reporter, anticipating the additional box office receipts from curious Americans.[38] However, local politics were not so straightforward. Vancouver had a large Chinese community, almost entirely anti-Communist. How would it react to this company from Peking? Niki and his board took no chances. In 1957, over a year before the first festival, Dean Geoff Andrew wrote to Niki in Toronto about his inquiries in the Chinese Canadian community, and reports from his contacts that 'the leaders of the Chinese Canadian Community would favour having the Peking Opera here.'[39]

With that encouragement, Niki pursued the possibilities with the Clearinghouse for International Cultural Exchange, located in Brussels. It took time, but gradually the plans came together. There was the vexing matter of the visas for the company members, but in spite of a change in government and the usual bureaucratic delays the necessary paperwork was done.

On the day of the company's arrival in Vancouver, unsigned leaflets were distributed in Chinatown urging a boycott of the show and telling the company members that they were 'welcome to come over to the side of freedom.'[40] At the same time, newspaper advertisements placed by a number of Chinese community groups from across the country labelled the company an 'instrument of Chinese propaganda.' Niki, anticipating protest, had been busy, talking to as many supporters as possible. The result was a full welcoming party at the station led by the mayor and a large number of Chinese community leaders showering the visitors with flowers and greetings, and a cavalcade of limousines and buses decorated with welcoming banners to take the visitors through the streets of the city to the hotel. It was a grand spontaneous parade and a public relations success, defusing the impact of the fifty protesters who stood in the sweltering heat (the hottest day on record in Vancouver) to shout insults at the company. Even the heat worked in Niki's favour as everyone, artists and protestors, soon went their separate ways to find a cold glass of beer.

The practical arrangement for getting the company to Vancouver had presented Niki with another formidable challenge. Scarcely two weeks before its scheduled appearance, Niki received a call from the company director, Chen Chung-Ching. 'We are in Cuba,' he said. 'And now, we are not sure how to get to Canada.' It was a dilemma. The United States would veto any suggestion that they fly over American airspace, and there was no time for a leisurely trip by sea through the Panama Canal and up the Pacific Coast. Niki was undaunted. As Shelagh says, 'Two things that Niki loves are travel and the telephone, so here he could use the one to organize the other!'

Niki was indeed on the phone at once, discovering a freighter leaving Cuba shortly for Halifax. With his usual persistence, he secured passage on that ship for the almost one hundred dancers, acrobats, instrumentalists, and singers, their costumes, props, and luggage, connecting with the train in Halifax that would bring them all across the breadth of Canada to Vancouver in time for their scheduled appearances.

Niki and the company members enjoyed each other tremendously, right from the start, in spite of differences in culture and practice! Niki recalls that in both weeks of their stay the director came to him near the end of the week, when banks in Canada still closed tight at 3 o'clock on Friday, with a brown paper bag full of cash.

Niki was astonished, but undismayed.

He told me that he had to change all these American bills into Canadian dollars so he could pay his company. It was more than $40,000. The first time we were out at UBC, and there was only the campus bank, and there wasn't much time, so I walked with him over to the bank and asked the manager there if he could change the money. Well, of course he could, but it was a great deal of money for that time for a small branch and it created a bit of a flurry. We had to wait for some time. But it was done. And all negotiated through the interpreter!

Although some critics did not quite know what to make of the eclectic mix of drama and comedy and music featured in the company's program,[41] the performances were a huge success, with tickets at such a premium that arrangements were hastily put together for an extra performance. So, Niki had taken another big gamble that had paid off, and made new friends in the bargain.

After the company left Vancouver to continue touring, Director Chen sent Niki a cable from Edmonton, saying 'Most greatful [sic] to your warm welcome and hospitality shown us during our stay in Vancouver. 1960 Vancouver International Festival significant cultural event ... Regretted passing by without meeting New York Philharmonic Orchestra directed by Conductor Bernstein and not hearing their beautiful performance ... Best regards to you and all the friends.'[42]

The Peking Opera headed back across Canada on a further tour, as the New York Philharmonic arrived in Vancouver (on its way to the Far East) for two concerts, one in the morning at the old Forum at the Exhibition grounds, for the young people, and the other a full evening program at the Queen Elizabeth Theatre.

At the Forum, Bernstein, the great communicator, enthralled his audience of 4500, most under the age of eighteen, and in the evening he thrilled the more mature audience, especially with his own playing of Beethoven's First Piano Concerto, and what Stanley Bligh in the *Vancouver Sun* called a 'brilliant' performance by the Philharmonic of Bartók's *Concerto for Orchestra.*

Altogether, the visit of the Philharmonic was an exhilarating finale to a dazzling season. Dilys Powell, writing in the *Sunday Times* of London, called the festival a 'remarkable enterprise in such a young city,' and went on to suggest that it 'is the fusion of this New World energy with Old World devotion that has made the festival possible.'[43] Others chided the city for its lack of on-the-street gala spirit. Humphrey Burton, while rhapsodizing about the festival as a whole, said that he 'didn't find this city in a particularly festive mood,'[44] and the *Vancouver Sun,* complaining about the dreary Union Jacks surrounding the terrace of the Queen Elizabeth Theatre, suggested that the city 'Run Up Some Festival Flags.'[45]

In 'doing it all' the 1960 festival ended with essentially a balanced budget,[46] but the issue of civic support for the festival became a large one in its fourth season in 1961. The overall shape was the familiar one, a few high-profile highlights, opera, popular specials, theatre, recitals, concerts, and film. The 1961 'popular' feature was a winner, a Military Searchlight Tattoo, with bands and Scottish dancers from Great Britain and across Canada that created an amazing spectacle and attracted a staggering 160,000 ticket buyers. Then there was the Red Army Chorus, which brought the audience to cheers, and tears, with its ringing rendition of *O Canada.* Making its Canadian premiere, the New York City Ballet gave eight performances of Balanchine's best-known works, while Glenn Gould was featured in two programs. On the first, an all-Bach evening, he played, conducted, and lectured on 'The Universality of Bach,' while in the second he played Brahms's Concerto no. 1 Opus 15 in D Minor, with the festival orchestra conducted by the twenty-four-year-old Zubin Mehta, described in the notes as 'A new star ... [who has]

rocketed into the musical world's orbit in recent months, and every opera glass is following his passage.'

But for Niki, the highlight of it all was the North American premiere of Benjamin Britten's new opera, A *Midsummer Night's Dream*, wich was first seen at Aldeburgh just one year before. Conducted by Meredith Davies, it starred famed counter-tenor Russell Oberlin, soprano Mary Costa, Milla Andrew, and another of Niki's inspired ideas, Joy Coghill as Puck.

'I had never paid any attention to opera until he cast me as Puck,' she says. 'Harry Horner was the director and it was very much in that Max Reinhardt style, all glitter and very dramatic. I learned a lot, and in fact from that I was engaged to play Puck at the San Francisco Opera, in quite a different style of production.'[47]

This opera, a departure from the standards of the repertoire, was more difficult for the Vancouver audience but nevertheless of the five performances one was a sell-out and two sold over 95 per cent of the seats.

But somewhere, at the centre of it all, rumblings and rumours of trouble at the VIF were beginning to surface. The press reports began to take on a defensive tone as though the reporters were expecting an outright attack on the festival while their commentaries continued to focus on the soaring attendance and generally optimistic prospects for a satisfactory financial outcome on the season.

Mike Tytherleigh, writing in the *Vancouver Province*, was complimentary to the festival, saying that 'there was something for everyone,' and everything had an audience, including the smaller, lesser-known events. And taking a larger view, he remarked that the opportunity for technicians and performers in Vancouver to work with top artists was a plus for the city. Altogether, in his opinion, Vancouver was fortunate, because 'the air fare to see these artists on their own ground would be exorbitant.'[48]

In early September the mood was promising as Niki announced next year's festival opener, Mozart's *The Magic Flute*. Niki was excited about the plans, and had consulted his mentor, Bruno Walter, about various aspects of the production, including who should conduct. Walter put down all of his thoughts in a letter written late in the fall of 1961.

Walter wrote that he was delighted that Niki was planning to do *The Magic Flute* and went on to say that he was willing to offer his own ideas and experiences with the work, including his last production with Harry Horner at the Metropolitan Opera. He then turned to the matter of a conductor.

'Besides the very rare qualification for Mozart's music,' he wrote, 'the "Magic Flute" asks for a musician with the deep understanding for the variety of its style, comprising phantastic elements, a droll kind of humor, a childlike hilarity and a most earnest lofty solemnity. Only a musician whose nature and talent combines all these elements can understand and perform Mozart's "Magic Flute." – I deliberated thoroughly and I believe I should recommend to you to undertake the task – yourself. I heard you conduct Mozart's "Don Giovanni" and found you fully at home in that task. I heard an excellent Bruckner under your baton.' And then the beloved maestro concluded with a particularly touching summation. 'I believe,' he wrote, 'that you have the inner qualities as well as the musicianship to live up to the unique demands of this unique work.'[49]

Niki treasures this last letter from his musical mentor, written just three months before Walter died in February 1962.

Meanwhile, events in Vancouver had overtaken Niki's plans for the next summer. In early November came bad news: the 1961 festival had lost just over $50,000. The unanticipated deficit came as a result of the two plays, the only offerings that failed to pull in a crowd. Jean Giradoux's *Men, Women and Angels* and Karl Wittlinger's *Do You Know the Milky Way?* were presented in the last week of the festival and had little profile. Most reviewers failed to mention them, and given their places in the line-up there was no time for special marketing or word-of-mouth build-up. This would have been especially important for *Milky Way*, a piece certainly outside the mainstream of theatrical realism and risky business for Vancouver at that time. On 10 November General Sir Ouvry Roberts, president of the Festival Society, sent a letter to the members of the festival saying that 'there is a good deal of misunderstanding about the Festival's operations' and therefore he was writing to give some facts.

He began with a comparison with the Edinburgh Festival and the more favourable position of the VIF's Scottish cousin in terms of grants, especially from the city. He went on to enumerate the many Vancouver organizations that benefited from the existence of the VIF. Then he dealt with some management issues, addressing the rumours blowing through Vancouver as the winter rains overtook the sunny autumn days.

No, the festival had not gambled on the weather with the outdoor Tattoo, having purchased the necessary insurance. No, the festival was not paying higher rates to popular attractions than commercial agents pay. No, the festival did not pay for Mr Goldschmidt's trip to Asia, it was at his own expense. Yes, the festival included some shows that make a profit to reduce the overall deficit based on other offerings.[50]

He had support. Harold Weir, writing in the *Sun*, said, 'Current gripes over the Vancouver International Festival's deficit do not appear to be wholly justified.' He warned against 'retreating from the cultural aims' of the festival, adding that 'the greatest danger that faces the festival is not the piling up of deficits ... but the temptation to lower standards of performance and presentation ... The festival is always going to cost Vancouver money. It is worth it.'[51]

However, even support from the press could not stop what now seemed inevitable. On 22 November the *Sun*, with two-inch headlines, announced, 'New Festival Boss Appointed in Shakeup,' with a subhead adding, 'Goldschmidt Drops Down.' The story following announced that at his own request Niki was giving over the role of Managing Director to Vancouver impresario Gordon Hilker, while retaining the title of Artistic Director. The festival's administrator, Peter Bennett, also resigned. The festival's president issued a statement from the board containing the usual tributes and thanks to 'these two enthusiastic and devoted workers for the Festival.' He suggested that people read the article by Harold Weir, adding that 'we have been criticized ... for putting on events that don't lose money – on the grounds that they could equally well be put on by a Commercial organization. Let me be quite clear that, for the time being anyway, we have to put on some of both the losers and the winners.' Apart from one phrase about maintaining 'certain standards,' the statement was all about money and management. It had a defensive tone, with nothing about the integrity of the festival, about the pleasure all those concerts and plays and films and the rest had given to Vancouver residents. It said nothing about future opportunities, great artists still to come and young talents to be discovered.[52]

For Niki, in spite of retaining artistic direction, it was in fact all over.

He had made his own decision, for two reasons, one that seemed like a detail but went to the heart of artistic judgment, and the other the larger issue of what the festival was about.

Well, I had been to see Darius Milhaud in California and asked him if he would come to Vancouver in 1962 and conduct a concert of his own music in honour of his seventieth birthday. He was very enthusiastic, but later he wasn't well, and asked if we could postpone it, because, as he said, 'My birthday goes on all year!' Of course it wasn't possible so that was that.

Then I received a letter from the president of the festival saying that they had decided to go ahead with the concert and had already engaged John Avison to conduct!

I was aghast. No offence to John Avison, who did a very good job, but the only interest in a program like that would be to have the composer conducting. I told them, 'You will have no one there,' and that is what happened. It was such an amateurish kind of decision.

And then the board really wanted to take the 'international' out of the festival and I was no longer interested. That's when I said good-bye.

Niki was in Vancouver for the 1962 festival, a much scaled-down affair. *The Magic Flute* was one of the few big productions, but Niki did not conduct. His audacious, daring occupation of the director's chair was finished.

So, for the sake of a shortfall that amounted to less than 10 per cent of the total budget for the year, the festival and the city allowed the foundations of what they had built together to crumble away in a series of misadventures, growing deficits, and bad press. The VIF shut down for good in 1968.

In his biography of Irving Guttman, David Watmaugh said that the festival succeeded in bringing Vancouver from 'cultural infancy to adolescence' and berated the 'small-minded Vancouverites' whom he held responsible for its demise.[53] George Zukerman recalls Niki's tenure with real joy. 'He gave us our first opera, he gave us our magnificent and extravagant first International festival. But most of all, he gave us a shared love of music and of early excellence.'[54]

Robert Creech, former musician and long-time arts administrator, puts it in a larger context: 'Today most orchestras and festivals survive because of large subsidies and sponsorship, something that was virtually non-existent in 1958 ... Of course, no one lasts in these positions forever, but if Niki had remained in control for a few more years, until someone else came along with the same vision and energy, I do believe that Vancouver would today have a summer festival which would rank with the best in the world.'[55]

In fact, a revival did take place in the summer of 2000. 'Festival Vancouver,' as it was named, looked surprisingly like the VIF, with a sweeping musical program including a Britten church opera and a tribute to Oscar Peterson, who had been on the bill in 1958!

John Friesen wrote a historical reminiscence of the VIF for the souvenir program book of the new festival. Acknowledging Niki's pivotal role in those summers half a century ago, when Vancouver's artistic life glowed as brilliantly as the sun over the Pacific, he summed up Niki's vision and what might have been, with a quote from Andre Malraux:

the mind supplies the ideas of a nation,
but what gives the idea its essential
force is a community of dreams.[56]

6

Celebrations East to West

It was the early 1960s and Niki and Shelagh were back in Toronto, in the gracious red-brick house on the hill. While Niki had no permanent position, in the brief hiatus before his next big undertaking they were never idle.

Guests came and went at Kineras, where there was always a warm welcome. For artists, tired from their incessant public appearances, the house provided a restful escape.

And such an array of visitors! Kerstin Meyer and Elisabeth Söderström, two famous Swedish singers celebrating the annual Festival of Light walking around the dining table with candles held aloft; Yehudi Menuhin doing yoga in the den, and playing his violin as he came down the stairs to join the other guests for dinner; George London, vocalizing, Aaron Copland, rather quiet compared to his old friend Leonard Bernstein. The latter was a guest one evening together with Glenn Gould. As usual when the pianist who dreaded the cold came to visit, Niki had turned up the heat and the room gradually became hotter and hotter. Perched on the back of a chair, Bernstein was holding forth in his ebullient way. Niki laughs at the memory of Bernstein, who never stopped talking. 'First he just mopped his brow with his handkerchief. Then he took off his jacket, then his tie, and he undid the top buttons of his shirt and finally threw that off too. Just about then Glenn remarked that the house seemed rather warm, and that was a very welcome signal that I could turn down the heat!'

Not surprisingly, among the many visitors Niki remembers singers most vividly, including the great Irmgard Seefried, whom he describes as the only singer who 'matched the glory of Lois Marshall.' Seefried was never as well known in North America as in Europe, but Niki speaks warmly about what he calls her 'special style' and the way in every song the words and the music matched perfectly: 'She moulded the words, like a sculpture, so that the music supported the projection. of the words. And you sensed this perfect balance; it was transporting, very touching. It brought tears to your eyes.'

The entertaining has never been limited, however, to famous artists. Groups of eight or ten good friends are invited often for good food and conversation around the oval dining table. Vincent Tovell has often been among the guests: 'Niki orchestrates it very carefully to have a nicely balanced table with people who are compatible. And Shelagh prepares a wonderful meal, simple but very elegant food. And the mix of people is always different; sometimes there are musicians, sometimes members of Niki's family from Belgium, so that often it is a bilingual occasion. It is always comfortable, and always stimulating.'[1]

But, their life was then and continues to be much more than staying home and entertaining. Both Niki and Shelagh are avid travellers; they have spent a lifetime crossing borders. During Niki's time in Vancouver he was always looking to what was happening artistically across the Pacific, frequently remarking that Vancouver was the only city in Canada to have this unique view, appreciating the potential of the 'Pacific Rim' long before that term became part of common discourse. He made several trips to Asia, one to Japan to investigate the two Japanese companies that appeared at the VIF (and where he made the contacts resulting in the loan of the costumes and wigs for *Madama Butterfly*). On that same trip William Judd from Columbia Artists commissioned him to reconnoitre the Japanese market to determine which big American artists would sell there.

In September 1961, before he had officially given up the leadership of the VIF, Niki and Shelagh made a special voyage to China in response to an invitation from the Chinese People's Association for Cultural Relations with Foreign Countries. Coming as a result of the friendships made during the North American premiere of the Peking Opera in Vancouver, it presented an extraordinary opportunity, since scarcely anyone was visiting Mao's China. It was sufficiently unusual that Norman Robertson, undersecretary of state for external affairs, wrote to Niki concerning the visit, noting that 'the appropriate officials in Hong Kong and Peking are being informed of your impending visit' and giving him the relevant names and document requirements.[2]

They entered China via Hong Kong and from there travelled by train to the border, where they met their interpreter and crossed into China on foot. 'Our interpreter was named Chu Chu, and I remember she wore a Western-style dress and hat, which we thought very strange at that time. We had our first big meal with her right there at the border and we were both struck by the fact that she gobbled it up as though she had not had such a big meal for a long time.'

In China the couple was warmly welcomed and ushered about by their hosts, eager to exhibit what they considered to be the best of Chinese arts.

The infamous Cultural Revolution was yet to come, so performances most often reflected Western influences. Niki brought back a tape of one performance of Beethoven's Ninth Symphony conducted by a Russian, with the chorale sung in Chinese. Vincent Tovell later used it on a CBC broadcast in which he and Niki talked about the arts of China.

Canadian Pacific Airlines was the improbable collaborator in another journey, the initial step toward a prospective new venture. The airline had covered the cost of transporting the costumes from Japan for the VIF, and in 1962 sent Niki on a festival fact-finding mission to one of its prime destinations, Hawaii. His job was to investigate the likelihood of mounting a festival on the island that would attract large numbers of visitors from abroad. Niki's report, reflecting his own natural optimism, proposed a festival 'To Display the Arts of the Pacific Basin on a Grand Scale.'[3]

He recommended a four-week affair featuring artists from over a dozen countries in an all-inclusive Festival of the Pacific that would showcase the best from all the countries touching the Pacific Ocean, including South Asia, Japan, and the countries of Central, South, and North America. Having learned from his previous ventures, he emphasized the importance of a pre-festival strategy to develop the essential local support. All the interested parties needed to be spoken to: politicians, tourist board members, press, leaders in the hospitality industries, facility managers, and leaders of the existing arts organizations to be featured within the festival.

The idea was well received by the airline and the local newspaper, which reported on the $300,000 plans of the 'Canadian impresario who thinks big.'[4]

Although it went as far as working budgets and schedules for 1964, the project never built sufficient local momentum, although it continued to be talked about over several years. In the 1970s there was an exchange of letters among interested parties wanting to reconsider the project for the 1976 American Bicentennial. Niki corresponded with

Senator Daniel Inouye, who acknowledged that he was 'intrigued' by the proposal but concerned about the cost, and, lacking influential backing in the islands, the idea faded from the scene.[5]

In spite of all this activity, the Pacific could never wash away Niki's roots in Europe; in the period after Vancouver he continued to make regular visits to the continent.

He was in Belgium in 1964 conducting Britten's *Rape of Lucretia* at Le Théâtre Royal de la Monnaie in Brussels, for which, the Canadian Press reported, he received 'rave notices.'[6]

Niki profited from his experience with student singers when he took on an ambitious conducting assignment offered by Maurice Huisman of Brussels's La Monnaie. Trainees in the young company came together with promising professionals for a production in Brussels that toured the Netherlands as part of the 1966 Spring Opera Festival. Niki conducted nine performances of the very opera for which Bruno Walter had said he was ideally suited, Mozart's *Magic Flute*.

Thierry Bosquet designed a simple unit set with dramatic lighting effects to create the many layers of mood and character that the opera demands. It was, in Niki's view, a flawless backdrop for the singers, including a dramatic bass brought by the director from Bulgaria, and a Queen of the Night that Niki remembers as 'divine':

> That was Christina Deutekom, who was later famous at the Met for that role. You know it was the time of student protests, especially throughout the Netherlands, but we went from Brussels to Eindhoven, Utrecht, Scheveningen, and finally to Amsterdam with no trouble. It was a wonderful production, just a simple set design that I wish more of our designers would use. The contrasts were stunning; all the scenes with the Queen of the Night were lit in dark blue, and with Sarastro he used brilliant golden light. Then he went to just stage lights for all the scenes with Papageno. With those voices, it was marvellous.

Altogether it was a great success, with Niki again receiving glowing reviews.[7]

In early 1964 Niki made a visit to one of his favourite destinations, India, where he was the Canadian representative to the East-West Music Conference.

> We have been four times to India and it is always a great treat. Our great friend there, Patwant Singh, whose father was head of the Sikhs, has often

been our host in New Delhi. I was pleased to be part of that conference, which was chaired by Yehudi Menuhin and by the head of All-India Radio and was called to explore how different countries developed their arts. It was fascinating, a learning experience. That was the first time that I heard Yehudi together with Ravi Shankar. And of course we were treated to one of those five-hour concerts of Indian music where people move in and out, in that casual way because it is so long. Then Shelagh and I travelled to the north where we saw the work of all kinds of artists, and a wonderful performance of Indian dance.

On the voyage home from that trip a letter was delivered to Niki's cabin on a stopover at Gibraltar that carried echoes of the Vancouver Festival and the ill-starred production of *Do You Know the Milky Way?* It also gave Niki the last laugh!

The letter was from a theatre company in Dublin that was planning a production of that play. I don't know where they got their information, but they not only tracked me to Gibraltar, they also knew that I had written the incidental music for the play at the Vancouver festival, and they wanted permission to use it. I had used a pseudonym so not even the board members knew I was the composer. In fact, when one board member asked me to bring the composer to a reception I had to tell her that he had already left town! Now Dublin wanted the same music, and of course I said yes, and asked for a royalty, which they paid with no question. It was the only time I ever received a royalty for writing music![8]

Back home in Canada, through the early years of the 1960s, Canadians had their eyes on one date, 1967, the country's one hundredth birthday. Plans for celebrations were underway, and in every province people were talking about what their communities should do to celebrate. As local citizens sketched out their ideas, the federal government appointed John Fisher, affectionately known as 'Mr Canada,' to be chief of the Centennial Commission, charged with organizing national celebrations. Niki had met Fisher when the broadcaster came backstage at the opera festival in Toronto to interview the young singers. In early 1964, Niki was summoned to Ottawa to discuss the possibility of heading up the performing arts section of the commission.

Niki found the bureaucratic approach unusual, to say the least:

I had been involved in a national study of arts facilities across the country so I knew many of the people. I went to Ottawa for one interview, and then they said they needed to discuss it. Robbins Elliott [director of the planning branch of the commission] invited me to his office for another discussion about this new position and right there in front of me, he made a call to another person and asked him 'are you interested or not in this centennial job?' It wasn't very tactful. There I was sitting, hoping to get the job, and he was making that call! I assumed that man said 'No,' because Robbins hung up the phone and said to me, 'Niki, the job is yours!' Isn't that an incredible way to hire someone? In any event he took me along then to meet with Mr Fisher, Claude Gauthier, secretary to the commission, and Robert Choquette, the deputy commissioner, a poet, and a most distinguished man. They asked me a lot of questions and I answered almost all of them in French. I think they were more impressed by my bilingual capability than my professional credentials!

Niki never did quite become accustomed to the Ottawa way of doing things. For example, he was offered the job in August 1964, officially welcomed to the staff by John Fisher a week or two later, on 10 September, and in November was still wondering when he would receive his first paycheque. He was surprised one day when his secretary congratulated him.

'For what?' he asked. 'You now have a number,' was the reply. 'Now you can be paid!' In fact it might have taken even longer, except for the intervention of Walter Gordon, the finance minister of the day and an acquaintance of Niki's, who made sure that the necessary paperwork was handed to secretary of state Maurice Lamontagne for signing.

However odd the recruiting process, out of it came a three-year artistic expedition that saw Niki crisscross Canada almost two dozen times, visiting large cities and tiny towns, giving him an extraordinary view of their artistic wealth and how it was valued by the residents.

After his first artistic reconnaissance trips across the country, Niki laid out his vision for the upcoming celebrations in his customary stirring style, making sure that the celebrations would have a bilingual title: 'Festival Canada' is planned as an expression of Canadian talent in a variety of entertainment from coast to coast,' he wrote '... to present a program that must be as diversified in content as it is wide-spread geographically. Above all monies spent must become an investment in the future.'[9]

He might have added, 'Not to be confused with Expo '67.' The Montreal World's Fair achieved international acclaim, presenting a full performance program, grabbing headlines, and fixing itself in the public memory as the most important artistic undertaking of the year. But residents of towns and cities throughout the country knew better. Canadians in 1967 engaged with their country in hundreds of ways. Some set out to visit every province and territory, others fulfilled their wish to see the northern lights, or the ocean, or the Rockies, or the prairies. Some recreated the voyages of the fur traders, paddling down rivers and across lakes, while others bicycled or even roller-skated the length of the Trans-Canada Highway. And hundreds of thousands celebrated in their own home towns with the performing artists who for twelve whole months brought to the nation's stages songs and dances and music and tales from around the world, and from their own country, and their own unique place in that country.

Niki, as chief of Performing Arts of the Centennial Commission, made the assumption that such an imposing title gave him the authority to make all the decisions for his section. Again, he had a lot to learn. Every single suggestion for performances and engagements and all plans, had to be approved by his superiors. His immediate supervisor, Mr Elliott, reported to the Management Committee, which in turn reported to the associate commissioner, who reported to the commissioner, who reported to the minister.

That chain of command, in Niki's mind an impossible barrier to making creative things happen, had to be overcome. He seized every opportunity. 'I took a few shortcuts. For example, I soon found out when the commissioner went out for lunch, and would be getting in the elevator. So if I had a very good idea, I would wait and try to catch him in the elevator and tell him my idea. And often he would say, "Niki, that's terrific, go ahead." And so I did. Sometimes he told me to forget about it, that it would be politically impossible, and I took his advice and dropped that idea.'

Budgeting is another Ottawa pastime, but it is one at which Niki can beat even the most accomplished mandarin. One of his first chores was to submit an estimate of how much money would be required to meet the commission's performing arts mandate for 1967. He was given three days to come up with a figure. Knowing the kind and scope of things they wanted to do, and working almost literally on the back of an envelope, Niki gave them the figure of $3.5 million. The bureaucrats took his rough estimates, went away to do the detailed work, and three months later were back with their number, $3.7 million; the gap between the two, less than 10 per cent! (Subsequently the allocation was increased to $4.1 million as more community projects were developed.)

Ottawa, like all capital cities, loves committees, and the Centennial Commission had its share. Numerous interests had to be represented in the planning: all disciplines, regions, private and public agencies and organizations, multicultural concerns, amateurs and professionals, an elaborate and complex assortment of organizations and coalitions, any one of which could derail the process, or significantly diminish its impact. Niki is not a committee man, but he knows that they can sometimes be useful. He proposed and received approval for a Programme Development Committee. Comprising regional representation together with distinguished representatives from the Canada Council and other major arts institutions, it was an excellent sounding board for ideas. Most important, the impeccable credentials of its members helped to defuse criticisms that inevitably arise within the frequently fractious Canadian federation.

Early concerns, for example, were raised from some of the provinces that did not want to have anything dictated from Ottawa. Eventually accommodation was reached, with the commission distributing funds across the country and the provinces adding to the pot through direct subsidy to their own companies, primarily to keep the cost of tickets within reach of the average citizen. Since attendance at arts events flourished during 1967, with ticket prices affordable for everyone, the policy worked. The provinces had the incentive they needed to get involved. Up until that time, arts groups across the country had been struggling to provide sufficient employment at reasonable fees to keep Canadian performers in their own country. Only two provinces, Saskatchewan and Ontario, had arts councils providing ongoing support; for the most part provincial support amounted to modest and sporadic subsidy for specific projects.

As Niki says, 'The centennial woke up a lot of people to the enormous amount of talent we had to offer, all over the country, and that it was worth seeing, and supporting. They just didn't know what was there. It was really what we always said it was, a plan for the whole country.'

One uncomfortable contretemps over federal involvement with the provinces happened in Quebec. Niki was on the official platform at the time.

The province of Quebec was given a substantial sum from the federal centennial fund toward the cost of the new concert hall at Mount Orford. The commissioner and all the officials were there at the ceremony when the announcement was made, and the federal minister handed over the cheque. The Quebec minister, instead of saying thank you, told everyone that Quebec really didn't need the federal money, they could have paid for it themselves. But he took the cheque anyway. It was very embarrassing.

And it was an action that appalled Niki, who understands very well the etiquette surrounding acknowledgment to supporters.

The planning for the centennial program continued at an ever-increasing pace as 1967 neared. Niki travelled everywhere, and under the auspices of the Canadian Clubs spoke to groups in all the major cities, with a twofold purpose: to promote already booked events, and to find out what else would be welcome.

One of his favourite encounters happened in Corner Brook, Newfoundland, where he met with the local arts supporters:

Corner Brook is not very large, and not a lot of professional theatres or music groups appeared there, especially at that time. So I proudly told the meeting that we could offer them an appearance by Sir Laurence Olivier and the National Theatre of Great Britain, doing *Henry the Fifth*. There was a lady who stood up and said, 'Mr. Goldschmidt, bringing Sir Laurence Olivier here will cost a lot of money. Why don't you just give the money to us and we will put on our own show, and we will be sure to sell out the house!' So I said to myself, well this is something I've learned. Olivier won't sell out in Corner Brook, but their own performers will!

The Programme Development Committee was in favour of inviting prominent artists from other countries to honour Canada in its great birthday year, but the word from the minister was that only the two so-called founding nations and the United States were to be invited, and only one company from each. Eventually they settled on the Roland Petit Dance Company from France, the New York Philharmonic, and the National Theatre of Great Britain. All three toured the country in 1967 to much acclaim, Corner Brook notwithstanding.

After a colossal amount of bargaining, sorting out which shows would actually be ready, who would pay for which expenses, which shows would go where, and how the outlying towns would be served, most plans were set by the end of 1966 for over 700 touring performances in 122 communities, including 40 in the northern territories. In addition there were local productions, popular and amateur entertainments, festivals, workshops, commissions, and special presentations for youth. *Anne of*

Green Gables, The Best of Barkerville, The Ecstasy of Rita Joe, and *Louis Riel* are only four among dozens of productions on the centennial roster that remain as outstanding names in Canadian arts production.

Among the 1967 commissions were eighteen new Canadian plays, a tremendous step forward, especially in English Canada, where there was, as the *Canadian Encyclopedia* says, a 'dearth' of original Canadian material for the stage.

An even more stunning array of new music works, over fifty, were realized in centennial year, with $60,000 from Niki's department. Canadians attended everything from chamber music to ballet to song cycles, written by a list of composers that comprises the who's who of Canadian musical composition for the second half of the twentieth century. In fact, from Niki's perspective it was the forerunner of what would be realized years later for the millennium.

The official centennial celebrations opened at 7:00 in the evening on New Year's Eve, 1966, on Ottawa's Parliament Hill in the presence of the prime minister and other government and centennial dignitaries. Designed to give the coming year a suitably momentous launch, it was an outdoor ceremony with the lighting of the centennial flame as the centrepiece, altogether an audacious plan in a city renowned for its severe winter weather.

Niki was to conduct his Centennial Choir in the Centennial Hymn written by Healey Willan with a text by Robert Choquette, while the Dominion carillonneur was at the ready to provide the musical accompaniment from his lofty place, high in the Peace Tower above the Centre Block of the Parliament Buildings. The afternoon rehearsal went well, but then the capricious winter elements intervened, upsetting the carefully rehearsed program:

> It was one of the catastrophes of my life! I was to conduct the two national anthems, and the hymn. Of course it is always difficult in the open air, and in winter, trying to hear each other with the carillon coming from above. We were very excited because the dress rehearsal was a huge success. We were well prepared. Except for the weather. Between the time of the rehearsal and the ceremony, the wind shifted right around, carrying the sound away from us, so when we came to perform there was this tremendous delay in the sound reaching us; we couldn't co-ordinate at all, and of course it was chaos. A disaster.

It was an imperfect beginning, but no one seemed to worry. The light was lit, the dignitaries had their moment in history, and across the nation the show, or shows, were set to begin.

The Canadian Centennial Choir could be called Niki's personal contribution to 'Festival Canada'; in terms of his own criterion that something should be left behind after all the celebrations were over, it met the challenge, since the choir is still in existence over thirty years later. No doubt it also satisfied his own creative urge to take part in what was happening, rather than just looking on.

Niki mobilized the entire capital region to form the two-hundred-voice ensemble, putting out a call to church choir directors, organists, and choral societies for people who could sing and read music. Given Canada's long choral tradition, it was not difficult to find willing volunteers, and before long the choir began rehearsing for its first appearance at the New Year's Eve ceremony. By all accounts none of the singers balked at the substantial commitment demanded to make it a success. Godfrey Hewitt, the choir's accompanist, described Niki's technique: 'He keeps them in good humor, but all the time makes them work hard – they all like him so much.'[10]

Young people made up an important part of the choir's forces, as they have in so many of Niki's projects, embracing that sense of urgency that he engenders. Many of them have gone on to successful careers in the arts, including Robert Cooper, choral conductor and executive producer at the CBC. He was a grade 13 high school student who joined the Canadian Centennial Choir for its first rehearsal in the auditorium of the old National Gallery, just down the street from the Parliament Buildings: 'We rolled up our sleeves, got out our music and started to work, on the Vivaldi *Gloria* and the Beethoven *Mass in C.* I didn't know these works before joining the choir; Niki brought so much music to Ottawa at that time, he was a real force. We sang at the various ceremonies, and did performances at the Cathedral and at the Capitol theatre. He introduced me to the excitement of the large chorus and the thrill of being involved in music-making on a grand scale, bigger than yourself.'[11]

The choir was busy. After the opening ceremony there was the commemoration of the fiftieth Anniversary of the Battle of Vimy Ridge in April, and the Canada Day festivities on 1 July, again on Parliament Hill, in the presence of the queen. For its own concerts the choir prepared a substantial repertoire. After their premiere appearance at the Capitol Theatre, for example, featuring the Vivaldi and Beethoven, the choir prepared Schubert's *Mass in G Major* and the Bruckner *Te Deum* for a concert later in the year in which Leopold Simoneau was soloist.

When Niki is excited about a project he wants everyone to enjoy it, and the choir was no exception. He organized a series of educational concerts for members of the choir, a practice that continued after centennial year. Touring the schools in the Ottawa region, Niki worked hard to make the concerts fun for the students without compromising quality. One report describes the program as a 'thumb-nail outline of the history of choral music,' covering everything from chant to carols, Bach to Britten, and described it as 'a unique musical history lesson' that drew 'enthusiastic applause.'[12]

Not only did the educational concerts continue into the next decade, but the choir made many prestigious appearances under Niki's leadership, playing in the presence of several foreign diplomats, as would be expected in the nation's capital. The representative of the Federal Republic of Germany attended a concert on 26 March 1970 commemorating the bicentenary of Beethoven's birth at which the choir gave a performance of the composer's oratorio, *Mount of Olives*. Broadcast on the CBC, that concert was only one in a busy year for the choir; one reviewer, commenting on what he called this 'renowned' ensemble, said, 'Mr. Goldschmidt, as usual, stressed clarity as opposed to the clamour which is often the temptation where such large forces are involved.'[13]

Niki enjoyed the choir, especially the contacts in the schools and with younger singers. His personal ease in relating to young people is captured in two charming letters from a pair of students writing to him regarding a bet they had made to fill the Capitol Theatre for the choir's concert on 19 April 1967.

'You may recall,' they said, 'that in February you were kind enough to grant Barbara and I an interview for our music project. At the end of the interview you made us a bet. You challenged us to fill the Capitol Theatre by arranging for buses.' The girls evidently worked hard writing letters and enlisting assistance, all of which paid off with a full house, as they pointed out:

We kept our part of the bargain! So ... ?
Yours sincerely,
Ann Gamey,
Barbara Eagleson
P.S. The bet was two passes to Expo '67.[14]

Niki kept his word. In the second letter the girls thanked Niki for honouring his debt and acknowledged receipt of a cheque: 'We will exchange [it] for two passes to Expo, and are looking forward to a day there.'[15]

Niki, apart from attending to these personal details, and his choir and the national celebrations, was also preparing his second production of *Noah's Flood*, again directed by Joy Coghill. Robert Cooper, who played one of Noah's sons, remembers it as a 'very big deal, with a marvellous big raked set.' That set was the first of several that William Lord would create for Niki. The Toronto designer devised a medieval scene starting with a large raked wooden platform, 'such as you might have seen in the twelveth century in the square in front of great cathedral,' on which the ark was constructed, explains Lord. All the other elements, masks and costumes, repeated the tones and style of medieval illuminated manuscripts, connecting the opera directly to its roots as Britten seems to have intended.

The production was a success on every level, but Joy Coghill says it took some hard negotiation before it all came together, including some heated discussion between her and Niki regarding the number of rehearsals; she finally was allotted more than the originally scheduled two weeks. She was insistent for reasons that Niki could understand, as she acknowledges: 'I said that I was not interested in just having the kids tramp down the aisle and sing the right notes. There is far more drama than that going on. And I think Niki responded to my demands because they were based on quality, which of course is always first with him.'[16]

Niki had hoped that Britten would attend that production, but unfortunately it was not possible. The composer wrote from Aldeburgh saying, 'I am delighted to hear that "Noye's Fludde" went well and had such a splendid reaction.'[17]

Meanwhile, across the country the centennial productions continued, and amid all the new works, and old, Canadians were gaining a deeper understanding of their own country. Both audiences and performers were seeing things they had never seen and feeling at home in places they had never been. Niki was pleased. 'For example, Monique Leyrac was one of the most famous chanteuses in Quebec, but she was rarely heard in the rest of the country. We sent her to Saskatchewan to give concerts and when she came back she told me the reception had been fantastic!'

Then there was 'One Hundred Years of Musical Comedy,' a revue featuring seven artists from British Columbia: 'They came and launched the show on Parliament Hill, and imagine, not one of those seven artists had ever been in Ottawa before. That whole group in a charter plane with the minister was flown to Labrador, where they gave a performance. So they saw Ottawa and the northland, that was the excitement. There were so many stories like that.'

By the end of the celebration there had been 690 Festival Canada On Tour performances, playing to over 650,000 patrons. 'The Best of Barkerville' did five performances in one week in November on the Canadian prairies, playing in small halls and selling almost three thousand tickets. The large companies like the Stratford Shakespearean Festival and the touring *Anne of Green Gables* played to sold-out houses everywhere they went. At the same time, 'Le théâtre flottante,' constructed on an old ferry, recreated the days of lively river traffic, taking theatre to the tiniest villages up and down the St Lawrence.

Of course, touring was important, especially in communities where local resources were limited, but original productions by resident companies were equally essential to the success of the centennial's artistic awakening.

The Centennial Commission primarily played its part in providing funds toward production costs for these works, supporting in a small but important way the communities and individuals with the vision to feature original Canadian creations for the birthday year. Five new operas were commissioned that year by local companies, all with subject matter inspired by Canada's history. The one that the provoked the most attention was *Louis Riel*, composed by Harry Somers with a libretto by Mavor Moore. In telling the story of Canada's legendary Métis leader, Louis Riel, the opera ventured into territory that was only just becoming familiar to Canadians as they began to explore the events that had formed their country. This was a project that had its origins in the imagination and commitment of individuals who believed in the excellence and vision of Canadian artists. Commissioned with a gift from the Floyd S. Chalmers Foundation, the opera was presented by the Canadian Opera Company, directed by Leon Major, and conducted by Victor Feldbrill with an all-Canadian cast. The Centennial Commission gave limited assistance toward the substantial production costs. *Riel* was a huge critical and box-office success and in 1976 was remounted at the Kennedy Centre in Washington, DC, as part of Canada's tribute to the U.S. in its bicentennial year.

Out on the west coast another premiere dealing with the life of Canada's Native peoples, George Ryga's play *The Ecstasy of Rita Joe*, summed up the spirit of 1967 and the importance of the federal involvement across the nation. The tragic story of a young Native girl on Vancouver's skid row, it had a rough ride to full realization. Joy Coghill received the outline her first day on the job as director of Vancouver's Playhouse Theatre, and was immediately committed to it. Then ensued the anxious wait for the finished script, which went through many iterations and was even misplaced for a time. Joy never lost faith: 'Sometimes board members or other people would ask me about the new play, and I always told them it was marvellous, even though I didn't see it until the day of the first reading. It was touch and go because I knew it would be expensive for us, about $100,000 to mount. The Centennial Commission gave us just $1000, but that was enough to lever the board to go out and find the rest. It wasn't just the money, it was about the seal of approval, the recognition that we were doing something very important.'[18]

Rita Joe opened on 23 November 1967, starring Frances Hyland, August Schellenberg, and Chief Dan George playing Rita's father. It was a moving experience, acclaimed by the critics. Mike Tytherleigh set the play in the context of the Native experience by quoting Dan George, who had spoken at an earlier centennial celebration. 'When I fought to protect my land and my home,' he had said, 'I was called a savage; when I neither welcomed nor wanted this way of life I was called lazy; when I tried to rule my people I was stripped of my authority.'[19]

Writing in the *Vancouver Sun*, Jack Richards called the play 'a thing of sorrow and anger deeper than mere tears,' reminding his readers that it was the first time such a story had been told.[20]

Among the outpouring of cultural expression of that year, *Rita Joe* exemplified Niki's conviction that the 1967 arts programs should 'generate mutual respect and understanding' and 'recognize the importance of respecting each other's culture ... and way of life.' With echoes of his beloved Uncle Paul, the diplomat, Niki wrote, 'Only then can we contribute to the peaceful co-existence (if that is the right word in this context) of our people as well as the peoples of the world.'[21]

However, not every project contributed to the lofty ideals of the centennial. There was the unfortunate plan for the 'Centennial Play,' which began as a straightforward suggestion to commission Robertson Davies to write a play to be performed by amateur theatre groups across the country. It was a good idea taken several steps too far, evolving into an unwieldy scheme for five one-act mini-plays, written by five different authors and knitted together into one production.

After a tryout in Lindsay, Ontario, the 'Centennial Play' opened in

Ottawa on 11 January 1967, where it was called 'A Centennial Bomb' by Ron Evans, writing in the *Toronto Telegram*. Niki agrees, and smiles now at the recollection, although at the time he felt anything but sanguine: 'Oh, my God, it was awful, the perfect example of art created by a committee! We tried to put regional representation together with the idea of a play, with an author from each part of the country. It just didn't work, and it was never done again.'[22]

Robertson Davies had bad luck with the centennial. He contributed a scenario for an enormous open-air spectacle planned for Parliament Hill, to be directed by Tyrone Guthrie. Niki's Centennial Choir was slated to be part of the affair, ambitiously intended to capture the whole of Canada's complex history right there on the parliamentary lawn. Production plans were well along when it was summarily cancelled. Davies was quoted as blaming an official in the Public Works Department.[23] Niki claims the opposition to the project was wider than that, involving conflicts of ego and influence typical of a place like Ottawa with its several layers of government and agencies all promoting their own interests.

Niki's only other disappointment was on a smaller scale, and possibly he was the only one who noticed that things weren't quite as expected. It is one of those stories that Niki tells on himself, with a chuckle.

> We didn't want to leave anything out of the program, so I had the idea that we should bring some Inuit throat singers to perform outside of their own community. My colleagues at the commission thought it was a good idea so we arranged to have an Inuit choir from Labrador come and do a concert in St John's, Newfoundland. Of course, it was an important event and I went to St John's to hear the concert. But the minute I looked at the program I thought, 'What have I done?' The whole program was Bach cantatas and the like. Not one bit of Inuit throat singing in the evening! It turned out that this particular choir had been trained by a German missionary and all its concerts reflected his background![24]

The program did not appear to have detracted from the evening in any way. Howard Taubman in the *New York Times* remarked on the choir's presentation, 'surprising the audience and itself with its success.'[25]

Taubman summed up the artistic accomplishments realized through the Centennial Commission's Performing Arts Division, saying, 'The scope and size of this effort are hard to believe,' adding that in reviewing Canada's commitment to subsidize an effort of this scope and size, 'one realizes how boldly the Canadians have planned and acted.'[26]

Looking back over three decades, Niki still can scarcely contain his excitement when he remembers all the successes of 1967. A speech he made right at the end of that year still resonates for him. He spoke of the 'cultural explosion' of centennial year:

> Yes, an explosion has taken place. And although we may have had some debris we also found a vault of hidden treasures. What is the debris and what are the treasures?
>
> The debris is the scattered remains of our cynics! ... The treasures, the artists, playwrights, composers choreographers, filmmakers, and educators who have been given the opportunity to shine ... in their own country and to carry their message far beyond the frontiers of Canada.[27]

Niki referred to the exciting stage presentations, but he did not overlook the contributions of special competitions, workshops, conferences, and educators to centennial year, each adding its own momentum to the future development of the arts in Canada.

Queen's University in Kingston was the site of a major conference where Niki had another one of those chance encounters that have continually defined the course of his career and his personal contribution to the cultural milieu.

Niki's old friend from Vancouver, Geoff Andrew, was the director of the Association of Universities and Colleges of Canada. Early in 1966 he proposed that the AUCC host a meeting in centennial year to discuss the role of universities as cultural leaders. Committees were put together, and Niki was enlisted to provide guidance on topics and speakers, especially from the arts perspective. The 1967 conference attracted participants from across the country, ensuring a provocative exchange of ideas that eventually produced over thirty resolutions affirming the positive role for academic institutions in the artistic life of their communities. It was a welcome outcome for the co-chair of the Planning Committee, Murdo MacKinnon, then dean of the Wellington College of Arts and Science at Guelph University. MacKinnon recognized that a small southern Ontario city like Guelph, lacking the artistic infrastructure of a large urban centre, needed the guidance and resources of the university to fill the cultural vacuum. In his quietly determined way, he was ready to take up the challenge and through the Kingston conference he found the perfect collaborator. In 1967 he and Niki began an association that was to last through two decades of music-making and festival-building.

In fact, their first undertaking of that kind happened in 1967 with the presentation of the National Vocal Competition in Guelph. It was one of three such nationwide events supported by the Centennial Commission and held under the auspices of Jeunesses Musicales. Guelph was chosen as the site for the vocal finals, because as the birthplace of Edward Johnson it was symbolically appropriate, and because MacKinnon and the Edward Johnson Music Foundation were in place to look after logistics like ticket sales and hospitality. Niki assisted with the musical requirements and jurors, and helped to stir up community excitement with characteristically spirited speeches to local service clubs.

Although the recollection is that the audience for the finals was small, and there was some embarrassment when the international jury refused to award the 'Grand Prize,'[28] the competition scored very high on one important test for measuring the success of Commission-supported efforts. What did it leave behind for the future? The National Vocal Competition left a group of committed citizens, volunteers, university officials, and supporters who, with Niki's artistic guidance, used the momentum of 1967 to establish an outstanding annual festival.

And so, Canada's giant birthday party wound down, and Niki and Shelagh were ready to leave their little apartment in Ottawa for larger vistas and new challenges. Once again they were on the move, this time on a grand trip around the world, assisted by the Canada Council and the government, who asked Niki to look at how Canadian cultural institutions and artists were being served by the country's overseas missions and embassies. It was perhaps another fallout from the 1967 celebrations; government officials had come to the understanding that Canada's artistic resources could be as important to our international commerce as lumber or minerals. Niki's visits were one small step in building a new Canadian artistic profile.

One of the longest stops on that trip was a return visit to India, where the press reported on his presence, and where he boldly wrote an article offering suggestions to the Indian cultural community on how it might celebrate its own arts.

Comparing India to Canada is tricky, a bit of a stretch, but Niki, never at a loss for new ideas, looked at it from the perspective of his recent experience. Here was a country with large geographical distances that were expensive to cross, tremendous regional and social diversity, local interests that had to be understood and accommodated, and like Canada, 'although known for its phenomenal natural resources, it has not yet produced an equal reservoir of cultural resources.'[29]

His blueprint for Indian cultural expansion not surprisingly included a series of regional contests leading to a national competition for young sitar players, culminating in a grand celebratory festival of Indian arts and artists, supported by widespread national promotion of all events, with the defining criteria always being quality of presentation.

He was equally adamant that any celebration include the widest possible representation of the country's artistic resources, and that their importance be recognized as more than just entertainment. The centennial program had convinced him that although both Canada and India were justifiably proud of their internationally renowned artists and institutions, and although 'they are the pride of our nations, this is not enough. What really counts in the long run is the awareness that a country's cultural resources are the strongest force in building harmony where there is strife, in creating a congenial environment instead of despondency, in arousing curiosity instead of complacency, and in creating genuine pride instead of doubt and envy.'[30]

Niki had given his best advice and then moved on, as he always does, returning home to new opportunities. He was in his sixtieth year, when retirement comes into view for many people. Not for Niki. He was about to embark on another career, his sixth or seventh depending on how you count, and he would have several after that. All would be informed by the same set of values put down in the article written in India. Celebrate the arts in the community, and always have the best, whether from home or abroad.

7

For All Seasons and for All Places

Guelph is a small city, one hundred kilometres from the centre of Toronto, just far enough to give it a distinct identity. It is solid and well kept, with handsome nineteenth-century limestone houses and business blocks, attractive churches from the same period, riverside parks, a spacious university campus, and a population that takes pride in its community. It is also the place where Niki's festival-making skills triumphed for two decades, inspiring Mavor Moore to advise anyone wanting to mount a festival to 'listen to the voice of the prophet Niki.'[1]

The thought that excellent artistic presentations could originate and flourish outside of high-profile venues in big cities was the sort of audacious idea that took hold in Canada as a result of centennial year. And the 1967 Kingston conference created the right climate for universities to step out from their marble halls and lead these new ventures. It also produced a dynamic collaboration of two men, Niki Goldschmidt and Murdo MacKinnon, each with a daring imagination and the will to turn their dreams into reality.

Murdo MacKinnon, tall, plain spoken, passionate about his Scottish heritage, embraced the challenges and the possibilities for real musical growth in Guelph as eagerly as Niki; neither saw any reason why it shouldn't happen. As Barbara (Wolfand) Little, who worked with them from the beginning (and later went on to be national head of festivals and special events for the CBC), says, 'They were men with no small plans.'[2]

The University of Guelph was in an expansionist mode, and Murdo, as dean of Arts and Sciences, had a budget to match. In 1966–7 he hired seventy-five new faculty, and in late 1967, with centennial year winding down, he appointed Niki as director of music, with the rank of professor of music reporting directly to Murdo.

The university was Niki's first permanent base in Guelph and it was the co-operation of the university with the Edward Johnson Music Foundation that allowed the Guelph Spring Festival to establish itself as a quality event where artistic surprises bloomed like May flowers.

The story of the Guelph Spring Festival has been admirably documented by Gloria Dent and Leonard Conolly; they have given it a historical context and listed the programs over the life of the festival. Niki's years at Guelph constitute a large portion of that account; at the same time they are part of the bigger story of Niki's influence on community artistic initiatives across the country.

In Murdo MacKinnon's view, Niki was the essential animator, and that talent was evident immediately at the university:

Niki taught conducting for credit, and on Monday nights gave an extension course for the community. He was always unique at the university; he didn't carry all the same mundane responsibilities as regular professors, but he was in charge of the music programs. He had to come to me for money, but otherwise he made the decisions, whether it was which artists to invite for the noon-hour series, or the repertoire for the choir. I had a parallel budget, apart from the regular departmental money, for cultural affairs, so whether it was a summer program, an art show, a choir tour, or a festival, the university could give it that necessary push to get it off the ground. And Niki had lots of ideas.'[3]

Niki described his duties at the university in a 1968 report written in typically non-academic language, emphasizing his goal of 'bringing students into an active relationship with the artistic life' around them.[4] His duties included conducting the University Choir, giving instruction in vocal literature, and 'acting as a catalyst for various activities in music and the arts.'[5] He remains very clear about his role at the university:

Murdo talked to me about taking on the music department and I said right away, 'I must warn you, I cannot be a regular professor type. I can give you musical activities, with lots of excitement. I think the students will benefit, and have a wonderful time. But I am not an academic.' And Murdo said, 'That's why I want you!' He is a wonderful man and he had an unusual idea for his new department. So I was appointed, and I became at the same time 'artistic consultant' to the Edward Johnson Music Foundation.

The university music program, with this man who never acted like a professor at its head, soon attracted new students looking to fill out their education. Among them was Robert Missen, who went on to a career as a singer, producer, impresario, and artists' manager. The choir was his first musical involvement at the university:

> Someone told me about the University of Guelph Choir. I was a tenor and played piano and could sight read, and had studied some languages, so I had the basics. Within two months Niki said to me, 'Young man, why don't you think about a career as a singer?' Well, that was the impetus I needed ... to be told that by Nicholas Goldschmidt.
>
> So I started to sing some solos in the choir, and Niki helped me to find extra employment so I could afford to continue to study. It was wonderful exposure at the highest level. I worked at the festival in the box office, and did management and front of house. And of course there were the great choir tours. I got to sing, and to learn the business. What could be better?[6]

The University of Guelph Choir, like the Centennial Choir before, and others that came later, had Niki's signature on it from the beginning. With his infectious enthusiasm, word soon spread about this new opportunity open to students, faculty, and anyone in town who wanted to sing and was willing to make the commitment to participate fully.

Every Wednesday night Niki boarded a train or the inter-city coach heading from Toronto to Guelph. Before getting down to work he made it a habit to have his dinner in the cafeteria. And again he behaved unlike other professors, as Murdo McKinnon recalls:

> He would go into the big cafeteria, where very few of the staff ever went, as it was really the student hangout. Usually there were few people around when he was there, about 6 o'clock in the evening. One time, he was sitting with his dinner, a group of students nearby, when he announced, very loudly, 'This food is not hot, it is not well cooked. Get the person in charge!' So one of the students went and got that person, whoever it was, and Niki told him that even plain food could be hot and well cooked. All the students cheered. It was typical Niki. He just fitted in, he was never intimidated and he just was himself, all the time.[7]

Robert and Margarete Goldschmidt, Niki's parents, 1900. NG's private collection.

Niki with his four older brothers, c 1913. NG's private collection.

Hon. Paul Hymans, Niki's 'Uncle Paul,' c 1920. NG's private collection.

Bruno Walter: snap taken by Niki in a train station in Europe, c 1935. NG's private collection.

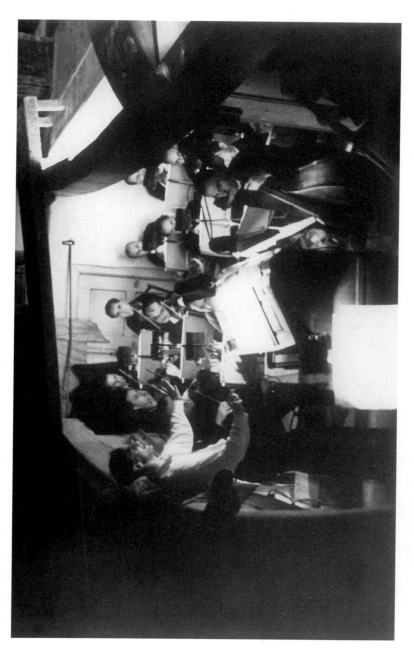

Niki conducting rehearsal in pit of theatre at Opava, c 1936. NG's private collection.

Joseph Marx

Niki in San Francisco, c 1940. NG's private collection.

Shelagh Goldschmidt, c 1945. NG's private collection.

Niki with students at Rollins Theater School, Lennox, Massachusetts, c 1947. NG's private collection.

Niki and Maureen Forrester at Vancouver International Festival, 1958.

Niki and Murdo MacKinnon, Guelph 1967. *Guelph Mercury.*

Robertson Davies and Niki, Guelph Spring Festival, 1972. Archival and Special Collections, McLaughlin Library, University of Guelph.

(Left to right) Barbara (Wolfand) Little, Mabel Krugge, Jon Vickers, Ruby Mercer, and Niki, Guelph Spring Festival, 1974. Archival and Special Collections, McLaughlin Library, University of Guelph.

Jon Vickers and Niki, Guelph, 1974. Archival and Special Collections, McLaughlin Library, University of Guelph.

Sir Peter Ustinov speaking with Scarborough students at rehearsal for *Noah's Flood*, in preparation for appearance in San Francisco for fiftieth anniversary of the United Nations. Private collection.

André Prévost, Yehudi Menuhin, and Niki, Guelph Spring Festival, 1987.
Archival and Special Collections, McLaughlin Library, University of Guelph.

Niki with Krzysztof Penderecki, c 2000. NG's private collection.

It was also typical of Niki's attitude toward food. He never feels he has to seek out the latest chic restaurant with a five-star rating and a price list to match. He is comfortable eating almost everywhere, but he does expect, perhaps from Shelagh's teaching, that even plain food can be well prepared. It is the same philosophy he brings to his concert presentations. The circumstances may be modest, but the performances should always be well prepared and only as fancy as resources allow.

Niki and his Guelph choir soon became regulars on the performance stage. They gave an annual concert in March to preview the coming of spring, and in early winter to enhance the pre-Christmas season; they sang for Convocation, participated in an inter-university choral festival, and became in the process a musical force across the southwest region. The repertoire was familiar in Niki's canon, but new to many of the choir members: Fauré, Schubert, Haydn, the great choral works that had inspired students in Toronto, Vancouver, and Ottawa.

Murdo MacKinnon was one of the choristers: 'The choir became very visible in the community, and attracted an extraordinary level of singer. I remember standing beside one young man, a baritone, and just being thrilled with his voice. He introduced himself. 'I'm Kevin McMillan.' He was studying agriculture then, but went on to have a big career as a professional singer. And there was Bob Missen as lead tenor, and Nick Kaethler, who was lead bass and the assistant conductor.'

Singers were enticed by the music and by the exciting opportunity to go on the choir's tours. Assisted financially by the university, and by Murdo MacKinnon with his talent for organization, the choir set out in the early 1970s on a series of summer adventures that took them to Scotland and the Edinburgh Festival fringe, the cathedrals of England, and to Canada's Maritime provinces.

As Murdo recalls:

Niki was so enthusiastic about the choir and said to me one day, 'We will make a tour, yes?' And naturally I said, 'Yes, of course.' Scotland was just great fun, and the choir was very well received. The tour in 1975 to southern England was especially successful. We sang in Canterbury on Bank Holiday, I remember, and we had fifty-five voices singing in the nave. Before the concert began the priest spoke to Niki about the difficulty of the acoustics, how hard it was to be heard clearly. Afterwards he announced that he wanted to apologize to Mr Goldschmidt. 'I didn't have to tell him anything about the acoustics of a cathedral. He knew just what to do.[8]

Niki was especially pleased that the choir gave a concert in the famous Orford Church so closely associated with Benjamin Britten's Aldeburgh Festival, before travelling on to the heart of London for a final appearance right across Trafalgar Square from Canada House at the Church of St Martin-in-the-Fields. It was a grand finale, with the noon-hour audience, customarily anxious to leave after the regulation fifty minutes, noisily applauding Niki and his company and demanding several encores.

Back in Guelph, Niki was present every Thursday at noon for the series of concerts that was causing a buzz around the campus. Students, staff, and townspeople came out regularly for an eclectic series presented by the university. While it was not really his series, he was close to the programming, on stage, or through artists whom he could attract. The choir always appeared at least once annually, and there were vocal recitals (among them Niki's own lieder recitals); once there was a joint lecture with Niki and his old friend Herman Geiger-Torel discussing opera, and the Czech Quartet, then resident in nearby Hamilton, made regular appearances. The Guelph audiences loved it, scrambling to find out what would be next in this eclectic mix.

Teresa Stratas gave a rare evening recital in a series that made Guelph a place 'worth a musical stop,' according to William Littler in the *Toronto Star*, as he noted that Ms Stratas was in 'especially good voice.' That same series, in the 1968 season, included an evening concert by the University of Guelph Rehearsal Orchestra, conducted by Niki, and the Jacques Loussier Trio from France. As Littler said, 'The former head of Festival Canada is nothing if not enterprising.'

While the university activity was expanding, Niki's enterprise was finding a more exciting outlet beyond academe. A number of individuals on the board of the Edward Johnson Music Foundation wanted to build a program to attract the citizens of Guelph, bring attention to the community, and make an artistic link between 'town and gown.' They supported Niki's idea for an annual festival, but it took more than one meeting and Murdo MacKinnon's Scottish fortitude before the matter was settled.

Murdo and Barbara Little and Edith Kidd, and Eugene Benson, were prominent among the supporters. The university was very important because it provided the initial finances as well as office space and that kind of help. It was a modest undertaking, with a small budget because fees weren't very high at that time, not like now. That first year included participation by many Guelph people, musicians, singers, actors, and others working behind the scenes. It was really a celebration in the city. And so it was launched.

The Guelph Spring Festival was initiated in May 1968, featuring a parade, clowns, dancing, games and bands in the park by the river, and a half-dozen concerts, two of choral music, and one a recital by Lois Marshall. Niki conducted the opening concert in St George's Church, and composer Charles Wilson presided over the closing when the Guelph Light Opera Company Oratorio Chorus sang his new work, *En Guise d'Orphée*, commissioned by the foundation. It was one of two commissioned works that year, the other was by Godfrey Ridout. They were the first of thirty-six Canadian works commissioned and/or premiered by the festival under Niki's leadership.

Niki insists that a successful festival must reflect the significant features of its place. No surprise then that the opening festival highlighted a celebration of the life of Edward Johnson, in an exhibition that was given the same production values as any other offering. Pictures from historic productions, letters, programs, and costumes were all cleverly displayed in a walk-through set created by designer William Lord, complemented by taped remembrances and the actual voice of Edward Johnson, giving the visitor a totally absorbing experience of Guelph's favourite musical son.

John Cripton, who later became an expert touring promoter and impresario, was another of a long list of professionals in the arts world who started their careers with Niki. He recalls that first spring:

Aside from programming concerts for students at the university, for which I often looked to Nicholas for guidance, I was hired by the festival as a sort of student builder and technician. I had no real knowledge of classical music and opera at that time, but I was building the exhibition panels and listening to the tapes of Edward Johnson and I fell in love with his voice and the music. That is how I discovered opera! And the next year I got to build that wonderful set that Bill Lord designed for *The Prodigal Son*. It was exciting, a great experience for a Canadian.[9]

The buzz of excitement gave the board the courage to commit itself to the future, and a program for the second year that typified Niki's direction of the Guelph Spring Festival.

The Prodigal Son was the first of Britten's miracle plays to appear at

Guelph, and was the centrepiece of the attempt in those early years to define each festival by a theme. 'Religion and the Arts' was the theme in 1969, followed by 'Beethoven and His Time' in 1970. But fitting artistic ideas and opportunities, budget imperatives, audience expectations, and artists' availability into a thematic box ultimately proved too limiting for Niki's expansive imagination, and that approach was quietly abandoned after 1970.

Nevertheless, although the programming, like Vancouver, included all the performing arts, together with film, visual arts, and lectures, opera was special.

> The Guelph Festival became known as the place where you could hear operas that you couldn't find anywhere else. (Except for *Hansel and Gretel*, which we did for the UN Year of the Child. With Maureen Forrester as the witch it was a smash hit.) We became known as a centre for Britten's chamber operas, *The Prodigal Son, The Burning Fiery Furnace, Noye's Fludde, The Rape of Lucretia, The Beggar's Opera, Curlew River,* and then all the new operas, some commissioned by the festival, and toured afterwards. *Seabird Island* by Derek Healey and Norman Newton, *Psycho Red* by Guelph composer Charles Wilson, a hometown boy, and *Postcard from Morocco* by Dominic Argento, who told me that it was the best production ever given his opera, and of course *The Lighthouse* by Peter Maxwell Davies, with Ben Heppner and directed by Canadian Robert Carsen. People waited every year to see what we would do next. It was very innovative and of very high quality. I am proud and happy about what we did at that festival. Early on, people had said it would be small, that we would have a mini-program, but I always said that a mini-program is no program.

Looking back from a new century at the operas on offer at Guelph, it is easy to forget just how adventurous the programming was. Contemporary or unfamiliar operas are a hard sell anywhere, anytime. Only the largest, richest, or most specialized companies take on the challenge, and then only occasionally.

In Guelph one venture taught staff and board very early on how difficult it can be.

> Just a few days before the opening of *The Prodigal Son* we had sold only about two hundred tickets for the three performances in the beautiful church on the hill, the Church of Our Lady. Everyone was upset and the board wanted to cancel, but I told them that would be impossible, it would

kill the whole festival. So I told them to just get out and paper the house and see what would happen. We gave away many tickets and through a lot of effort on the part of Murdo and the board members and volunteers we sold the rest for the first performance, and had an audience of close to nine hundred people. And for the next two performances it was sold out, because there were such good notices, and everyone was talking about it. It was so different, a medieval parable with Britten's music. When the audience saw it they understood it and they loved it.

The critic for the *Financial Times* of London wrote an extensive review, calling it 'a powerful and moving experience,' and describing the expectation in the audience. 'The large church was packed, and since the audience gathered long before starting time, an unusual degree of anticipatory tension was built up.'[10]

John Kraglund, writing in the *Globe and Mail*, echoed Niki's belief in what a festival must be. 'It must present the rare, new, the unusual,' he said. And he cautioned that the standard should be equal to anything that the audience can see during a regular season. Guelph's *Prodigal Son* 'met the most stringent demands with flying colours,' he told his readers.[11]

It was a defining moment for Niki:

From that time on the Guelph Spring Festival was established and I am happy to say became a centre for these works for small forces by Benjamin Britten.

It was also the year when I established my credo. That is, the board will tell me how much money they can give me for an artistic program, and I will tell them what the program will be. Unfortunately the dollar is often the limit. I love to let my imagination fly, and say that the sky is the limit. But I have to be realistic and make my programs within the boundaries of the resources available to me. That philosophy has stood me in good stead for many years.

The Guelph Festival was more than opera, however. There was always an essential mix of concerts and special events. In 1969 Jon Vickers sang to a sold-out house in the university's War Memorial Hall, another example of Niki's ability to persuade his far-reaching list of friends and colleagues to come and work with him, for very modest fees.

The 1969 festival carried out its theme of Religion and the Arts with films on religious art, choral music, and a production of medieval drama in another form, this one about King Herod, told in old English. The playbill is instructive: here was one 'Trish Nelligan,' better known to audiences now as film star Kate Nelligan, and 'Bob' Thomson, none other than one of Canada's leading men of theatre and film, R.H. Thomson, showing that Niki's festival featured important young talent not only in music but in other art forms too.

The board and the patrons of the festival were delighted with the success that year. Barbara Little recalls what it was like for the dedicated volunteers who made it all come together:

Niki was the man with the ideas, and with the artistic know-how in terms of which artists to invite. He really was the right man in the right place for the right reasons. But someone had to look after all the details. I lived in Guelph at the time, and so I was invited along with Edith Kidd, and Murdo, and Eugene Benson, to help out. I was primarily responsible for all the promotion and publicity. At first I was really in awe of Niki because I had never done anything this big, and I often didn't know what I was doing. (I left Niki's name off of the front of the first brochure, and soon learned that it was bad form not to put the artistic director's name out front!) Niki trained me, and I went on to a career at the CBC because of what I learned from him. For example, it was always hard to estimate how many seats exactly to sell in the churches, because how many people can you fit in one pew? I mean, it depends on their size! Edith Kidd, who looked after the box office, used to say that Niki would sell the altar! But he knew that we could oversell because there would always be people who wouldn't show up. And if we were truly over capacity the board members just had to give up their seats![12]

As planning went forward for the future, Niki, careful and cunning, would try out his ideas on a core group of influential board members, getting support and dealing with questions and problems before going to the full group that set the final budget. His 1970 plan was based on the Beethoven theme, which could have been constricting. But once again Niki's imagination was working full out; the offerings under that motif were surprisingly expansive. It is instructive to look at the program in the context of the time. Canada's Orford Quartet performing Beethoven's great string quartets later became familiar and valued fare to chamber music audiences around the world, but in 1970 the quartet was in the early years of its long career. It was something completely new for the audience to hear them perform Beethoven and two new Canadian works, one by Guelph composer Charles Wilson, the other by Gerhard Wuensch entitled *Music without Pretensions* for string quartet and accordion. Joseph Macerollo, accordionist and native of Guelph, joined the Orford for that performance, which certainly was innovative festival fare. Kenneth Winters in the *Toronto Telegram* applauded the players after their first concert and urged his readers to 'hurry and stand in line to get tickets for the next.'[13]

The choice of opera in 1970, to accommodate the Beethoven theme, was unconventional, and something of a stretch. Niki conducted *The Village Barber* by Johann Schenk, a teacher of the great master. While the production received generally good marks, the work itself was not a favourite of the critics.[14]

Altogether that year was another success, living up to the expectations of the city as expressed in an editorial in the local paper. The writer was confident that performers, critics, and audiences 'will come to Guelph from around the world,' stressing that there were nearly three hundred citizens who were patrons and donors. The editorial assured readers that the local contribution brought further support from the senior levels of government, and offered the opinion that 'the grant of $6000 from the city council was fully justified, and perhaps in future years our city fathers can be even more generous.'[15]

And every year Niki's festival, like the spring rush on the local rivers, brought excitement and surprises. In 1971 Beverly Sills was forced to cancel her scheduled appearance, causing some panic in the office! Barbara Little recalls that she had built the entire season's subscription sales around that one concert. Now what was she to do?

'I waited for Niki to arrive from Toronto,' she says, 'and I told him what had happened. Before I could say another thing he was on the phone to New York. After a couple of calls he told me, "Well it's okay. We have Jan Peerce." I wasn't convinced that an aging tenor would satisfy an audience expecting Beverly Sills. But Peerce came, and everyone loved him. He was so endearing, and sang all their old favourites. It was marvellous, and Niki stood in War Memorial Hall just beaming, for good reason. His artistic instincts had served him well again.'[16]

Ravi Shankar came in 1972, and Marilyn Horne the same year. 1973 featured a double celebration; first there was Benjamin Britten's sixtieth birthday, and the North American premiere of his song cycle *Who Are the Children?* followed by Jon Vickers with Richard Woitach in a tribute to Edward Johnson (this time for the fiftieth anniversary of his Metropolitan Opera Debut), with an introduction by Robertson Davies.

The opera that year, *The Consul* by Menotti, had less profile than the big celebrations, although it was directed by Niki's old friend and colleague Herman Geiger-Torel and featured a remarkable Canadian cast including Milla Andrew, Jan Rubeš, Alan Monk, and Judith Forst.

As usual, Niki made every effort to extend the experience of the festival to the broadest possible audience in the community, and in this case it was a rehearsal attended by students that featured more than music, as Murdo recalls: 'It was a dress rehearsal, and we had all these students there. The cast was taking a break, so Niki decided that he should speak to the students, I guess to give them a little background. At the same moment Herman decided that he would do the same. Here were these two, at opposite sides of the auditorium, both talking, neither giving way, and the mystified students not knowing what either had to say. But it was all okay, no hard feelings, I think.'[17]

The following year Yehudi Menuhin made his first visit to the Festival, playing a special commission by Canada's Harry Somers, titled simply *Music for Solo Violin.* Niki loves to tell the story of how that commission came about.

> Yehudi was in town for a concert with the symphony in the early seventies, and we asked him to come for dinner. We were sitting in the living room and I was telling him about the festival and that we often commissioned new works. I said to him, 'Maybe you will come and play a new piece by a Canadian composer.' He was young at heart and he said that it would interest him very much, perhaps a joint commission, for solo violin.
>
> Right away I suggested Somers, and I went to the telephone and called Harry. I asked him, 'Would you like to write a violin solo?' He said he really would like to but he just had no time. So I said, 'It's too bad because Yehudi is right here and he would like to talk about it.' Well, before I had hardly said those words, Harry responded, I could hear the excitement in his voice. 'I'll do it,' he said. So he came the next day and we talked and that is how it happened.

The year 1974 was the year of *The Rape of Lucretia* with Jon Vickers, Patricia Rideout, Lyn Vernon, and Alan Monk, all directed by famed Britten director Colin Graham.

William Lord travelled to the Aldeburgh Festival to see Graham at work. Lord appreciated Britten's dramatic genius, and especially liked *Lucretia.* 'Of all the designs I did at Guelph,' says Lord, 'I am most proud of *Rape of Lucretia.* We had that terrible problem of the stage in Ross

Hall [where many of the operas were performed]. It is so wide and so shallow, like a letter slot. I sat with Colin in a pub in England and told him the problem and he found a workable solution. It was a perfect example of Niki hiring the person who really was the best.'[18]

Colin Graham directed twice at Guelph, for the Britten and later for Mozart's *La Finta Giardiniera*, both conducted by Niki.

Graham writes, 'They were both quite magnificently cast (by Nicky) and he was always a delight to work with. It was only Nicky's "undeniable charm" that had us all eating out of the palm of his hand – and for peanuts! But therein lies his genius: my admiration for his determination, energy, courage, and that CHARM, is unbounded.'[19]

Niki needed all his charm to dispose of one final bureaucratic detail after *The Rape of Lucretia*. Actors' Equity, the union governing contracts for singers and actors in Canada, complained that Jon Vickers was not one of its members, a situation that could compromise relations between the festival and other artists. Mustering up all his diplomacy, Niki explained the situation to his star singer and then wrote to Vickers, summing up the discussion. Clearly he had waited until the opera was safely launched.

'The officials of Actors' Equity understood that I did not want to bother you with this before the premiere,' he said. He went on to explain that, as agreed, $171.00, representing the initiation charge and dues, would be deducted from Vickers's fee and sent to Equity along with the required contract. He ended the letter with appropriate appreciation of Vickers's appearance at the festival. 'We all realize what a magnificent performance you have given, what a strong influence you have had.'[20]

The year 1974 had been a big one for the festival. It was also Niki's final year on the faculty of the university, since he had reached mandatory retirement age. At a luncheon given on 15 March in his honour he penned a seven-stanza ode of farewell. In his amusing verse he acknowledged the work of Murdo MacKinnon and other volunteers and the university's unique contribution to the festival. He concluded in true Niki style:

Let me leave you with a message of hope
Which is: for the arts there is unlimited scope,
As long as you at this University
Remain the proud keepers of true quality.
So may I thank you on this special occasion

For all you let me do even without persuasion;
But beware of the Ides of March, I say,
Don't worry! I will not fade away –
As I intend to remain young and healthy ... anyway![21]

Niki's good humour helped him deal with the inevitable criticisms. The Guelph festival had arrived at that point faced by many arts organizations, dealing with not always very logical demands for more 'popular' offerings. Never mind that the program is varied, box office returns are solid, and public opinion is supportive; voices are raised, responses mandatory.

An article in the Guelph student newspaper condescendingly accused the festival of having 'disgustingly little to offer the average citizen.'[22] In a surprising, one might say contradictory, twist, it went on to suggest more jazz and classical ballet, two art forms that traditionally attract their own, often small, specialized audiences, and are notoriously difficult to sell to a broader public.

Murdo, ever with his ear tuned to the sound and fury around him, anticipated the criticism and handled it smoothly. He wrote to the board in February of 1974 with a list of items that he said Niki had been asked to consider, and that the board would discuss at its March meeting. The issue of broad 'family appeal' came at the end, following carefully phrased questions such as 'Can we find an event of quality and appeal ...? Can we find a blockbuster like Menuhin?' and 'Can we do more with the film festival for youth?'

Niki's programs over the next several years show that he heard the concerns and was prepared to make some concessions, but not at the expense of high standards or his overall artistic vision. He added jazz, but only those artists and names that he knew, like Oscar Peterson and Moe Koffman. Ballet was a problem, being so expensive to tour; Rudolf Nureyev on film was Niki's solution, but later he brought Les Grands Ballets Canadiens, and in his final year the National Ballet of Canada with its two great stars, Karen Kain and Veronica Tennant.

The dazzling list of solo singers continued, with Jon Vickers returning in 1975 to sing Janáček's *The Diary of One Who Has Vanished*, with mezzo-soprano Janet Stubbs and pianist Rudolf Firkusny. John Kraglund found the concert, titled 'The Czech Composer,' somewhat 'out of context' among the usual fare at the festival; he failed to make the connection with Niki's own Moravian roots, shared with the composer. Nevertheless, Kraglund praised the event and all three performers, saying, 'They made an impressive team in this exceptionally beautiful and intensely moving composition.'[23]

Marilyn Horne's second appearance in Guelph was an artistic triumph, but one of those events that concert organizers remember with dismay, and a little humour only if enough time has lapsed.

On her first visit to Guelph Ms Horne sang at the charming War Memorial Hall. But Niki and the board, ever budget-conscious, knew they could sell many more tickets, so her return engagement was booked into the recreation centre at the university, the dreaded gymnasium with which North American touring artists are all too familiar. Unfortunately, Guelph was having an early heat wave that year, and the place was stifling. Murdo MacKinnon was the designated volunteer to look after this most important of artists, as he vividly recalls:

> She arrived, firing rockets before she was within twenty feet of me. Why couldn't she sing in that 'lovely hall?' How could she sing in this heat? And so on. The treasurer produced the cheque for her fee in advance, to placate her as much as we could. Of course her performance as a singer was fantastic, but she complained from the stage about the heat and refused after to go to the dinner for a group of donors, to which she had agreed. She just went back to Toronto. Of course, it was all reported in the press, but later I received a letter from a music lover in the US who told me that she had frequently sung in gymnasiums, and in the South where it was certainly hotter than our gym could ever be.[24]

Stephen Godfrey in the *Globe and Mail* was less charitable to the festival. He reported that Ms Horne exhibited great discomfort, telling the audience that 'I've never been to a jungle ... but it can't be worse than this.' Godfrey went on to describe her discomfort and exhaustion with the heat, which 'by the second half was affecting her pitch ... and emotional expression,' and concluded that if the festival wanted to attract artists of Ms Horne's calibre it would 'have to try to minimize a repeat of Saturday night.'[25]

Crises, large and small, are all part of organizing a festival in a small community with very few resources. It was a challenge for everyone, all of the time. Edwina Carson was Niki's long-time right hand in the publicity and public relations function, and she recalls how they managed: 'The festival was brilliant because every year the programming was fresh. But that also posed some difficulty because every year we started from zero with our target audience. It wasn't like selling a Bach festival every year. But I learned many skills from Niki, the most important being how to grab a vision and implement it using whatever tools are at hand. And I was able to succeed because Niki gave me confidence, he trusted me.'[26]

Out of the festival's tiny office, the staff, with Niki's encouragement, learned how to get the best deals on everything from airline tickets to flowers, and how to talk tough with New York agents. The latter skill they picked up from listening to Niki on the phone. As Edwina Carson tells it: 'He was the master manipulator, and I mean that in the kindest way, in the very best sense of that word. "We have nothing," he would say, on the telephone to some agent. And then he would mention one of the big names he had already lined up. "Madame So and So is coming, and for a very modest fee. I know your artist will want to be there with her." It worked and it was wonderful.'[27]

Niki used the hour or more travelling time from Toronto to make plans and suggestions for the regular festival staff meetings. Marilyn Crooks, administrator over many years, remembers:

> He would arrive with a lot of notes scribbled on the back of an envelope and I would have to read them, sometimes with great difficulty. Or Niki would interpret them, and fill in the blanks for me. He was always bursting to tell me anyway, especially whenever he had a new idea, which was nearly every time.
>
> Then while I sorted things out he would reach for the phone, and we would be in business. We had a lot of fun in that office because we were creating something so special. It was like Salzburg in southern Ontario; we were missing Mozart but we had Edward Johnson, and we had Niki to give it life.[28]

Marilyn Crooks's careful notes of each planning session capture that spirit. Every agenda item was recorded and numbered, including questions of fees ('Jessie Norman, $20,000 – unlikely'), problems of exclusivity in artists' contracts, tentative programs for future festivals, and matters of acoustics. Someone mentions that the St Andrew's Church may not be the best for the upcoming *Curlew River*, to which comes the reply from Niki: 'anything is better than Ross Hall; not to worry.' Later, Niki is complaining about the planned poster, saying that the 'artwork is dreadful.' Then it is back again to whether Richard Woitach will be available for a concert with Gilda Cruz-Romo.

The numbers of letters and notes are prodigious, some labelled simply 'ideas' most of which were never realized. One great diva was not available, another was too expensive, funding requests for commissions occasionally were not forthcoming. There were countless obstacles, but no time was wasted on regrets. Disappointments are noted, followed immediately by a fresh list of possibilities.

The premiere of *Seabird Island* by Derek Healey and Norman Newton brought considerable attention to the 1977 festival. While the reviews were in some cases contradictory (William Littler in the *Toronto Star* thought that the west coast Tsimshian legend 'failed to come alive as musical drama,'[29] while on the other hand Jamie Portman writing for Southam News Service said that 'the point about Healey is that he has a remarkable sense of musical drama')[30] Niki's faith in the piece was well placed when his proposal for a national tour was realized the following year. A chance conversation on a plane gave him the idea when his seat-mate told him there was to be a heritage festival in Vancouver, celebrating the two hundredth anniversary of the arrival of Captain Cook. Niki, ever alert to the artistic possibilities offered by an anniversary, immediately contacted the Vancouver group and suggested that they present *Seabird Island* as part of the festivities. At the same time he was immediately on the telephone to potential funders and sponsors; before long there was a string of dates in hand and the tour was a go, to Ottawa, Montreal, Banff, and ending at the west coast.

Psycho Red, the 1978 opera commissioned from composer Charles Wilson and librettist Eugene Benson, was a psychological thriller that threatened to become a metaphor for itself during the few weeks leading up to opening night. It was an extraordinarily complex work, described by William Littler as 'a 20th century work that has been forced into a 19th century theatrical frame.'[31] And that frame was supported by the limited resources of a small festival, with a budget that had no room for extended rehearsal time, an inadequate facility, and principals who had other professional obligations to fulfil. The musical structure was time-based, one second to a beat, and the libretto was anything but linear in its structure. (Critic John Kraglund couldn't figure it out. 'If I had discovered what the piece was all about,' he wrote, 'I would offer a brief synopsis.')[32] Brian Macdonald, who has met more than his share of artistic challenges, remembers it as being 'indescribably complicated,' and William Lord, whose students at York University were building the set, had difficulty giving them a clear design concept. 'I couldn't hear any colours in the music,' he says. 'It was difficult for anyone, singers, dancers, anyone to connect to the opera.'

Production problems were compounded drastically when the lead singer became ill, unable to carry on with the heavy demands of trying to learn the unfamiliar score and the complex staging demands. A replacement was found who made an extraordinary effort, even turning up for rehearsal at 7:00 in the morning at Murdo MacKinnon's house. But he gave up after a few days, recognizing that there was not enough time left to do justice to the role (and undoubtedly to his own professional reputation).

An emergency meeting was held to decide what to do. Niki had several ideas, the most practical, he thought, being to put the whole thing off for a year. But Murdo and the other board members involved said 'No' to that idea. After all, these were Guelph artists, the premiere had been advertised, funding had been received. In Murdo's view it had to go forward. He remembers that emotions were running high.

'We did not think we could cancel. But we discussed all the options and then Brian told us, "Go away, give me an hour." When we came back he said that he thought he could restage it so that the central character could sit at a desk for the whole opera, giving him the opportunity to have the score in front of him. So, after several phone calls we were able to persuade our baritone to return, and with a delayed opening and fewer performances we went ahead.'[33]

Niki frowns at the memory of the débâcle. At least he was not conducting, having turned that role over to the composer. (Robert Cooper, the young singer from Centennial Choir days, by then launched on his own career, sat in the orchestra shadowing Wilson's beat and cueing the singers.)

Wilson remembers it as a 'hair-raising' experience, and feels that Niki was 'negative' about it, but he praises Macdonald's direction, and acknowledges that the festival overall was good for Guelph artists and for his own music, several pieces of which were programmed there over the years.[34] Surprisingly, the critics were not unduly negative. Avoiding the temptation to report gossip, they generally praised the festival and the artists for taking risks and bringing high professional standards to the stage. So, in spite of the anxiety, arguments, and disastrous box office, the festival escaped relatively unscathed from what Niki still refers to as a 'terrible failure.'

And undaunted he continued, year after year, to tantalize his audience with operatic surprises from an astounding diversity of periods and places; the world premiere of Menotti's *Chip and His Dog* in 1979, followed the next year by Smetana's *The Two Widows*, Britten, Argento, and Gluck.

One of the happiest experiences for everyone came with the 1986 presentation of another psychological music drama, Peter Maxwell Davies's *The Lighthouse*.

> I was determined to do it, so I went to New York to see a production by the Fires of London (and by the way to get the Canadian rights). Andrew Porter was also at the performance and he and I agreed that it was a very exciting work, but the performance in New York was only so so! I came back to Guelph and told the board about this terrific piece. 'We have to do it,' I said. 'And it won't be too expensive, only three singers.'
>
> Of course I had no tenor, and that was crucial. One evening I was at home listening to the radio, and heard *Messiah* from Vancouver and I said to Shelagh, 'Listen to that tenor, God, what a voice!' The announcer said at the end that it was Ben Heppner. So I got in touch with him and told him what I had planned. He came to the house with the director Robert Carsen and Michael Eagen, the designer, to discuss the project, and we talked and then Ben said that he would do it. That was the beginning. Christopher Cameron [bass] and Cornelius Opthof [baritone] joined the cast, an all-Canadian team. I took one look at the score and said this wasn't for me to conduct so I invited Stuart Bedford, who was splendid. It was a terrific production and of course it was Ben's operatic debut.[35]

This was a risk of a different sort. The work had already been given several productions internationally by directors of the stature of Peter Sellars, and among the small but fiercely opinionated followers of contemporary opera its nuances were much debated.

Into this company strode Niki and his intrepid Guelph team, with the opera's Canadian premiere.

The critics were ecstatic. William Littler said it was the Guelph Spring Festival 'at its enterprising best,' and Andrew Porter, writing in the *Financial Times* of London, praised the production, saying 'the three characters, and the tensions between them, were defined more sharply than in other productions I have seen.' He applauded the singers. 'All three sang very well,' he said.[36] The only surprise in the laudatory reviews was that none singled out for special mention the great tenor voice that had caught Niki's attention on a radio broadcast and that in a few short years would be heard from the great operatic stages of the world!

This was one of those cases where Niki knew he had an extraordinary event planned and saw the possibility to exploit it fully. With his customary zeal he assembled the resources for a western tour of *The Lighthouse*, ending on stage in the Canada Pavilion at Vancouver's Expo '86. The newsletter for opera lovers in Vancouver called it 'by far the best operatic evening of the season in Vancouver.'[37]

It was the kind of success that inspired the small staff and the board members at Guelph, who were kept busy looking after the arrangements and comforts of dozens of artists every year. Siobhan McKenna starred as Sarah Bernhardt in the world premiere of John Murrell's *Memoir*, and was accommodated in the home of a board member who had to ensure a regular supply of Irish whisky.

Maureen Forrester appeared in 1974, and caused a minor flurry, mitigated by the good humour that always surrounds this beloved Canadian artist. Murdo remembers it well:

Her program was advertised as 'old favourites,' art songs and opera with which the audience was familiar. But at the last minute she changed the program, and sang mostly late nineteenth-century French repertoire. It really was marvellous and different. At the reception afterward a few of the more conservative types were upset. Niki, at his most mischievous, walked up to Maureen and announced, 'Miss Forrester, I am the artistic director of this festival and you have let me down. I show my back.' He turned and walked away a few steps, then turned back, laughed and gave her a big hug.[38]

There was, however a subtext to that incident. Murdo received a letter from a professor in the Department of Philosophy explaining that his students had been discussing whether 'an artist generally had to fulfil the expectations of the public.'[39] Agreeing that artists have to follow their own creative needs, they nevertheless concluded that once a program was advertised it took on the nature of a promise and to change it was 'unethical.' On a less philosophical note, they added that in their opinion a New York audience would not have been 'cheated' in this way. The professor added a personal note at the bottom of the letter, to Niki, thanking him for his excellent work over the years.

Niki finessed the question neatly in his reply, telling the professor and his students that there was a 'dilemma.' He had been advised of the change only a day or two before the concert and did not want to risk a program that 'perhaps would not have done justice' to the evening. He went on to assure the professor that it would not happen again.[40]

Of course there were unavoidable cancellations and changes, but if the headlines tell the tale, no one was unduly put off. 'Masterpiece,' 'triumph,' 'captivating,' 'engrossing,' the superlatives continued. There were singers, Nicolai Gedda, Martina Arroyo, Pauline Julien, Catherine Robbin, Lois Marshall, the Bach Aria Group; chamber groups—over a dozen of the world's finest appeared at the festival; symphony orchestras, dance groups, comedy and drama, and always the special event, the risk that made the treasurer nervous and everyone else sit up and take notice.

In 1976 Niki persuaded Polish composer Krzysztof Penderecki to come to Guelph as conductor of his own work. Niki assembled a stellar group of Canadian performers[41] for a concert that drew a standing ovation from the Guelph audience and signalled to music lovers across the country that they should pay attention to the little city in southwestern Ontario if they wanted to keep up with what was happening on the concert scene.

But it wasn't all serious music-making. At Niki's seventieth birthday party in Guelph, complete with sparklers and singing, composer Louis Applebaum, then executive director of the Ontario Arts Council, called him the 'youngest pixie in the world,' no doubt thinking of all the times Niki had popped into the council's offices 'just to explain his latest idea,' as he would always say – in the process generating so much enthusiasm that when he came back later asking for financial assistance it was impossible to say 'No.'

Not all his ideas were brand new. Some were firmly rooted in the festival's beginnings, the 1967 vocal competition, and the educational mandate of the Edward Johnson Foundation. Local and regional competitions, vocal and instrumental, became part of the festival early in the 1970s, and in 1977 Niki reinstituted the national vocal competition, to be held every five years. As usual he did it with class, calling on his worldwide contacts to gather jurors of the highest reputation: Leopold Simoneau, Rose Bampton, Theodore Upman, Heather Harper, the Earl of Harewood.

Vincent Tovell was the non-voting chair of the jury in 1987: 'Niki was always looking for opportunities for young people. He knew that whatever he did had to be well structured, and there had to be some idea of where they would go next. He used his festivals, through the competitions and through performing roles, to give opportunities to young artists, always making sure that they were well cast.'[42]

Once only, in 1980, the festival co-operated with the Royal College of

Organists to present an organ competition as part of the festival's celebrations for the Healey Willan centennial. There were national events
honouring Canada's best-known composer and organist. At Guelph,
Niki mixed innovation, quality, and fun to overcome any perception
that this was to be a year of solemn church music. The opening concert
featured Lois Marshall and the Elmer Iseler Singers presenting the premiere of Harry Somers's irreverent *Limericks,* commissioned for the
occasion, and commemorating Somers's last meeting with Willan, at
which they had exchanged humorous verses.[43]

A 'first' that was more difficult to sell was an evening devoted to Austrian composer Ernst Krenek on the occasion of his eightienth birthday.
He was almost unknown in Canada, and the premiere of his *Concerto for
Organ and String Orchestra* was not the kind of fare that had people lining
up at the box office for tickets. Nevertheless, Krenek praised the result,
writing to Niki, 'I especially enjoyed conducting the fine Kitchener-
Waterloo Orchestra in my Organ Concerto,' and remarking on the success of the symposium held in conjunction with the concert.[44] All these
programs led up to the competition itself, with finals being held in St
George's Church, where the capacity audience, including Lieutenant-
Governor Pauline McGibbon, sat on the hard flat pews through an
exceptionally long evening before the winners were selected.

Although the organ competition was never repeated, Murdo felt it
was worthwhile: 'It was one of those events that Niki plans that had
many benefits for the community. The jurors came from all over, they
were very distinguished, and gave master classes, and played recitals in
the local churches, even in towns outside of Guelph.'[45]

Since Niki's days at the conservatory in the 1940s, Canada's artistic
institutions had been growing exponentially, in both quantity and quality. At the same time, at least until the end of the 1980s, there was a parallel growth on the bureaucratic side. Arts councils and government
departments responsible for culture were established federally and in
most provinces and territories. Advocacy groups sprang up, and the arts
became a lively subject of the public discourse. While Niki was never a
central figure on the policy development side, working as he did on the
front line where performances happened, he nevertheless was profoundly interested in the public debate. He is most proud of his years as
a member of the Canada Council (Canada's federal agency for arts support), to which he was appointed in 1980, and where he served two
terms of three years each. It was an experience which he enjoyed and to
which he brought his unique style of deliberation.

The role of working artists as members of grant-giving bodies is always fraught with ambiguity and, occasionally, charges of conflict and favouritism. Tim Porteous, director of the Canada Council during Niki's tenure, says it is the price to pay for the knowledge such people bring to the table: 'It is a matter of balance. In Canada we always have to consider the regional interests, as well as a board that reflects the community we are trying to serve. Artists bring an understanding to the board that is unique and very helpful to the deliberations. In Niki's case, of course, he was frequently an applicant, and a brilliant one. We managed to work around that, and in fact he didn't always receive what he thought he should have, particularly to support tours. He didn't like it, but it never caused any problem.'[46]

Niki often acted as the council's ambassador in small communities, explaining the important elements for a successful grant application (quality programming, evidence of fiscal viability, and strong community support), and urging his listeners to travel, especially across Canada, and attend performances, be informed, hear what was going on.[47]

He was a loyal attendee at the Canada Council meetings, where he served under three chairpersons, Charles Lussier, Mavor Moore, and Maureen Forrester:

It was tremendously illuminating, it gave me insight into how support worked, and about arm's length. Although the appointments to the board were made through the political process (one member during two years never asked one question, a poor example of patronage!), generally they were very interesting people. The staff department heads attended the meetings, which made the meetings interesting, lively, because they knew their field and fought for the applicants and for their disciplines. There was no political patronage on the staff side; they were very professional. The Canada Council is a fabulous institution that has been central to the development of the arts in Canada. I am sure that less than half of the arts organizations across the country would exist today if it had not been for the council.

In 1984, when the council was locked in a controversy with the government over proposed legislation designed to increase government's control over Crown corporations, Niki made the trip to Ottawa to attend the Parliamentary Committee hearing. Council presented its arguments that it be excluded from the legislation. Niki had no part in the proceedings, but he was happy to be there, to show the committee members that as an artist and member of the council he was confident that it was a fully accountable body, and that the legislation would only compromise its independence from political influence over artistic decisions.

In spite of Niki's strong belief in council, he reserved the right to question policies that he felt were not in the best interests of the artists, or of the country. He paid particular attention to the practice of awarding grants to young artists (especially singers) to study abroad. He feels strongly that assistance of that kind should be given only for training opportunities not available in Canada, to perfect skills, not simply learn the basics. He made this point in a larger report, prepared at council's request, on the benefits that might be realized from a closer relationship between Canada's arts community and Austria.[48]

After meeting with a long list of contacts in the diplomatic and arts world in Austria, he suggested ways in which Canada and Austria could enhance their cultural ties. Better information supplied to the Canadian Embassy staff was essential, in his opinion, and, no doubt anticipating long months of committees and task forces while the situation steadily deteriorated, he insisted that improvements needed to '*be done right away.*' His report also offered practical advice to artists wishing to appear in Europe. Good management, contracts settled one and a half to two years in advance, attractive programming, excellent promotional materials supplied in a timely fashion, and realistic expectations about fees, which in Europe were not high (for example, Radio Vienna was paying the equivalent of $1000 for a string quartet, $250 for a solo pianist), those were the basics.

On the 'question of students abroad' he reported on his meetings with twenty Canadian students, instructors at the Hochschule für Musik, and other experts. His conclusions were unequivocal. Although Europe offered a rich musical environment, he was disappointed in the general level of training available in Vienna.

Despite his affection for the city, he said frankly that the standards were not what they had once been. After attending performances and classes, and talking to the experts who had seen and heard student performances in Canada, Niki suggested, in his most diplomatic way, that Canada already presented excellent opportunities for young artists to learn their craft, and that there were other centres besides Vienna where high-quality training was available. He urged prudence: 'I believe that many students go over to Europe much too early. They should be well prepared in order to understand better their new environment, and understand the true meaning of Master Classes, which is to take advantage of the "Master's" expertise. Study abroad should be considered part of graduate work. One does not go to Vienna to *learn* more about the German language – one goes there to *perfect* it; only then is one ready to study Lieder from an expert.'

He was firm in the view that all possibilities be explored. 'Maybe the time has come to consider reversing the flow of talent,' he wrote. 'It might be more beneficial ... to bring outstanding teachers over to Canada for short residencies at the various universities from coast to coast. I believe that twenty concentrated hours of teaching by a great expert in Canada could do more good for a student than six months with some on and off teaching abroad.'

He concluded with some powerful, and generous, remarks on this subject:

> In short, it is my strong belief that the Canada Council and all other grant-giving agencies should be truly more selective; talent one is born with; but initiative and perseverance are as essential to a career as continuous hard work – and more work and more work.
>
> For those who make the grade the Canada Council will always be gratified to have given its support. For those who do not succeed, the Canada Council would at least be glad to have given the opportunity.

Nothing in the record indicates that Niki's report was immediately embraced or changes in policies effected. However, Mavor Moore calls it an 'important piece of work,' and former staff and members of granting juries acknowledge its contribution to the improvement of procedures with respect to sending Canadian artists abroad.

He had less success, however, on another subject on which he argued with Council for several years. It all started with the Menuhin commission for a work from Harry Somers, for the Guelph Spring Festival. Niki called the Canada Council's Music Section to ask for assistance with this project, in Niki's view unquestionably deserving. After all, here was a leading Canadian composer, an internationally renowned performer, and a festival with a proven record of excellence. In Niki's mind, support should have been almost automatic. But he was told that, like every other proposal for commissioning new work, the appropriate application would have to be submitted, along with examples of the composer's previous work, and the final decision would be made by a jury looking at all current submissions.

Niki was annoyed then and continues to be so:

> I don't think anyone has ever really looked at that policy. It happened to me again, with the same composer, when I asked Harry to write the Children's Hymn for the United Nations. When they told me I would have to ask him to send in tapes and scores I just said, 'Over my dead body!' It seems to me that senior composers should be exempt from this competition process. A certain amount of money should be set aside for commissions in that category, and then it could be reviewed every three or four years. We should not put our senior artists who have proved themselves in the same bag as someone absolutely new.

Grants officers and arts bureaucrats acknowledge the logic of Niki's position, but insist that, given the increasing demand for funds from credible organizations and gifted composers, the present system is the fairest. And so this is one argument that Niki has not won.

Characteristically, he never allowed his disagreements with 'the system' to slow him down, or get in the way of his participation in the artistic life of the country.

The debates in the Canada Council's boardroom often focused on the question of excellence, and here Niki's respect for serious artistic effort was evident. One granting program designed to encourage new work and relatively unknown artists in all regions of the country had Niki's full support. Some members of council felt that this 'Explorations' program, as it was called, ran counter to the goal of supporting excellence in the arts. Niki spoke out strongly in its favour:

> I told my colleagues that excellence can only be achieved by progressing, by experimenting. We need to let artists try, and perhaps try again. If they have the basic talent and sound training in their field, whether it is music or dance or any discipline, they should be assisted to do their work. Perhaps the first time it may be a flop. Even the second or third time, but out of that experimenting will come excellence. I came from a part of the world where one could say 'excellence' in the arts of Western Europe had already been achieved. But nothing can be static; it cannot stay stuck in that time and that place. We have to develop our own artists with their own artistic expression. Art must be dynamic or it dies.

Throughout those interesting years as council member, Guelph remained Niki's artistic home, until in 1986 he announced that the 1987 season, his twentieth, would be his last. It turned out to be a superstar of a festival, with a familiar format and favourite artists, and some rare treats! It was a year's worth of concert-going packed into three weeks.

Jon Vickers opened the festivities on 24 April, his sixth appearance on stage at the festival, treating the ecstatic audience to a program featuring music that Niki so loves, lieder and opera. The hall was absolutely still, no one moving, as the great *Heldentenor* delivered a gripping performance of the third-act soliloquy from *Peter Grimes*. The entire evening was electric, with Vickers turning 'songs into dramas full of meaning.'[49]

Chamber music lovers, savouring Niki's last program, flocked to hear the Orford Quartet, now in the third decade of its career, perform the full cycle of Beethoven String Quartets; residents and visitors hurried to buy tickets for everything on offer, among them pianist Angela Hewitt, the National Ballet of Canada, and the Canadian Brass .

The opera was another Canadian premiere, this time not a contemporary drama but Mozart's youthful romp, *La Finta Giardiniera*. The production, with an all-Canadian cast headed by Donna Trifunovich and Mark Pedrotti, conducted by Niki, was a triumph. (The following summer Niki and the singers gave a semi-concert version of the opera in the Chatauqua auditorium at the Colorado Music Festival. The critic there declared that 'If singers like this grow on the trees of Ontario, I want a job with the Canadian forest service.' He praised Niki, calling him the 'No. 1 hero of the production, the master of both cast and orchestra.')[50]

Niki was especially moved by Yehudi Menuhin's participation in the 1987 festival. His old friend came to help celebrate Niki's final season, bringing with him the International Soloists of the Camerata Lysy Gstaad, a chamber orchestra made up of the stars of Menuhin's academy in Switzerland. Here was a musical icon, playing and conducting with talented youth, on a program that was a mix of the old, Bach and Mozart, and the new, a commission from Canadian André Prévost. It was a quintessential Guelph special, as were the master classes given by Menuhin for gifted young Ontario violinists. Niki sat in the hall each day, listening and observing intently as one after the other the aspiring musicians played for the master. And afterward, Niki and Menuhin took time to go off together for a visit to the market, or a quiet meal with Shelagh.

Niki had worked for two years, using his many contacts across the country and his considerable persuasive powers, to facilitate a tour by

Menuhin and his orchestra to smaller communities such as Thunder Bay in northern Ontario and St John's, Newfoundland, as well as larger centres, enhancing Guelph's reputation beyond its own region and attracting private sponsors and governments to support the project to extraordinary levels.

Menuhin wrote to Niki just before returning home: 'As our Canadian adventure reaches its terms [*sic*] I feel a growing gratitude to you for our experience which more than any other has revealed to me the great heart of this youthful and giant country.' He went on to praise the young players he had heard, one as young as six, and offered the opinion that 'there is such good teaching in Canada that unless it is for a particular experience ... it is quite unnecessary to send people elsewhere.' And he concluded, 'Dear Niki and Shelagh, again my thanks and love to both of you for your remarkable companionship which made our tour unforgettable to me.'[51]

That letter with its warm sentiments of friendship was repeated over and over again in the sheafs of messages received at the gala dinner given in Niki's honour at the close of the festival. Artists, festival staff and board members, patrons, government officials, and friends, amid balloons and bubbly, applauded as eloquent tributes and thanks were given for twenty years of artistic magic. They all wished Niki well for his future ventures, because of course he was only in his eightieth year and was already involved in realizing his next 'good ideas.'

It had been a remarkable two decades, but not without its bumps. It was probably time for Niki to move on. At the beginning of the 1980s he had expressed some impatience with the programming of the festival, wondering if it had become dull, predictable. Certainly the musical scene was changing and the festival, once unique, found itself competing with an extended season in Toronto and festivals springing up in other towns across the province. But Niki, never at a loss for ideas, met the programming challenge and audiences continued to wait expectantly for the annual announcement of what was in store for the next spring. On the financial side, however, it was not so easy. Although ticket sales (with the exception of a few events) were always strong, costs escalated during that inflationary period and soaring interest rates combined with a stalled economy made it difficult to meet budget targets, leaving the board to wrestle with finances and wonder whether they could find the resources and the individuals with the energy to continue in the tradition established in the 1960s.

At the end of the 1983 season the board had taken drastic action, cutting costs wherever it could, including halving the salaries of the artistic director and the director of publicity. Edwina Carson, who held the latter position, was understandably indignant: 'We were not at the meeting when the board took that action, and I felt hurt, that I could have been part of the solution, because we had just had a blockbuster year in terms of sales, and I knew there were other things to do. I wanted to quit but Niki said, "No, just be like the willow, bend with the pressure, and then come back when it is time." It was another one of those lessons I learned from him.'[52]

Others wanted to learn from Niki too. As the 1980s unfolded, bringing an expansion on the artistic scene across the country, Niki became a kind of 'Mr Festival' in Canada. He was called on by communities across the country to tell them how to do it ... how to make a festival successful as Guelph's.

On the east coast, on Prince Edward Island, for example, he was invited to investigate the feasibility of a putting in place a small festival, called Music in Charlottetown. Niki's report showed his experience in dealing with various and often conflicting community interests, and his basic formula for success. After a brief run-down of the various festivals across the country, including jazz in Fredericton, and teaching/festival combinations at Banff and at Courtenay, BC, he listed the various interested parties he consulted, the clear message being that before anything could happen it was important to enthuse, reassure, one could say co-opt anyone who might be affected by the project. In this case he reported after his consultations with Island residents that they would welcome any new arts activity as long as it didn't conflict with the summer performances at Charlottetown's Confederation Centre of the Arts.

His conclusion: that new activities on the university campus and in churches could only enhance the festival spirit. But he cautioned: start on a small scale, have a committed person in place as director, combine music instruction and performance, and be sure that quality is the only criterion for presentation.[53]

Niki's involvement with PEI extended only to the report, and the festival idea never did take hold. However, a request from Yarmouth, Nova Scotia, for a similar report did have good results for the community, because, in Niki's view, it had the essential ingredient: 'At least one person who is committed to it, the guiding light.' And there was one other non-musical element that in Niki's view guaranteed success in Nova Scotia. 'We had every day the fresh lobster right from the sea. It was marvellous.'

Not long after he had taken on Guelph, in 1969, Niki was invited to be artistic consultant to a Canadian festival in the northern Ontario city of Sudbury. More famous for its nickel mining than its arts, this bilingual community nevertheless had a history of choral singing reflecting the diverse ethnic mix of the region, a strong music teaching tradition, community and youth orchestras, and an accordion orchestra.

The first festival focused on choral music, coinciding with what turned out to be the founding conference of the Ontario Choral Federation, and featuring Niki's Centennial Choir together with local groups.

Niki's post-festival report declared that the entire event suffered from administrative confusion, lack of strong leadership, or a clear plan and no influential, committed fundraising committee.[54] Even the musical co-operation was not there: 'The first time I went there it was fine, but when I came the second time I found that there was conflict among the choirs. You can't have a festival like that. It just won't work.'

The second year was no better than the first, it seems, and the entire enterprise collapsed under the weight of its own deficit.

With changes in society after the upheavals of the 1960s and early 1970s came a new consciousness about community. Universities were offering courses on the evolution of society and community development, but Niki didn't need a degree to tell him how the arts can flourish. His experience had given him a finely honed sense about the elements needed to successfully launch and maintain any artistic venture. In 1974 he wrote a report for Robert Sunter, then music officer of the Ontario Arts Council, regarding the feasibility of establishing an Affiliate Artists Program in Ontario. The US model had gained acclaim, placing young artists in communities as musical ambassadors and animators.

Niki's report identified the two possible goals for such a program, to develop the young artists, or to further the cultural development of the community. 'Ideally it should do both,' he wrote, 'but you must decide at the beginning which is most applicable to Ontario.' He outlined a possible program of activity, then turned to the matter of local support. Having looked at four different regions, he emphasized the need to find a forceful and well-connected business person to raise funds for the program and suggested that a pilot project would be the prudent way to start.[55]

Niki had done his job, and although Ontario never embraced the Affiliate Artists idea, it did have a framework for assessing upstart ideas in future.

But of course, Niki was doing much more than just writing reports. Every year he travelled to Europe visiting family and taking in performances, always with an ear to what would be exciting (and affordable) at home. And always willing to take a risk, he participated in some extraordinary undertakings. In 1972, at the request of John Godfrey, son of his old friend Senator Godfrey, he went to Dalhousie University to give one of the most unlikely lectures of his career. Seven hundred and fifty history students were gathered in the student union building for a 'Niebelungathon,' a non-stop, twenty-four-hour multimedia presentation that included filmed productions of Wagner's *Ring Cycle* and related texts and of course the music. Niki's job was to introduce the whole affair, give it some context.

'Niki did a great job,' says Godfrey. 'He's a great showman and he really had their measure. He displayed his real professionalism; it is really attitudinal. It is this huge enthusiasm mixed with shrewdness. It goes beyond the music, but music is the force.'[56]

Niki's recollections also focus on the music: 'I told the students that I couldn't possibly tell them all about the *Ring* in one hour. All I could do was give them some clues, some keys, what to listen for. So I didn't go into a long analysis, but I did tell them to listen carefully to the first twelve bars of *Das Rheingold*, then they would know not only what orchestration is all about, but they would be taken down into the deepest part of existence.'[57]

At the other end of the country, on Vancouver Island, Niki took on a different challenge in the 1980s. At the Courtenay Youth Music Centre, a summer program of teaching and performance, set in a stunning landscape of mountain glaciers, roaring rivers, forests, and ocean, where sailing and hiking feel more relevant than concert-going, he helped fashion an opera and choral program. It brought together young professionals with seasoned pros in a mix that was vintage Goldschmidt. On soft warm summer evenings he lured residents into the modest Civic Centre for a 1984 production of Mozart's *Marriage of Figaro* that the local critic said 'brims with excellence.' And the next year he returned for *Die Fledermaus*, which the same paper termed a 'joy.' The director of the Centre, Robert Creech, described Niki's contribution in broader terms:

Niki first came to the CYMC in 1980, for a very modest fee. He is very good at promoting in a community; he formed and inspired a local amateur choir that learned an amazing amount of music. I remember among the highlights a very creditable performance of Brahms's *German Requiem* in 1983 and the following year an excellent performance of Bruckner's *Te Deum*, again quite a feat for a small community.

As for the operas, he coached and imparted a knowledge of the work, and conducted some of them; they were all done on a small budget, but were always successful, reflecting his enthusiasm and love of music.[58]

Niki was thrust into a location and a project of a different cast in the late 1970s, that has been a part of his professional life for over a quarter of a century. Sault Ste Marie, Ontario, a town of approximately eighty thousand, sits beside the swirling rapids of the St Mary's River where giant lake freighters churn into view as they line up to pass through the locks between lakes Huron and Superior. Turning 180 degrees, the view is dominated by the sprawling industrial site of Algoma Steel, and the rise of the trees and rock of the Canadian Shield beyond. This is a northern town with the air of the frontier. The *Canadian Encyclopedia* describes its cultural life as consisting of Sault College and Algoma University, winter carnival, hockey, boat tours of the locks, and wilderness tours to nearby Agawa Canyon. Not one mention of the painters drawn to the region's exotic beauty, or the long and diverse choral tradition, the enthusiastic bands and local orchestras and the tradition of music teaching that began early in the twentieth century and saw dedicated music teachers placed in the town's schools as early as 1920. And no chronicle of the Algoma Fall Festival, founded in 1973 after a group of eager citizens from that area had approached the Ontario Arts Council about starting a summer festival.

Naomi Lightbourne, the officer responsible for community-based arts at the council, was deeply committed to the expansion of arts activity beyond the major centres and wanted to help. 'We knew that they had never talked to anyone who had run a festival,' she says, 'so we thought it would be wise to send Niki up to look things over. He not only told them the realities of how a festival could work, but the greatest thing he did for them was to give them confidence. They came in saying that they wanted to do something but had no idea how to do it. He gave them ideas about what could be done and they just went full steam ahead.'[59]

His initial meeting in the Sault was not auspicious, but the northerners were persistent, and Niki as usual had an open mind and a keen eye: 'The founding of that festival I think is a lovely story, I would call it romantic. I first went up in early August of 1972, and I met with an assembly of people, and we began to discuss their plans. What kind of a budget were they thinking of? Oh, about $750,000! "Well that's quite a plan, I said. How will you raise it?" [No doubt he was mindful that Guelph's budget was under $200,000!] From the three levels of government, they thought.'

Niki smiles at the audacity of the plan. He reminded them that without local support from the community and local business the governments wouldn't give a cent. They were surprised to hear that, but took note and the discussion moved on to other matters.

It was terribly hot so I asked if they had an air-conditioned facility. 'No.' They didn't have that so I pointed out how difficult that would be for the musicians, to say nothing of the audience. And speaking of audience, I asked about who would they expect to attend the concerts. They told me that most of the locals, certainly the community leaders, the business people and so on are always out at their cottages in August. 'But,' they told me, 'We have lots of tourists.' 'And what do the tourists do?' I asked. 'Well, they come for the fishing and camping.' So I had to ask them, did they really think that those tourists, after a day of fishing, would come into town and sit in a hot auditorium to listen to a concert? I didn't want to disappoint them, but they had to refine their ideas. So I went back to OAC and told them that there was no chance.

Several weeks later, Niki received another call from the Arts Council asking him to go back again and give it another try. So at the end of September, as the trees were turning from green to flaming red and orange and yellow, he flew north again, and this time, before the plane had even landed, he knew what could happen in the Sault.

I looked out the window of the plane and I saw this carpet of colours, that I had never experienced before, it was gorgeous, just unbelievable. Meeting me was Mrs Harriet Black, who was really the soul of the whole plan, and we drove together into town. She said to me, 'Well, what about it, do you think we can have a festival?' I told her 'Of course, you have it!' She was startled and looked at me. 'What do you mean?' 'Look out the window, look at these colours. That's it. You have the Algoma Fall Festival.'

And within a year, beginning on 21 September 1973, they did, with a modest budget of about $35,000. Niki acted as artistic consultant, but did not take over artistic responsibility for the festival until two years later.

While Algoma has an eclectic mix of presentations that might be

called the Goldschmidt trademark, it has never been a carbon copy of
Guelph, or of any other of Niki's undertakings. Programming has always
been heavily dependent on which artists and ensembles are already
touring in any one year, in order to keep the crushing costs of travel in
the north to a minimum. Limited facilities and a smaller potential audience than in the more populous south have also influenced the choices.
But these constraints have only challenged Niki's ingenuity, and a review
of the programs tells the tale. Over half a dozen orchestras, including
the BBC Scottish Symphony and the TSO, have appeared at the festival.
An equal number of chamber ensembles, including Niki's old friends
the Orford Quartet and the Canadian Brass, a dozen dance companies
from across Canada and from as far away as New Zealand, instrumentalists, jazz artists, among them Wynton Marsalis and Dizzy Gillespie –
concert-goers have seen and heard them all. Families came to see shows
by the likes of Nova Scotia's Mermaid Theatre, the Canadian Mime Theatre, and the Chinese Magic Circus; others attended the regular film
offerings.

Perhaps because of the landscape, the light, the shapes and colours
that suffuse the region, the Sault has always attracted visual artists, and
their work has had a prominent place in the festival since the beginning.
Robert Bateman, Ken Danby, Dora de Pedery-Hunt, Ken Bradford,
David Milne, Lawren Harris, and dozens more have been featured in
special exhibitions. Many community leaders credit the festival's commitment to visual art as the foundation on which they were able to build
support for the establishment of the Algoma Art Gallery.

Niki has always wanted his projects to have the widest possible impact
on the community, and in the Sault, with teachers and parents pushing
to take advantage of every opportunity, the festival's education program
is exemplary. Special performances and workshops by festival artists,
artists-in-schools residencies, tours, and talks have given the students
of the Sault a collective artistic experience not always enjoyed in more
so-called sophisticated centres. The 1997 program shows how it has
developed.

John Leonard, artist in residence, worked with a group of senior students on a mural project; Martha Johnson gave a special concert for primary listeners while Quartetto Gelato gave a performance and question-
and-answer session for intermediate and senior students.

Two luminaries of Canadian theatre, Martha Henry and Rod Beattie,
appearing at the festival in A.R. Gurney's *Love Letters*, gave senior drama,
art, and English students the benefit of their long theatrical experience
in a lecture demonstration 'On *Acting*.'

A master class by I Musici encouraged budding instrumentalists, and *The Shooting of Dan McGrew* by Theatre Orangeville brought a little fun and history to the intermediate grades. And will the students of English literature ever forget Timothy Findley giving a special reading and a question-and-answer session, just for them? Altogether over seven thousand students participated in these remarkable artistic 'extras.'

Timothy Findley is only one of the Canadian authors that Niki has offered his audiences. Northrop Fyre, Robertson Davies, Mordecai Richler, W.O. Mitchell, Jane Urquhart, and Michael Ignatieff all have appeared at the Sault and been welcomed by enthusiastic audiences each year.

Of course there has always been music, and Niki understands that choral music is one sure way to a community's heart. In 1974 he formed the Algoma Festival Choir with nearly a hundred members from every part of the community, steelworkers, teachers, anyone who loved to sing. Many participated in their church choirs, and Niki laughingly says that when they came together with him 'it was the first time that the Anglicans sang with the Catholics, and they all got on very well!'

Niki flew back and forth from Toronto to prepare the choir for its debut at St Luke's Cathedral in a program that featured Bach, Handel, Schubert, Mozart, and Vaughan Williams. Local critics described the evening as being a 'delightful surprise,' spoke about the 'superb style,' and said it left the audience wanting more. And they were not disappointed. The choir became a fixture. A typical program and one that illustrates how Niki has blended community performers with touring artists was given in 1983 when the Festival Choir was joined by Toronto's Tapestry Singers and the Sault Symphony together with the Canadian Chamber Ensemble from Kitchener for a concert at Central United Church featuring Handel's *Passion of Christ.* One writer said it was a highlight of the festival and a 'triumph for the entire ensemble and conductor Goldschmidt.'[60]

Could an ongoing community festival directed by Niki continue without featuring *Noah's Flood* at least once? In fact, Niki has presented it twice in the Sault, giving two generations of children the opportunity to don the animal masks and enter into the drama of the piece. The first production came early in his tenure, in 1976, and was directed by his dear friend and collaborator from Vancouver, Joy Coghill. The second was in the year 2000, with friends and family filling the pews, joining in the traditional hymns that are woven into the Britten score. It is a work that still generates a sense of awe, a mythic story, the voice of God, and a cast of children concentratring hard to do it right. One, 'Jason, the buck,' was so enthralled with his role that he wrote to Joy Coghill expressing his feelings when it was all over. 'I cryed so much that I could have made lake superior look like a paudal.'[61]

Original production of opera was not a regular feature of the Algoma Festival. In 1977 Niki risked doing two Menotti operas, *The Telephone* and *The Old Maid and the Thief*. In 1982 he mounted another favourite, Humperdinck's *Hansel and Gretel*, a production that was repeated the following year at the Bermuda Festival. The witch was played this time by Sister Barbara Ianni, a Sault Ste Marie native whom Niki had first met when she was performing in Toronto, and who had sung at Guelph in the production of *Seabird Island*.

In describing the background of the Bermuda production, one reviewer mixed up Niki's several enterprises to describe it as involving singers and staff from 'the Algoma Fall Festival of Guelph, Ontario.' She did, however, go on to praise the 'outstanding' Mark Pedrotti and the witch, 'hideously well-played and sung to great effect,' and said that Niki managed to conduct 'with a minimum of effort and a maximum of good.'[62]

The financial fortunes of the Algoma Festival have fluctuated with the economic ups and downs of the city, always dependent on the state of the highly volatile steel industry. As the festival budget grew until it hovered around the $200,000 mark, there were years with surpluses, while others ended with deficits. The board has struggled with how to maintain box office receipts, generating the inevitable arguments about more 'popular' programming, with Niki always defending quality, and (on a more practical note) promoting the collaboration with community arts groups that is favoured by funders. Niki knows how it all works. In his non-stop negotiations with artists and their managers he is always definite about the restraints of a small northern festival in terms of the fees it can pay. His approach to these business matters is well known and even admired. As a New York agent said to one of Niki's colleagues, 'When I think about Niki Goldschmidt I think about going through a revolving door with him. When you come out, your pocket has been picked, and you say "Thank you!"'[63]

For all its ups and downs, the Algoma Fall Festival has continued into the new millennium, and retains Niki's strong affection. At the celebration of its twenty-fifth anniversary, the Algoma Festival Choir joined with the Sault Symphony in a joy-filled concert at which Niki conducted. He was especially touched by the fact that thirty-two choristers that evening had been with him from the start, and one had flown from Ottawa especially to mark the anniversary. At the civic reception honouring the festival, the crowd of well-wishers and performers heard letters of congratulation from the governor-general and other Canadian officials, and from artists residing all over the world! Niki was presented with a painting of the Sault all dressed in its autumn colours, and from the choir an Inuit sculpture that now has a place of honour in his Toronto home.

It was an event that summed up the spirit not only of Algoma but of each of Niki's community undertakings, and recalled his 'message of hope' to the University of Guelph, that for the arts there is 'unlimited scope.' He speaks of Algoma with great affection.

> The Sault is a wonderful community, the people are passionate about the festival, they are excited about meeting the artists, people like Karen Kain, who came more than once, and Jon Vickers, and so many others, the most wonderful people. It has made an enormous impression on the community and as always when festivals are strong and inspirational something remains. When the festival started the only thing happening was what the Columbia Artists sent around on their touring circuit. And people wanted something of their own. Now there are many activities during the season. That festival will go on. Maybe not always the same after I'm no longer associated with it. But, the important thing is that it really belongs to the city and those people who have put so much into it over all these years. It has become one of the most important arts activities in the north and I am very proud of it.

North or south, west coast or east, Canada had become Niki's country. All of his associations, in Ottawa with diplomats and bureaucrats at the highest level, in towns and cities with volunteers, and everywhere with the artists, gave him an extraordinary sensitivity to the arts in the community. As he moved on from Guelph, his experiences reinforced his conviction that the arts will always flourish where there is an undertaking to promote excellence, take risks, and treat the community with respect.

8

Something up His Sleeve, and More

It was autumn, 1982, and Niki was in Paris when he picked up a copy of *Le Monde* and read of Glenn Gould's death. He was immediately struck by the importance given the front-page article, by how seriously the French press treated this tragic event.

Niki had known Gould since the famous pianist was a teenager at the Royal Conservatory, and from their later collaborations at various festivals. They had shared a fondness for offbeat ideas; Gould had once persuaded Niki to consider a 'Legacy Spoof,' a recital to be performed in a trapper's cabin or other unlikely northern venue as part of the centennial celebrations, although he eventually thought better of that plan.[1] After Gould's death, Niki could not stop thinking that something must be done to mark the life of this great artist, and was surprised, on his return from Europe, that there were no special plans being put forward. 'I said to myself, "We need to have an event that will be very important, something that the whole world will be aware of." And that is when I thought of a competition in which pianists would play Bach, which was so identified with Glenn. I knew there was no such thing, it would be unique.' It would also tie in with the Bach tricentennial in 1985, the kind of association that Niki always looks for to enhance the appeal of his projects.

This one had to move forward quickly if it were to succeed. Two years' lead time is the bare minimum for putting together a complex artistic venture, especially one with no history. And in this case there was a major impediment to success.

Glenn Gould hated competitions. In a biting essay written in 1966 he complained that the very idea of a competition eliminates what he called the 'notion of ecstasy' in music, and 'leaves its eager, ill-advised suppliants forever stunted, victims of a spiritual lobotomy.'[2]

Niki, convinced that the ultimate benefits from the competition transcended even Gould's persuasive arguments, pressed on with his plans for what was originally to be called the Glenn Gould International Piano Competition. But the executors of the pianist's estate, who were careful to guard against any exploitation of his famous name, were reluctant to see it attached to an event of a kind that Gould had held in such disdain.

Here Niki's mastery of powerful persuasion and diplomacy were challenged, and he moved quickly, on two fronts.

First, he knew that the plan needed high-profile names attached to it, so opening his little brown book, which contains all the important telephone numbers of his life, he began putting together an honorary advisory board. Leonard Bernstein was the first, accepting the title of honorary president. Then came Herbert von Karajan, who wrote to say that he was deeply moved by Gould's death and would be pleased to put his name to the event in his honour. Yehudi Menuhin was next, followed by conductor Zubin Mehta, who wrote to say that 'of course' he would be happy to serve as a member of the Honorary Advisory Board. He added a personal note to Niki, wishing that the latter could be 'posted' to Tel Aviv, saying, 'I do feel that someone of your stature could do an immense amount of good in the Middle East.'[3]

By the end of January 1983, Andrew Davis, Maureen Forrester, Lois Marshall, Seiji Ozawa, Murray Perahia, Rudolph Serkin, and Rosalyn Tureck had filled out the gilt-edged list, giving the project real distinction. But Niki knew that he needed more than international names. He needed influence, and money, from the community, and that meant a solid working board headed by a prominent citizen.

David Leighton, formerly head of the Banff Centre, had recently relocated to Toronto as chair of Nabisco, the food giant. He and Niki had struck up a friendship at Banff when Niki was awarded the Donald Cameron Prize. Niki paid him a visit. 'I explained the whole idea, that I wanted to have a piano competition to raise money to establish a prize in Glenn's name. He agreed to chair the board even before I finished talking, he was so excited by the idea. And he was able to gather an excellent group to raise money and give the plan credibility with all the donors and government funders.'

It was a key appointment. Leighton had stature in both the business and arts communities and he was able to convince members of the Glenn Gould Memorial Foundation that this was a unique proposal run by people with impeccable credentials. After a series of meetings an agreement was reached in November 1983, with one important change to the original plan. The competition was to be called the 1985 International Bach Piano Competition. Glenn Gould's name would be mentioned only to explain that proceeds from the event would go toward the establishment of the Glenn Gould Prize, to be administered by the Canada Council.

In the meantime, Niki, ever optimistic, was proceeding with the organization of the competition itself. It was complex. Publicity was critical to attract the best pianists throughout the world, but difficult for a one-off event; generous prizes, both in terms of money and performance offers, were essential. But it was the jury that would bring artistic credibility to the whole. It had to be truly international, comprising knowledgeable, prestigious, and demonstrably fair members, while at the same time not being too large. Once again Niki was on the phone to his network of contacts, signing up first Olivier Messiaen from France, along with his wife Yvonne Loriod, and ten others, all with flawless reputations, representing five countries on four continents, and chaired by Canada's Gilles Lefebvre.

Administrator Sarah Pugh had travelled to Europe to observe how others organized their competitions; one challenge was to attract a strong field without having large numbers of hopefuls turn up who would fail to make even the first cut. Prescreening was the answer. Niki persuaded three eminent Canadian musicians, Helmut Blume, Valerie Tryon, and Leonard Isaacs, to undertake the daunting task of listening to 166 audition tapes, from which they selected 41 to enter the first round of the competition (32 eventually appeared).

To have attracted that number of entrants meant that the publicity had paid off. Early in the process Niki had wanted to stage the competition at the Guelph Spring Festival (and indeed as late as December 1983, when the first government grant of $70,000 was received from Ottawa, the letter referred to the Bach Piano competition to be held in Guelph). He sent Edwina Carson, Guelph's publicist, on a tour to develop awareness of the competition outside of Canada. She had never done such a job before and recalls that it had a certain off-centre quality.

'It was typical of Niki,' she recalls, 'who just always thought that anyone could accomplish anything they set out to do. It was great to have that vote of confidence. So there I was, like an inexperienced and nervous salesman, carrying a suitcase overloaded with brochures and falling apart. I mistakenly thought that Niki would call ahead, set things up for me. He didn't, and in London my contact at the Embassy didn't even know I was coming. I called him too early in the morning, and presented him with many problems. He was very gracious and helped tremendously. Later Niki just said, "I told you he would look after you, and he did!"'[4]

In Paris, Moira Johnson, cultural attaché to Adrienne Clarkson, then agent-general for the province of Ontario in the French capital, went to work, contacting press from major European capitals. She successfully overcame the customary European indifference to things Canadian; the resulting coverage not only attracted entrants but also focused international attention on the competition. She did everything she could to help, arranging to be the repository for audition tapes from France and Italy, and persuading presenters to offer concert engagements for the winner.

Johnson had first met Niki when she worked at the Canada Council's Touring Office and he was on the board. She respected his knowledge and his determination, recognizing that he can be demanding. 'I worked with him later, on the choral festival. You never say to Niki that something cannot be done, but the other side of that is that although he doesn't always know that you are doing, he gives you confidence that things will work out well!'[5]

And for the Bach Competition they certainly did. The board did its work, attracting major sponsors who donated everything from airline tickets to pianos. Most important were the major prizes, $15,000 from the Continental Bank for the first prize and $10,000 from Sony for second. Together with promise of a recording with Deutsche Grammophon and engagements in Canada and abroad, it was an enticing prospect.

Andrew Stephen documented the competition in the *Sunday Times Magazine* of London,[6] capturing all the tensions and triumphs, beginning with the first round on 1 May through to the finals on 11 May in Toronto's Roy Thomson Hall. (It had outgrown the capacity of the Guelph festival to act as host.) Describing what he calls 'the climax of this fraught fortnight,' when the chairman announced that Canadian Angela Hewitt had won, he tells of the crowd going wild, and of the universal consensus that she was 'a worthy occupant of the Glenn Gould throne.'[7] What he couldn't see was Niki's immense sense of accomplishment, of pride.

The finals were thrilling, because it had become much more than a Canadian event, it was truly international! When Angela won, everyone knew it was a most distinguished jury from all over the world who had chosen the best. It was a huge success. And do you know, with all the support we received, and the sell-out tickets, the residual after everything was paid was $148,000! That went to the Glenn Gould Foundation toward the establishment of the prize in his name.

Angela Hewitt went on to her first post-competition engagement, at the Guelph Spring Festival, Glenn Gould's father wrote to Niki to say how delighted he and Mrs Gould were to be part of the festivities,[8] and the press reported enthusiastically on the proceedings, avoiding any further reference to Gould's dislike of competitions. Niki had had his way, and the result exceeded even his optimistic predictions.

During this period Niki continued to direct the Guelph Spring Festival, but already fresh ideas were occurring to him. He does his thinking whenever he has a minute to himself, in his morning bath, on the subway or on a plane, or just sitting looking at the view on his annual visits to friends in Europe.

His imagination was no doubt fuelled by the success of the Bach Competition, so that when his resignation from Guelph was announced he told one reporter that he was too superstitious to outline all his plans, but there was more than one project 'up his sleeve.'[9] And the first one came out of his lifelong devotion to choral music.

'Of all the gifts of nature that humans have had to fashion into musical instruments, none have proved more versatile and sublime than ... the human voice.'[10] Words written by a reporter, in another context, but they could have come from Niki; he has a natural affinity for choral music and as he says,

> Wherever I had worked, in Vancouver, in Ottawa, everywhere, I had always organized choral concerts. It's been a central part of my musical life. So, when I was thinking about what to do after the Bach, it was natural to think, why not do a big international choral festival. They are quite common in other countries, and in Canada in the late 1980s there was a great deal of activity in the choral community. Choral associations had been formed, assisted by the granting agencies, so it was the right time to focus on choral music in a big way.[11]

There was a practical factor too. Niki knew that enthusiasm for the art form was not enough to ensure success of any project, large or small. He took to heart the advice he had so often given to others: local support from community members backing the project with personal involvement, and with money, is key. After the success of the Bach Competition, the Continental Bank (later Lloyd's Bank) was eager to continue its sponsorship in the arts. Recognizing that corporate commitment is difficult to find, Niki was not about to let it get away. The national enthusiasm for choral singing ensured visibility for a sponsor, and so, bringing all these interests together as skilfully as he blends voices in a chorus, Niki initiated the 1989 International Choral Festival, 'The Joy of Singing.'

Planning a month-long array of concerts by choirs from around the world presented a confusion of challenges. Availability of choirs, of conductors, and in some cases of soloists was an intricate puzzle to solve. If tenor A sang at one concert, then Niki would have to find tenor B for another. Would conductor X draw an audience without his own choir? Repertoire was a continuing question. Programs had to be exciting and appropriate for the venues selected, whether it was a large concert space like Roy Thomson Hall or a neighbourhood church. Audiences, and funders, expected to hear music from diverse backgrounds and styles; everyone wanted the highest possible quality, and the board wanted the budget to balance. Furthermore, there was no administrative structure in place to immediately handle all of the details that expanded exponentially every day.

Cathryn Gregor began working with Niki in 1987, taking the notes he made on the backs of envelopes and shaping them into an operational plan. His first budget estimate was drawn up that way (just as he had done for the centennial). Niki gave Gregor his rough estimate, worked out in his head; she laboured over the numbers, calculating every detail on her spreadsheets. On a total budget of over $3,000,000 the difference between the two drafts was less than $2000!

Niki travelled abroad, seeking out choirs. In early 1987 he visited Bulgaria, Austria (from which he reported that the fee for the Vienna Boys' Choir was 'totally out of proportion in comparison to other organizations'), Switzerland, Spain (to hear the Boys' Choir of Montserrat, which eventually made its North American debut at the 1989 choral festival), England, Wales, Scotland, Finland, and Russia. His handwritten notes reflect his non-stop planning; he was busy persuading embassy officials to help with transportation costs for their choirs, trying to put together mini-tours within Canada in order to spread the expenses around, and continually looking for any possible source of subsidy to reduce the cost to the festival.[12]

At home there was an ongoing round of budget meetings, program committee meetings, and technical planning. Niki and Cathryn Gregor comprised the total staff until late 1988 when Moira Johnson came on as director of marketing and a skeleton staff was gradually added in the office. In 1989 Great World Artists, led by John Cripton, was brought on to provide production and tour management, while Jean Latrémouille and assistants from the Canada Council touring office arrived to handle soloists, conductors, and the logistics of moving members of over thirty choirs around the city, being sure to get them to the church, or hall, on time!

Discussions at the board, chaired by Robert Bandeen, often reflected nervousness about the expanding size of the festival, given that there was no ongoing organization to carry, and recoup, any deficit. Gregor recalls that Niki was masterful at handling the unease. 'He always began his reports with positive news,' she recalls. 'A special choir that had been confirmed, or a famous conductor or soloist. Everyone would feel the enthusiasm and be ready to tackle the difficult issues.'[13]

One 'difficult issue' was the festival's plan to produce *Apocalypsis*, an immense music drama based on the Book of Revelation, and written by Canadian composer R. Murray Schafer. Employing multiple choirs and conductors, speakers, dancers, and musicians, 450–500 performers in all, the production logistics are considerable, but the result is compelling, a piece unlike any other scheduled for the festival. Up until that time it had been presented in its entirety only once, at Centennial Hall in London, Ontario, in 1980. With the arts councils guaranteeing grants amounting to $100,000 for this second full production, Niki engaged Brian Macdonald to direct, and the process of putting the piece together began. All the details relating to a major production had to be settled. Finding an appropriate venue was especially vexing, given the need to move large forces around the hall to meet the theatrical and musical images required from Schafer's score. It was well into 1988 before the production group settled on Convocation Hall at the University of Toronto. In addition, outside rehearsal space had to be found, banners and costumes rounded up from storage, paint shop space acquired, complex rehearsal schedules for the various choirs arranged, all within a reasonable cost. This was more than simply presenting a choral requiem, this was music theatre on a grand and complex scale. A meeting of the production group in October 1988 confirmed the participants, a who's who of southern Ontario choirs and conductors; preliminary plans were considered for seating, rehearsals, and how much time the singers needed to memorize, since Schafer vetoed the use of music stands.[14] Technical planning continued well into 1989, with costs estimated at over $325,000. In early May of 1989, less than a month before the festival opening, the board voted to cancel the production on the grounds that even though grant monies had to be returned and participants paid for the work already done, the savings and elimination of any further risk justified their action. Writing to Schafer, Niki expressed his regret, at the same time taking responsibility for the decision. 'You know, of course, how persuasive I was with the board in allocating more and more monies in order to do the work justice. Finally it came to the point where additional funds could not be made available and I had to put my foot down regretfully.'[15]

Cathryn Gregor confirms that the decision was entirely based on the financial risk, with Niki's commitment to the work, artistically, never wavering. It was a difficult decision, unpopular with composers and funders who wanted to see more, not fewer, major Canadian works featured in this high-profile festival. The festival offered a number of commissions, including one from Schafer for the BBC Singers, and twentieth-century music figured on many programs, but none so dramatic as *Apocalypsis*. Difficult as it was, the decision was taken, and everyone, including Niki, put their energies toward the immanent opening.

Moira Johnson, who was director of marketing for the festival, agrees that Niki always spoke for the artist at the board, while at the same time giving pointed attention to the dollars, and dedicating as many of those as possible to the artistic budget. She had to argue persuasively for sufficient resources to meet the demands of a project that required daily advertising informing ticket buyers of the more than seventy events, who was performing, what they were singing, in which of forty possible venues, and at what time of day or night. She also recalls using her own brand of psychology with Niki, who resisted her idea to sell T-shirts printed with the festival's elegant logo, 'The Joy of Singing.' Too commercial, in Niki's opinion. But Johnson persisted, making two shirts up for modelling at a board meeting. The members were enthusiastic, immediately ordering over a hundred; Niki, typically ready to alter course when it is fitting, jumped aboard with an order of his own for half a dozen.[16]

But all the discussions and arguments and apprehensions gave way as the sound of choral music took over Toronto, beginning with the 'Festival Overture' in Nathan Phillips Square at City Hall, featuring a massed choir of several hundred schoolchildren, and continuing with the gala opening at Roy Thomson Hall featuring the Poliansky Choir of Moscow, the Obretnov Choir of Bulgaria, the Boys of St Michael's Choir School in Toronto, and the Toronto Symphony, all conducted by Gennady Rozhdestvensky. It was a powerful evening in every sense, setting a larger than life tone for the next four weeks. The dedicated choral enthusiast could go from concert hall to cathedral to school auditorium, hearing everything from Bach to barbershop. And at every stop, whether it was a concert at midday, or late afternoon, early or late evening, there was Niki, most often accompanied by Shelagh, bounding down the aisle, smiling broadly, and asking anyone within earshot, 'Isn't it marvellous?'

His energy was prodigious. Jean Latrémouille recalls that Niki rarely missed an event, and always turned up for the receptions to talk with the artists, not just the celebrated 'names' appearing in the prestigious venues; he mingled with as many groups as possible, talking about their music-making and offering his congratulations.

Audiences turned out in unexpectedly large numbers. They filled the hall for Helmuth Rilling conducting Bach's *Mass in B Minor*, and to hear Winnipeg's Mennonite Festival Chorus with the Toronto Symphony all under Robert Shaw performing Beethoven's *Missa Solemnis*; they flocked to St Paul's Anglican Church to hear Paul Winter's *Missa Gaia/ Earth Mass*, and back to Roy Thomson Hall for Charles Dutoit and the Montreal Symphony Orchestra and Chorus performing the French music for which they have become famous, in this ease Berlioz's *Damnation of Faust*. Throughout the city, as part of the festival's special section dedicated to the community, devotees of choral music attended over twenty performances by Canadian and foreign choirs (including featured ensembles from the main festival) given in local churches and schools.

Critics raved throughout the month, heaping one superlative on another, but the most gratifying notices, for Niki, came in the form of letters from participants and from listeners across the country who had heard the performances on the CBC. One came from a woman in Vancouver, who had sung in the choir at the Vancouver International Festival when Bruno Walter conducted. She thanked Niki 'from her heart' for the festival performances. Others spoke of specific concerts, large and small. The boost given to the community brought some especially warm comments. A typical letter came from the director of the Norfolk Singers in Simcoe, Ontario, a small community north of Toronto, who wrote that his choir's appearance at the festival had given it a new cachet with his own audience and sponsors.[17]

And so it ended, where it had begun, amid the glitz of Roy Thomson Hall with Charles Dutoit conducting the Toronto Symphony and the Tanglewood Festival Chorus in the great Verdi *Requiem*.

In placing the festival in a historical context, Ken Winters reminded concert-goers that it was the most recent in a long line of vocal music-making in Canada. In fact, he said, the 'indigenous peoples' own singing reaches into the very cauldron of genesis.' In Canada, he wrote, 'the first warrior sang his aggression, the first hunter his kill, the first lover his heartbreak, the first mother her lullaby.' And the music continued, until 'In this great festival, the choral singing of the world brings us together.'[18]

Niki was ecstatic; another surprise pulled out from his sleeve had captivated the community. And it was a resounding financial success. When the statements were tabled in the summer of 1989 they showed a result almost unprecedented for an artistic undertaking of that size and kind; there was a surplus in the range of a quarter of a million dollars! The board was faced with a dilemma; what to do with the money?

'Well, we couldn't give it back,' Niki says. I asked the board, "Who can you give it back to? The governments? All those departments and councils? The sponsors?" There were so many. And what about the ticket buyers? We discussed it, and in the end it was decided that the money should be kept to be used toward a second festival that would take place in 1993.'

Niki began planning almost at once, while at the same time he was pulling together the final plans to mark another milestone, the two hundredth anniversary of Mozart's death in 1991. The shape of the festival, which ultimately came together under the title 'The Glory of Mozart,' was more diffuse, organizationally, than Niki's previous undertakings, and not the kind of expansive 'all over town' celebration that Niki had in mind at the outset. Initially a number of the large arts organizations in Toronto were thinking of a giant extravaganza, a co-operative venture that would attract artists and audiences from around the world. But as the 1990s were overtaken with an economic reality much less promising than the previous decade, plans were scaled back. The final configuration involved a small administration in Toronto managing one or two aspects of the whole while various companies presented their own performances loosely marketed under the festival's umbrella and designed to showcase Mozart's music in all its forms and through every medium.

Niki persuaded Cinemathèque Ontario to screen a series of Mozart-related films during one week of the festival, in June of 1991. The concert line-up commenced with Elly Ameling in recital, followed by choral and chamber music, including Niki's old friends, the Orford Quartet, making their farewell appearance. The Canadian Opera Company mounted three Mozart operas that spring and the Toronto Symphony with Helmuth Rilling performed choruses and interludes from *Thamos, King of Egypt,* music so obscure that it certainly filled Niki's precept that a good festival should include less well known fare and provide some 'firsts' for its audience.

The two components of the festival, however, that were really dear to Niki's heart and in which he was more involved were the dance program and the international competitions, especially the chamber music and piano competitions, which were, in fact, held far from Toronto, in St John's, Newfoundland, and Joliette, Quebec, respectively.

Originally the National Ballet of Canada announced it would present a major triple bill as part of its season, to honour the Mozart year; however, in January of 1991, less than six months before the celebrations were to take place, the ballet cancelled its plans. Undaunted, and showing a confident public face, Niki told the press that he would put together another program that would surprise the audience. And he managed it, with a different kind of triple bill that opened in mid-June at the University of Toronto's MacMillan Theatre. Heading the program were artists of the National Ballet of Canada, with Karen Kain in the world premiere of a new work by James Kudelka, set to Mozart's Quintet for Clarinet and Strings. The musicians, James Campbell and the Orford String Quartet, were as celebrated as their dance colleagues. Next came another first, a new work by choreographer Robert Desrosiers, entitled *Full Moon,* danced to excerpts from Mozart's *Missa Solemnis,* and the evening concluded with the Toronto Dance Theatre presenting David Earle's *Sacra Conversazione* (based on Mozart's *Requiem*). Finding artists to create new works and put together a balanced program in such a short time was a coup, and by most accounts a successful one, although the reviews were mixed. Both the major Toronto critics praised Kudelka; William Littler in the *Toronto Star* called his piece a 'fascinating exercise,' while Robert Everett Green writing in the *Globe and Mail* asked, 'Is there any more musical mind working in the dance today?' He was less kind to the other works.[19]

However, it was the international competitions, including the vocal contest conducted in Toronto by the Canadian Opera Company, that particularly excited Niki, who always looked for the participation of young people in his festivals. The fact that two components were held outside of the province of Ontario gave the festival an additional cachet beyond provincial borders, while assuring the essential funding from the national government! That had not been easy; the government insisted that it would not provide funds to an event in one part of the country if its programming was the same as an event being staged somewhere else. The funders were looking for originality, unique programs. Once again Niki needed all his persuasive skills to satisfy everyone's needs. An exchange of letters with his old friend Hamilton McClymont, who was co-chairing a group in Nova Scotia planning its own Mozart Festival, resulted in an agreement about who would do what in 1991. Niki then wrote, 'I saw the people at the Department in Ottawa and they are, I think, ready to go for both of us, but the ladder of bureaucracy is getting longer and longer.'[20]

The piano competition took place under the banner of Quebec's Lanaudière Festival and was won by a San Francisco pianist. An American also won the vocal competition in Toronto, while a quartet from France took first place in the chamber music division. Unfortunately, and perhaps understandably, these events never attained the stature of the Bach Competition, although the critics turned out for each winner's concert in Toronto. The highest-profile Canadian group to receive a prize was the brand new St Lawrence String Quartet, whose second-place standing gave them a boost with the hometown Toronto audience. Altogether, although 'The Glory of Mozart' is not one of those festivals that readily comes to mind when concert-goers discuss Niki's successes, it gave audiences their choice of engaging evenings in the concert hall, it generated new work, and the competitions gave exposure to young artists with a reach well beyond Toronto. Niki was not unhappy; as he said at the time, although it hadn't been easy, the results justified the effort: 'A true festival is a genuine attempt to bring the arts together in a concentrated space of time. The artistic quality must be high and the event must have the support of the community ... It is love of the arts that should motivate the idea.'[21]

During those years in the early 1990s Niki had his eye on 1993 and his ear to the telephone as he put together the plans for his second major choral festival.

Times had changed, though, in the brief period since 'The Joy of Singing' had burst on Toronto. The city's ethno-cultural mix was changing, making it one of the most diverse cities in the world. The funding agencies were looking for programs to reflect the new reality, while audiences, accustomed now to the big entertainment shows, sought out the spectacular, the 'big names.' And all of this was against a backdrop of economic restraint, everywhere. Grants, corporate sponsors, individual donations, all were difficult to find.

Niki, unfailingly optimistic, went ahead with his planning, travelling everywhere in search of the best choral singing in the world. He and Shelagh flew to Soweto, South Africa, to hear the Imilonji Kantu Choral Society, a visit captured on film for the Canadian Broadcasting Corporation.[22] There is Niki, standing in the hot sun, bareheaded, wearing an open shirt and casual trousers, singing along exuberantly as the choir performs Beethoven's *Ode to Joy*. 'Bravo, Bravo!' he says, grinning broadly. But he wants African music, and after long and lively consultation with the choir's director he hears another performance, again in the sunny courtyard, the choir in its colourful mix of nine different tribal costumes, singing and dancing in a semicircle around him.

Niki loved it, and his excitement was shared by the concert-goers in Toronto, where the Soweto choir was one of the hits of the festival.

While in South Africa Niki did not forget business. He took the opportunity to meet the Canadian ambassador, looking for financial help from the Department of External Affairs to bring the choir to Canada. Using his best persuasive skills to sell the ambassador on the importance of the festival, beaming with pride, showing clippings from the 1989 success, revealing surprises already lined up for 1993, Niki made his pitch. 'You like it, yes? It's marvellous, yes?' and finally, 'What are you going to do for us?' It worked. A textbook lesson from the master in how to capture supporters: know who has the money and/or the power, tell them your story in the most positive terms, and don't be afraid to ask!

The festival opened on the afternoon of 29 May with an extravaganza of massed choirs in Metro Square just across from Roy Thomson Hall, where that same evening the Toronto Symphony and the Toronto Mendelssohn Choir performed Mahler's great Symphony no. 8, the 'Symphony of a Thousand.' A sensational beginning to a festival that resembled its predecessor in size but exceeded it in variety. It was another musical marathon; choirs from fourteen different countries and five continents giving more than eighty concerts, singing repertoire as varied as Latin American folk music, Jewish music through the ages, and a specially commissioned oratorio, *Jezebel*, composed by Derek Holman with a libretto by Niki's long-time friend, Robertson Davies.

The Prague Philharmonic Choir was a special thrill for Niki, a part of his own heritage making its North American debut in his adopted homeland, at his festival. On the night of the concert Niki read from the stage a letter from Czech President Václav Havel, who expressed his country's pride in its cultural traditions and his delight that the choir would appear in a festival that 'offers a splendid cornucopia of global culture and an unforgettable adventure in musical exploration.'[23]

Urjo Kareda's review in the *Globe and Mail* described the Czech choir's singing as 'luminous.' Commenting on what he called 'Nicholas Goldschmidt's almost wilful programming of unfamiliar works' for the festival, he went on to say that the relatively unknown *Stabat Mater,* by Dvořák, although not a classic choral treasure, 'when championed by singers with the voice and soul of the Prague Philharmonic Choir ... leaves you more moved and shaken than many a better-made masterpiece.'[24]

Britten's *War Requiem,* Handel's *Israel in Egypt,* and finally, Beethoven's great Symphony no. 9, favourites of Niki's and of his audience, rang through the city during that exciting month. The rave reviews and the letters of congratulations rolled in, but none so welcome as the testimonial from the Board of Education in North York, a sprawling, diverse region now part of the City of Toronto. Six of the choirs featured in the main festival gave concerts for more than 2500 students. The Schola Cantorum de Caracas with their accompaniment of mandolins and percussion, the Cantemus Children's Choir of Hungary performing in traditional costume, choirs from Finland and the Philippines and from Howard University in Washington revealed their own unique style and sound, creating 'their own special magic,' and demonstrating to the excited students the discipline and 'the universality of singing as a form of communication and literacy,' the Board's music co-ordinator wrote.[25] Once again Niki had followed his own precept for a successful festival, expanding the reach of the artists' contribution beyond the concert hall, into the community.

Unhappily, the 1993 'Joy of Singing' left another legacy, a deficit of over $250,000. Why the outcome should have been so drastically different from four years before has been a matter for debate. Robert Cooper, recalling 1989 and the emotion of listening in the studio to the terrible news of the massacre in Tienanmen Square and the healing effect that same evening of the Tibetan Temple Singers, and still later, the Poliansky Choir singing the Rachmaninoff *Vespers,* says that a second festival could never recapture that magic. Magic or just plain show business, some supporters have said it was just too soon, that there wasn't the same buzz on the street, that events did not sell out. But the box office revenue for the second festival was approximately $800,000, roughly the same as for the 1989 event. Although the costs for the second festival were $600,000 less than for the first, government grants were down by nearly 50 per cent, and donations and other income dropped by over 25 per cent. So, the enthusiasm of the choral music buffs could not overcome the general economic malaise of the time, and Niki and his board were left with a major financial headache.

Their remedy was an enormous fundraising gala, 'A Night in Old Vienna,' billed as a 'Tribute to Nicholas Goldschmidt,' with proceeds to benefit the establishment of a Royal Conservatory of Music Nicholas Goldschmidt Chair for Vocal Studies, the Toronto Symphony Youth and Education Programs, and the International Choral Festival. Initially the idea was to celebrate Niki's eighty-fifth birthday, but December in Toronto is a month for parties with friends and family, or flights to warm climates, not ideal for fundraising galas. It was put off until the more appealing 10 April 1994, when a stellar line-up of Canadian artists, all of whom had worked with Niki at one time or another and gave their services gratis, presented a program of music and dance. It was led off by the Toronto Symphony, conducted by Raffi Armenian, and included all of Niki's favourites: Gluck, Mozart, Schubert, Brahms, and a grande finale of excerpts from that most Viennese of operas, *Die Fledermaus*. It was all good fun and celebration and it achieved its goal. The bills were paid and Niki could move on with confidence.

And this time his artistic antennae were out, focused farther ahead in time than was his custom, to the year 2000. But before giving his full attention to millennium celebrations, he had one more unexpected project to announce.

The year 1995 marked the fiftieth anniversary of the signing of the United Nations Charter in San Francisco, and there was to be a celebration in that city. Niki's response to this milestone was defined by his own background, his Uncle Paul's life work in international affairs, his world travels, which continually reinforced his conviction that there was a pressing need to embrace international co-operation, and his belief that children must be the voice of peace for the future. To Niki, that voice could be heard most compellingly through the dramatic themes of the children's opera that he loved, Britten's *Noah's Flood*.

Once again he assembled a board (this time chaired by businessman and philanthropist James Fleck) from his apparently inexhaustible list of contacts, to ensure the necessary support. In 1993 they received the endorsement of the Canadian Committee for the Fiftieth Anniversary of the United Nations to present the Britten work as 'the focal point of Canada's cultural program in the UN/50 celebrations.'[26]

The real excitement for Niki was putting together the cast; he was thrilled when Joy Coghill for the fourth time agreed to bring her inspiration and her exemplary standards to this high-profile undertaking.

Finding the choir was another challenge, and there were some false starts. One school district that initially accepted Niki's proposal to have its students participate ultimately withdrew on the grounds that there was concern for children of a variety of backgrounds and religions singing in an essentially 'Anglican' work, in an Anglican church. Niki was dumbfounded: '"My God," I told them when I got the call. "Isn't that what the UN is all about?" I just couldn't believe how narrow-minded they were. What kind of a lesson is that to teach children?'

Fortunately in short order Niki found a more adventurous school district in suburban Scarborough, where 120 students representing forty ethnic backgrounds signed on to the project. Under the direction of Lee Willingham they made the not inconsiderable commitment to attend all the rehearsals, and do the hard work necessary to represent Canada proudly in San Francisco.

All the forces gradually came together, with baritone Gary Relyea as Noah, Marcia Swanston as the feckless Mrs Noah, and Canadian actor, author, and arts advocate Mavor Moore in the commanding role of the Voice of God.

Sir Peter Ustinov, world citizen, long-time spokesperson for UNICEF, and honorary chairman of the San Francisco celebrations, was sufficiently impressed by the project that he paid a visit to the children's school, where he spent much of the day with the cast, watching them rehearse, telling jokes, examining their masks, and inspiring a renewed dedication in every theatrical creature of land and sea. Later, in an introduction to the celebrations in the Golden Gate city, he compared UNICEF to an ark, saving children from dangerous waters. 'The Ark is underway again,' he wrote. 'NOYE'S FLUDDE ... is an inspired work and here receives treatment worthy of that inspiration. The Ark navigates anew. May God bless all who sail in her, from Captain N. Goldschmidt ... to the splendid singers, players and choristers, and not forgetting for a single moment, the souls she saves!'[27]

Choral conductors, singers, musicians, designers, technical staff, all worked feverishly on a shoestring budget to ensure that the result would do justice to the occasion. With funding finally in place, and everyone as prepared as ever they would be, on 9 June 1995 Niki raised his baton and Noah and all the rest made their debut at St Anne's Anglican Church in Toronto, before moving on to Montreal, Ottawa, and finally San Francisco. It was a triumph; the *Toronto Star* called it 'Glittering

Goldschmidt,' and the *Montreal Gazette* critic said that the production was 'a chance to know how a great story that has been taken for granted can be fully refreshed.'[28]

There was one point of disagreement among the critics. Wanting to add an original Canadian theme to the program, Niki had commissioned Harry Somers to write a special 'Children's Hymn to the United Nations,' with a text by Victoria poet P.K. Page. It was sung at the end of the evening as a contemporary and specific tribute for the occasion it marked. Robert Everett Green, writing in the *Globe and Mail*, called the Somers hymn an 'afterthought' and expressed regret that Niki had not chosen a Canadian work that would have been just as pertinent to the anniversary as the Britten.[29] It was the only negative voice, however. Most critics felt that the hymn worked well, and appreciated the universality of the opera's theme and its appropriateness to the occasion.

The San Francisco trip was an unqualified success, drawing raves in the press. The critic for the *San Francisco Examiner* began his remarks by referring to the 'riot of art' that made up the UN/50 celebrations, and telling his audience it needed a 'sacramental heart' that it had found in the production from Canada, mounted in the First Congregational Church. He praised all aspects of the performance, using every superlative in the critic's lexicon, asserting finally that, 'While "Noah's Flood" almost always "works," it rarely surfaces at this level of musical mastery and theatrical forthrightness.'[30]

The San Francisco production of *Noah's Flood* was very special in the mind and imagination of Joy Coghill. She is definite about its impact:

> It was the best we had ever done. The animals were terrific, and the soloists were so sensitive, they knew exactly what was in the music. It is hard to explain but Niki had a different approach for that production. He never became impatient with the children, or anyone. He wasn't just doing it as an artistic director because it would fit on a program. He was really doing it for the piece itself and what the anniversary of the United Nations means. At the parents' run-through in Toronto he had tears in his eyes, he was genuinely moved. Later he asked me to do it again but I said, 'No. What we had in San Francisco was unique. We can never repeat that.[31]

Getting rave reviews for the Britten was only part of the excitement of the trip to San Francisco. Niki remembers it all with pride:

> It was an enormous undertaking with over 150 people, including children,

to move around. As we were flying west the children all began to sing, and it was so moving, like a wonderful euphoria filling that plane.

When we arrived of course they were all excited about the city, and they went around, singing wherever they could. But the biggest thrill was the invitation to appear at the official Commemorative Celebration in the San Francisco Opera House. It was June 26, I never forget. President Clinton was there, of course, with Bishop Tutu and ambassadors from over 140 countries, a momentous occasion. And there were our kids, standing in front of the great chorus from the opera, singing the closing number from *Candide*, by memory. It really was a magical occasion, the entire trip, and I am certain that those children will never forget it.

As Joy Coghill said, the 1995 UN project was more than just another exciting idea from Niki's musical storehouse. In his first proposal for a celebration of the United Nations anniversary, Niki had wanted to include a series of lectures and seminars with the aim of better understanding the UN, particularly as it relates to youth. The talks never materialized, at least not in conjunction with Niki's Britten production. If he was disappointed, he doesn't say. *Noah's Flood* is a piece that he cherishes, written by a pacifist and brought to life by the instrument that touches his innermost sensibility, the human voice. Britten's dramatic score ideally expresses Niki's own deep convictions about peace and the common humanity for which the UN stands. Taking it to the United Nations anniversary was a tremendous endeavour, and it left Niki optimistically looking forward as he made his plans to greet the new millennium.

9

'Where is the song before it is sung?'

When it comes to anticipating significant anniversaries, Niki is like a musical clairvoyant sensing the possibilities less visionary mortals have not even imagined. But the celebration of the millennium, the modulation from the 1900s to the year 2000 was a worldwide happening. It was impossible to escape the blare of the media, the image makers, the merchandisers who very early on began the countdown to midnight, 1999. Surely everyone would want to be first in line with proposals for millennium grants!

But the 1990s in Canada saw governments preoccupied with reducing deficits, and arts organizations struggling with the costs of day-to-day operations. A generally puritanical air had settled over the land. Public displays were frowned upon as frivolous and wasteful. When the federal government announced its Millennium Fund, it was without the usual fanfare, or the clamour to take advantage of this new largesse.

Niki, in the ninth decade of his life, had a larger vision: 'I was excited about the possibilities, especially because of my experience in 1967. The centennial celebrations had a huge impact on the arts, people became aware of the enormous resources that Canada had to offer. I thought it could be the same in the year 2000, that we could show how far we had come, and help create an exciting future. But only if the people in the arts were prepared, if they made their plans early.'

As it turned out, Niki was the first to think far enough ahead. His idea came to him in San Francisco at the UN anniversary. Perhaps it was the children's excitement, or the beautifully simple harmonies of Harry Somers's *Hymn*. Whatever the trigger, at that moment Niki began to sketch out his ideas for the millennium.

In July of 1995 he laid out the possible scenarios for a celebratory program in a report to a group of potential supporters. Titled 'The Second Millennium – the Year 2000: An Opportunity Not to Be Missed,' it focused on new creation and Canadian talent and threw out a bold challenge: 'Obviously, the Millennium Celebrations, depending on available funds, will either be a skimpy affair, a modest nod, or a dramatic display of our artistic and cultural resources on a scale never attempted before. This celebration gives us the tools to promote Canadian artists and make governments ... aware that the arts are of great importance in a democratic society ... Let us do it right – and be daring!'

Once again his enthusiasm built momentum around him, and within a year he had the format. It was to be a salute to the creativity of Canadian composers, heard from coast to coast through a series of new commissions. And so, Music Canada Musique 2000 was born. It was the first organization to present a fully realized proposal to the federal government for millennium funding, acknowledged with a $600,000 grant.

Following the model of the centennial year, Niki wanted to use the funds to stimulate others to participate. Through invitations to orchestras, opera companies, and music and dance ensembles across the country, Niki used Music Canada Musique 2000 as a catalyst to initiate projects, while he avoided a lot of headaches:

> My idea was to put composers on the map, but certainly not to choose the composers myself. They were to be selected by the organizations that would perform their work. Can you imagine the headaches if I had tried to choose who was to write what? No, that would not have worked. The board and I stayed completely clear of any charges of favouritism or patronage. The organizations sent us the name, I spoke with the composer about what they were planning, and we included it in the program. There was only one work that we commissioned directly, that was the oratorio by Derek Holman set to a collection of poems by P.K. Page and performed by the Toronto Symphony.'[1]

While government support was reasonably easy to obtain, private funding was another matter. The Roy Thomson Hall Founders' fund shared in the cost of the Holman piece, foundations helped with others; but it took all of the tenacity and skill of the board members and Niki himself to convince donors that this was a worthy and rewarding place to put their money. In some cases the 'hook' to attract dollars was peripheral to the actual commission; it might be a patron who admired the guest artist booked to perform the new work, or a fan of the hometown organization commissioning it. Gradually the sources of support were uncovered, and in the end Music Canada Musique 2000 amassed revenues of over $2,000,000, stimulating the creation of musical works of every genre, premiered from sea to sea.

> Some of the stories were wonderful. For example, I was in Vancouver very early on and I was introduced to the president of the Trans-Canada Trail Association. He said they would love to have a musical illustration of the trail. I asked him if he thought Oscar Peterson would be the right person, and he was just astounded. So when I got home I went to see Oscar, and after discussion, he agreed. So we have this delightful piece illustrating all the provinces that was recorded with Michel Legrand.

The trail is a cross-country environmental project passing through every province and territory in Canada. Niki knew Peterson's earlier work *Canadiana Suite* and persuaded his old friend that he would be the ideal composer to build on that concept for the millennium.

The musical realization of the *Trail of Dreams* was premiered in Toronto, and later Niki and Peterson attended the formal opening of the physical trail at a ceremony in Ottawa that featured the Ottawa Children's Choir singing one section of Peterson's opus given lyrics by Niki's long-time colleague P.K. Page. Both Niki and Peterson were disappointed with the ceremony, Niki because he felt the composer was not given appropriate recognition, and Peterson because it was largely ignored by Canada's media.

Disappointment aside, the story of the trail and Oscar Peterson's involvement is one example of how Niki's network of friends and associates across Canada assisted him in the kind of audacious undertaking that Music Canada Musique 2000 became. Every contact he made, in whatever circumstances, has been recorded in his little book. It bulges with over a half-century's worth of connections.

And during all of his years working in Canada he has kept track of more than names of personal contacts. His papers are replete with clippings of speeches, quotations from prominent politicians, announcements of new programs, and directions in public policy, including a copy of Canada's Charter of Rights and Freedoms. They are the working papers of an artistic director who keeps track of where the sources of support are, and at the same time they reflect his interest in politics and public affairs, inspired decades earlier by his beloved Uncle Paul.

Apart from the Canada Council, Niki has sat on a number of boards and committees: advisory committees to any number of organizations and granting bodies, the Olympic Arts Committee, the board of Roy Thomson Hall, and the Canadian Music Council, to name only a few. His travels often precluded attendance at meetings but his papers show his keen interest in the decisions of these bodies. Minutes have his handwritten comments, sometimes indignant exclamations to himself regarding actions he feels are inappropriate; in other cases he writes down suggestions to be brought forward for future consideration.

He never offered his advice in a vacuum, however. Niki is a prodigious reader of any newspaper he can get his hands on. When he is abroad he regularly reads all the prominent foreign papers in three languages, English, French, and German. When he is travelling within Canada he not only looks for the large Toronto dailies, but he actively seeks out the local papers, dailies and weeklies, and he reads them from front to back, getting a feel for the community, what is going on, and what grabs the interest of its residents.

He remains committed to the principle of public support to the arts, a conviction that is perhaps stronger now that the conventional wisdom as expressed in the media is that the arts are a frill, or just another form of commercial entertainment that can be looked after by the 'private sector.'

At the same time Niki's philosophy of public largesse is very much tied to his belief in hard work and quality effort:

> Grants have to be earned, and in the case of the individual artist, they should not be given too early. To be most effective the councils should encourage artists' development, but only as they prove themselves. The wonderful thing about the Canada Council, especially in its glory days, was that it was flexible. Now it has become more difficult to break through all the rules, for all government funding. You need to be flexible so that great ideas can be supported, even, or I should say, *especially* when they don't fit the criteria.[2]

Just as Niki's experience on boards, at festivals, and as a consultant expanded his already formidable list of contacts across the country, his growing list of honours helped his efforts on behalf of Music 2000. It began with the Centennial Medal in 1967, given for his service to Canada in that birthday year. Many awards specifically conferred for his service to music followed that first national recognition: the Canadian Music Council Medal in 1976, and in 1979 the University of Alberta's

National Award in Music; special citations from the Association of Canadian Choral Conductors and Orchestras Canada ('for his unique millennium project'), and the Diplôme d'Honneur from the Canadian Conference for the Arts.

In 1978 came perhaps the most prestigious of his honours when he was made a Member of the Order of Canada, which recognizes 'people who have made a difference to our country.' In 1989 he was elevated to its highest rank, Companion of the Order of Canada. Announced on the final jubilant day of the 1989 choral festival, that recognition of Niki's lifetime achievements provoked a flood of congratulatory cards and letters from around the world. Two Toronto colleagues, pianists Bruce Ubukata and Stephen Ralls, tied together the long threads of Niki's life in their note, which referred to 'recent honours' and went on to say how deserving Niki was, especially in view of the festival that had just concluded. 'Your vision and enterprise ... provided unforgettable memories for thousands of people. Such spiritual philanthropy is rare and surely in the great tradition of Adalbert von Goldschmidt's gifts to Hugo Wolf.'[3]

The card referred to 'honours' in the plural, and it indeed had been a season of tributes to the eighty-one-year-old musical powerhouse. In the same month as choirs and soloists were sharing the 'Joy of Singing' he received the honorary degree of Doctor of Music at the spring convocation of the University of Toronto. It had come about when one of Niki's 'ideas' was given a new twist. Several months before, Niki had paid a visit to Carl Morey, then dean of music at the university. He wanted Morey to propose choral conductor Robert Shaw for an honorary degree, knowing it would give the upcoming choral festival added profile and be a generous gesture to a visiting artist. But Morey realized at once the person most deserving was Niki himself.

As Morey explains, 'Niki often came to talk to me about his ideas, usually for some project of his. But this time he wanted a favour for someone else and had no idea that I was proposing him until he received the letter from the president.'[4]

At the ceremony, Morey traced the diverse paths of Niki's career and described the experience of dealing with him: 'Those of us who might receive a phone call or a visit from him know that we are about to agree to something without being entirely clear what we have committed ourselves to – but we can be sure of three things: that it will work, that it will be part of a grand scheme, and that it will absolutely and only be in the service of his commanding passion which is music.'[5]

The University of Toronto was not the first academic institution to confer an honorary degree on Niki; the University of Guelph took the initiative in 1984, followed three years later by the Royal Conservatory of Music. On 17 June 1999, York University presented him with an honorary Doctor of Laws at a ceremony in which the citation echoed his favourite themes. He 'has led a charmed life,' it stated, 'for the fates and the muses have allowed him to play the role of a modern Orpheus. He has been given the mastery over the art of music, and he has used that power to affect, and change for the better, the lives of all who have heard his song.'[6] His commitment to excellence, to young people, and to Canada, and his role as an animateur, all were cited as qualities deserving recognition.

Niki's response, at York and from other podiums, began with his favourite quote from Beethoven: 'It is the arts and sciences that indicate a higher life and give us the hope of attaining it.'[7] The speech continued, brimming with admonitions to his listeners to live that 'higher life,' through imagination, curiosity, and the optimism that nourishes the inquisitive mind. Add the practical traits of self-discipline and craftsmanship, and there is the Goldschmidt alchemy, conjuring a balance between exciting future technologies and all that is stimulating and inspirational in the arts. 'The arts must never again be considered as a frill,' he admonished, 'nor must they be reserved for the so-called elite (I hate that word). The arts are the possession of us all, just as public libraries, hospitals and the majestic Rockies are.'

These speeches are not long, perhaps ten minutes; the language is direct, with no fancy phrases or the jargon of 'artspeak.' The tone says, this is a man having a good time, pleased to receive these honours, enjoying his subject and happy to be communicating his vision to the young people before him.

The honours continued to roll in from governments wherever he had touched down. Both Toronto and Sault Ste Marie acknowledged his contribution to civic life with their highest honours, and there was the Order of Ontario, the Governor-General's Performing Arts Award, and the Queen's Jubilee Medal. The two countries in Europe that have been central to his life joined the list as he received the Ehrenkreuz Erster Klasse fur Kunst und Literatur, from Austria, and the Commander of the Order of King Leopold II, from Belgium.

Honours are received with gratitude, but to Niki the music means all. As he continued to harmonize the different voices that would bring Music 2000 to its full voice, he took on anther venture with a less happy outcome.

For two years in the mid-1990s Niki was artistic advisor to the National

Arts Centre's summer festival. There was talk around the sprawling grey building by the canal in the heart of the nation's capital that it was time to revive its prestigious summer festival. In the late 1970s the NAC was a favourite stop for summer visitors with its offerings of splendid concerts and opera productions. But since 1983 the centre's halls had been dark through July and August except for a handful of touring shows or modest concerts. Niki was invited by the centre's board to plan a series of events, and when John Cripton joined the NAC as director-general he encouraged his long-time friend and advisor to expand his vision, to create something that would be important, be noticed, and give the NAC new cachet.

In June of 1997 Ottawa marked the launch of a new month-long celebration of the arts ambitiously called Festival Canada, a name that had been attached to events and grand plans for the arts in Ottawa off and on since Centennial Year. The opening was a glittering one, as the cream of Ottawa society led by Governor-General Romeo LeBlanc took their seats for a performance of Berlioz's *L'Enfance du Christ*. It is one of Niki's favourite works, and one that he had presented in Guelph in a production that employed giant puppets to complement the musical telling of the story of King Herod and the flight of the Holy Family into Egypt. Niki had been waiting for the opportunity to repeat that earlier success, but as the drama unfolded he felt disappointment, then distress. On the large stage of the NAC's Opera, the dramatic effect was lost, the earlier magic was gone, and although musically the performance was stellar, the audience and the critics were lukewarm in their response. Unhappily, it set the tone for that festival, from which it never did recover in the minds of the public.

Even the presence of excellent performers and special festival fare could not attract audiences large enough to fill box office expectations. There were arguments within the artistic team over who was responsible for what, just one aspect of the NAC's internal financial and governance problems. It was no surprise when the board decided to discontinue the summer festival.

Niki regrets the outcome, but in his usual fashion prefers to remember the success:

In 1997 Brian Macdonald staged an absolutely marvellous production of *The Prodigal Son*. Of course it was not in the NAC itself, but in St Andrew's Church. With Gary Relyea and Gary Rideout and Benoît Boutet, it was a wonderful cast. Everything was perfect, just as it should be for Britten. The

audience was thrilled, gave it a standing ovation. It was certainly the highlight of the festival.

I was very sorry that we couldn't make things work out well in Ottawa,
but not everything succeeds, you know. And so you just have to move on.

The decade and the century were drawing to a close, and Niki turned
all his considerable energies to gaining the collective Canadian ear for
Music 2000. The sounds were sweet indeed when it all began to come
together, and the office fax began to hum with the press notices.

The diversity of expression was remarkable. Several composers took
the opportunity to explore and mix musical idioms from East and West,
and from Aboriginal cultures. R. Murray Schafer's *Four-Forty*, premiered
in Vancouver, inspired the critics to talk about humour in the concert
hall; one described it as a 'send-up ... a piece that is wild and clever.'[8]

And understandably, in a year that marked the end of one thousand
years, the composers turned to history for their themes: Devastating
tragedy was relived on 7 December in Toronto's old Massey Hall at the
premiere of *Fourteen Remembered*, Ahmed Hassan's requiem for fourteen
young women students killed eleven years earlier in a massacre at Montreal's Ecole Polytechnique.

In Canada's most easterly province the tone was more upbeat,
reminding Canadians of an event not always recorded in the history
books, and, what is more, one that belonged to the very beginning of
the millennium. Michael Parker with librettist John Steffler marked the
one thousandth anniversary of the Viking discovery of Newfoundland in
their chamber opera *The Visitor.*

Upper Canada's *Last Duel* was recalled in all its dark detail in the
opera of the same name by composer Gary Kulesha and librettist
Michael Patrick Albano. It debuted at the University of Toronto's Opera
Division.

And for millennium year, surrounded as it was by all kinds of portents
and prophecies, Pacific Opera added a measure of fantasy with its ambitious production of *Erewhon,* an opera with music by Louis Applebaum
and libretto by Mavor Moore. Based on the novels of Samuel Butler, the
opera had been through a long development process; the composer
was too ill to travel from his home in Toronto to attend the opening,
and rewrites and adjustments were being agreed upon over the long-
distance phone until the last minute. When opening night finally
arrived in Victoria's Royal Theatre, Niki was happy. Music 2000 had
been able to give a major grant toward the production costs, and the

work of two senior and respected artists had been given its place in this national celebration.

And wherever he went, to Windsor, or St John's, or Calgary, or Quebec City, Niki was beaming.

> I was getting rather bombastically proud. I felt that Music 2000 was one of my most important achievements. I think I attended almost forty premieres, and I can say honestly that there may be only two or perhaps three flops!
>
>   Those composers that write from their own heart with a craft that they have refined over time, in their own style, not what will just get a grant, their music will last.
>
>   And I think there are at least ten or perhaps a dozen that are true successes, which will really last, that we will hear again. That is a very good record by any standard. There were so many wonderful moments. Works for children, chamber music, dance, and three operas. There has never been a celebration of new compositions like that anywhere. Andrew Porter told me that we put his home country, England, to shame!'[9]

Music Canada Musique 2000 made a substantial addition to the growing library of Canadian music. Whether it will live on, whether these works will find other performers and new audiences, is for the future. The consensus of composers and conductors, singers and instrumentalists seems to be that the progressive series of premieres across the country brought attention to musical expression and its creators, generating a new awareness of Canada's absorbing and varied musical voices. Conductor Victor Feldbrill assessed it this way: 'It was a good idea to put this focus on Canadian music under one umbrella. It gave the music and the composers a new profile, new importance in their communities. How many will last? That will be decided over time. Look in Groves [Dictionary of Music]. There are biographies of composers on page after page, but how many do we know now, how many do we perform? It's the same in every age, but it doesn't mean that we shouldn't keep encouraging the composers to write.'[10]

And so what began in the icy cold north at a festival celebrating the longest night of the year concluded more than a year later on a warm summer evening at Quebec's Lanaudière Festival, with François Morel's *Piano Concerto for Two Left Hands*. Music 2000 added over sixty new works to the repertoire, and on the business side it ended with a small surplus. It gave Niki enormous satisfaction, and hours on planes to peruse newspapers and magazines, to keep current with what was happening around the world, and to think about what he was going to do next.

Certainly it was a time when his colleagues voiced their measure of the man and his work.

Many people refer to Niki from time to time, affectionately, as 'Saint Nicholas.' But they do not describe him as being 'saintly.'

Robert Cooper, conductor and CBC producer, has worked with Niki from Cooper's student days in Ottawa, at the Guelph Spring Festival, at the UN celebrations, and at the choral festivals. Niki has been a valued mentor and sometimes critic:

> Niki has an innate sense of what is right, which voice will be best for which part. Once when I was conducting the Opera in Concert Chorus I added some voices to support the tenors. Niki said that the colour was all wrong, and he was right.
>
> His approach is not always the most scholarly, but it is natural and it works. He can be irascible, and sometimes people say that when they are doing a piece with Niki they suffer through it, but afterwards they say it was a success. It works. It comes from inside him. He has given me, and many others, opportunities, he has opened doors. I always enjoy his calls and visits because he is always stimulating, wanting to make something good happen. There is no one to replace him right now.[11]

Mavor Moore echoes Cooper's sentiments, pointing out that Niki's persistence, his refusal to accept that something is impossible to accomplish, and his promotion of his own projects are necessary traits in a freelance artist, which Niki has been all his working life.

Joy Coghill, who has worked with Niki since his Vancouver days, in large communities and small, sums up Niki in one word, and then expands:

> He is 'incorrigible,' and I say that with great affection. I visited Delphi in Greece and saw a statue of a figure that the guide explained embodied the 'spirit of enthusiasm.' That is Niki. He has these great wells of energy and determination and courage that spring from his own vision. That is the incorrigible part.
>
> You know, Canadians are suspicious of people who enjoy the limelight, who stand up and say, 'This is my vision and I am right.' Niki is very persuasive and occasionally he is insensitive when another person might say that something can't be done. But that is part of how he must focus. And when

someone like me says, 'No, we won't do it that way,' he stops, and we argue, but we get it right together.

He has made a transformation in many people's thinking and in their lives. And he has done it all across this country.[12]

In such a long life there have inevitably been celebrations and written accolades, many of which are preserved among his papers, and in 'birthday books.' The artists have been most eloquent, and in the collection from his ninetieth birthday celebration is a handwritten note from soprano Teresa Stratas. Its tone is a glowing example of how so many artists express their affection: 'HAPPY BIRTHDAY,' it announces at the top of the page, and continues:

> Dear Teacher, Dear Friend. Dearest Niki
>
> Your influence and impact on my life have been enormous.
>
> You are the most positive human being I have ever met.
>
> The generous way you share your many talents, your wisdom, your wit, your love and enthusiasm for music, for people and for life – can you begin to imagine how important that was to me as a young student in Toronto?
>
> I celebrate you. I feel blessed to know you ...[13]

While Niki's life has been with the artists, he puts the value of the arts in the larger context. Over and over, in communities from east to west, he has talked about the place of music and dance and film and all the rest in the life of the community at large. As always, there is a philosophical message, with a practical edge.

> I will say one thing that I think that many people do not realize. The arts community is not only *us*, the performers, producers, actors, singers, painters, writers, and the rest. The arts community includes every ticket holder to a concert or a play or a dance performance, every visitor to a gallery, and there are millions of them. It is important to remember that, especially when we talk about government support for the arts. All those audience members are voters, and supporters. If there were no grants the ticket prices would be prohibitive!
>
> But most important, after all, is why we produce the art, to communicate with others, to share our vision and our talent. And the depth of the talent in Canada is terrific. We want to see and hear the work of these Canadians, not out of a feeling of nationalism, because that just kills all spirit, but because of patriotism, because we love our country and we want to share

the best of our artists and with them see and hear the best from the rest of the world.[14]

As he looked forward from the early months of the new millennium, as usual his mind was busy, thinking about that wider musical world. The result was what he called his 'Last Hurrah,' although that prediction was met with some cynicism. Appropriately, it was another choral festival, titled 'The Joy of Singing within the Noise of the World.' He freely admits to lifting the latter part of the title from a newspaper article he read while travelling on the train from Vienna to Salzburg. Its relevance, in his view, increases with every daily newscast.

Of course, before any announcement was made or contracts signed he was out raising the money and his first stop was Ottawa. With over a half-century of experience, and with his network of contacts, Niki starts at the top, not the bottom. As Dr Shirley Thompson, director of the Canada Council for the Arts, laughingly told it, 'He came to my office first, then to the Chair of the Council and then the section heads. And over at the Department of Canadian Heritage they were ready. There was a buzz in Ottawa, "Niki is in town."'[15]

He found his support, both public and private, and at a press conference in the sunlit lobby of Roy Thomson Hall on 7 November 2001 Niki announced the program for the following June.

Long-time colleague and friend Krzysztof Penderecki was heard on tape speaking from his native Krakow, announcing that he would conduct his *Credo* and compose a new work for the opening gala. Niki stood at the podium, excitedly reading from his notes. Once again he assembled a list of Canadian and international stars so numerous that even he was hesitant to start naming names in case someone was forgotten.

The format echoes former triumphs. Niki wanted an event with a shape and character with which he was familiar, understandable at age ninety-three and after more than half a century of working with the musical community. But while the organization echoed former festivals, the specifics were up to the minute: twenty-one premieres, twelve choirs from abroad and many more from all regions of Canada, children's choirs, free concerts, and an education program, all topped off with a closing night gala starring the great Canadian tenor Ben Heppner in the Toronto premiere of Franz Schmidt's *Book with Seven Seals,* written by the Austrian composer in 1937.

'True Festival fare,' said Niki, and at the announcement no one disagreed. The crowd of artists, supporters, colleagues, and press

applauded, posed for pictures, and smiled knowingly at the announcement that 'tickets for the new Joy of Singing are on sale.' They had
already begun to sort out their choices, what they must hear, what they
can pass, all the while feeling slightly inadequate, knowing that Niki
would be everywhere, in every hall and church, hearing every note.

This very likely was the last 'biggie,' as Niki calls his major festivals.
But already the telephone rings, bringing requests for his assistance and
expertise for projects beyond 2002. How will he respond? Niki loves his
leisure. He enjoys a glass of good scotch, and always the Belgian chocolate! On television, a well-written detective mystery or a classic movie of
the *Casablanca* era will hold his attention, but he admits to being too
impatient for long novels! He is at his core an uncomplicated man who
does not need extravagence, in any of its manifestations, to make him
happy. But in spite of his satisfaction with his life, he is restless, spending
much of his 'free' time mulling over ideas for new ventures, or the musical work at hand. It is a lifetime habit, begun as a small boy, and as he
says now when asked about retirement, 'Well, you don't expect me to sit
here with my knitting, do you?' It is a good-natured comment. Niki is
confident that finding things to do will never be a problem for him.
There are still concerts to hear, new voices to discover, advice to give,
projects to animate.

'The Joy of Singing within the Noise of the World' was the dream and
the reality created from the experiences of a professional life that has
spanned the length of two or even three typical careers. It was built on a
plan with which Niki is familiar, one with which he can work easily. But
the details were particular to this festival; each choir, each soloist, each
venue, and each piece of music had to fit with all the others. Schedules
changed, the value of the dollar was fluctuating and the budget with it,
adjustments were necessary, always with an eye to box-office appeal, and
the final arbiter, quality. Niki travelled every day by subway to the downtown office tower where he did all the planning, settling all the details
from a small cubicle crowded with a desk and a telephone and piles of
paper, publicity material, and CDs of potential participants in his festival. Every morning he began his never-ending round of calls and meetings and instructions to his busy assistant. Now in his nineties, he
maintained a pace and an enthusiasm that amazed almost everyone who
came in contact with him. Were there doubts in his mind? Were there
dark days when he despaired about the future or the past, wondering if
it had all been worthwhile, or indeed if this next adventure would succeed? The answer is in his lifetime of doing. From his childhood run-

ning across the Moravian countryside catching butterflies, to his first engagements learning his craft in the small theatres, to finding and creating opportunities in a new world, Niki has focused on what lay ahead, believing always that it would be splendid, and prepared to move on even if it did not meet expectations.

Alexander Herzen, man of letters, asked the question, 'Where is the song before it is sung?' Philosopher Isaiah Berlin answered: 'Where indeed? "Nowhere" is the answer – one creates the song by singing it, by composing it. So, too, life is created by those who live it, step by step.'[16]

Since his birth, far away in time and place, on St Nicholas Day, Niki has created his life, each step made from a fresh idea, a compelling vision.

He has given energy and excitement to the musical life of his adopted country, and heard the voices of Canada in its smallest towns and grandest concert halls.

Niki has composed his own life, from his roots in a realm that no longer exists, from all that the larger world has offered, and from all the songs that have touched him. Niki Goldschmidt is the resonant sound of a life lived gloriously one new day, one new place, one new song at a time.

Abbreviations

CC	Canada Council
COC	Canadian Opera Company
EJF	Edward Johnson Music Foundation
NG	Nicholas Goldschmidt
NLC	National Library of Canada, Music Division
RCOM	Royal Conservatory of Music
TFO	L'Office de la télécommunications éducative de l'Ontario
VIF	Vancouver International Festival

Notes

Prologue

1 Nicholas Goldschmidt, interview with Susan Hayes and Maria Muszynska. Unless otherwise noted, all recollections of NG quoted in text are from the same source, which comprised a number of interviews over a period of time, in 1998–9.

1: 'Tempi passati'

1 NG, interview with author, Toronto, 29 December 2000.
2 Ibid.
3 Ibid.
4 Ibid.
5 Ibid.
6 Frank Walker, *Hugo Wolf: A Biography* (London: J.M. Dent and Sons, 1951), 53–5.
7 Ibid., 53.
8 Satcheverell Sitwell, *Liszt* (London: Columbus Books, 1955), 346.
9 Henry Pleasants, ed. and trans., *The Music Criticism of Hugo Wolf* (London: Holmes and Meier Publishers, 1978), 278–9.
10 Walker, 53.
11 Kurt Stern, quoted in Roger Vaughan, *Herbert von Karajan: A Biographical Portrait* (London: Weidenfeld and Nicolson, 1986), 100.
12 Walter Taussig, telephone interview with author, 9 March 2000.
13 NG, interview with author, 5 January 2001.
14 Ibid.
15 Ibid.

16 NG, interview with author, 31 January 2001.
17 Shelagh Goldschmidt, interview with author, October 1999.

2: Upbeat and Down in an Old World

1 Francis Paul Walters, *League of Nations – History* (London: Oxford University Press, 1960), 33.
2 Ibid., 117.
3 Gary B. Ostrower, *The League of Nations from 1919 to 1929* (Garden City Park, NY: Avery Publishing Group, 1996), 8.
4 NG, interview with author, 4 October 2000.
5 Madame Thérèse Hymans and Jan Paderewski, exchange of correspondence, 1929. NG's private papers.
6 Sir Rudolf Bing, *Five Thousand Nights at the Opera* (New York: Doubleday and Company, 1972) 51–2.
7 NG, speech given at Royal Conservatory of Music, 28 November 1987.
8 Robert Jacobson, *Reverberations: Interviews with the World's Leading Musicians* (New York: William Morrow and Company, 1974), 201–2.
9 Rudolf Serkin, letter to NG, 30 December, 1982. NG's private papers.
10 Joseph Horowitz, *Understanding Toscanini* (New York: Alfred A. Knopf, 1987), 157.
11 Mathilde Kopetzky, letter to NG, Vienna, 17 April 1948. NG's private papers.
12 Henry Pleasants, ed. and trans., *The Music Criticism of Hugo Wolf* (London: Holmes and Meier Publishers, 1978), 273, no. 110.
13 Ibid.

3: New World Overtures

1 Jacobson, 167.
2 Humphrey Burton, 'An Interview with Aaron Copland,' *BBC Music Magazine* 9:2 (October 2000), 33.
3 *New Grove Dictionary of Opera*, ed. Stanley Sadie (London: Macmillan, 1992) 3:460.
4 *San Francisco Conservatory of Music: A Brief History*, http:// www.sfcm.edu/ history.html.
5 Alfred Frankenstein, 'Goldschmidt's Recital Lauded,' *San Francisco Chronicle*, 19 November 1938.
6 Alfred Frankenstein, 'The Function of Criticism,' *The Voice of America Forum Lectures Music Series No. 3* (United States Information Service, 1959), 8.

7 Alfred Frankenstein, 'Goldschmidt – Musician!' *San Francisco Chronicle*, 17 January 1940.
8 Aaron Copland and Vivian Perlis, *Copland 1900 through 1942* (New York: St Martin's/Marek, 1984), 258.
9 Virgil Thomson to Aaron Copland, Paris, 20 March 1939, in Gertrude Norman and Miriam Lubell Shrifte, eds., *Letters of Composers* (New York: Grosset and Dunlap, 1946), 379.
10 Alexander Fried, 'Second Hurricane,' *San Francisco Examiner*, 2 March 1941.
11 NG, interview with author, 16 March 2000.
12 NG, interview with author, 4 October 2000.
13 John Beckwith, interview with author, 15 March 2000.
14 'Two Misers Presented,' *New York Times*, 9 December 1943.
15 NG, interview with author, 22 December 1999.
16 'Goldschmidt Heard in Lecture Recital,' undated and unidentified newspaper clipping. NG's private papers.
17 *Musical America*, undated and untitled clipping reporting recital given 27 April 1945 by Nicholas Goldschmidt. NLC.
18 New Orleans Opera website, http//:Neworleansonline.com/perfart.htm.
19 Leopold Simoneau, letter to author, April 2000.
20 Ibid.

4: New Home, New Voices

1 *Encyclopedia of Music in Canada* (hereafter *EMC*), 2nd ed., Helmut Kallmann and Gilles Potvin (Toronto: University of Toronto Press, 1992), 1298.
2 *History of Concerts and Performers*, 2nd ed. (Toronto: Women's Musical Club of Toronto, 1997).
3 Carl Morey, former dean of music, University of Toronto, recalls that the TSO's pops concerts featured a serious and substantial repertoire that went beyond the film music and Broadway tunes of today's pops series. Interview with author, 14 October 2000.
4 *EMC*, 1302–3.
5 Ibid., 1154.
6 Ezra Schabas, *Sir Ernest MacMillan: The Importance of Being Canadian*. (Toronto: University of Toronto Press, 1996), 73.
7 Ezra Schabas and Carl Morey, *Opera Viva: Canadian Opera Company, The First Fifty Years* (Toronto: Dundurn Press, 2000), 7–12.
8 Ibid., 14–15.
9 Ettore Mazzoleni, *Opera School Flying High* (Toronto: Royal Conservatory of

Music, 1962), pamphlet condensed from article in Opera Canada, 1962. NG's private papers.

10 Arnold Walter, letter to NG, 26 September 1946. Uncatalogued records of University of Toronto, Faculty of Music.

11 A.D. Adamson, immigration inspector-in-charge, Department of Mines and Resources, letter to Arnold Walter, 7 October 1946. Ibid.

12 Arnold Walter, letter to A.D. Adamson, 16 October 1946. Ibid.

13 Arnold Walter, letter to Felix Brentano, 9 September 1946. Ibid.

14 John Beckwith, interview with author, 23 March 2000.

15 George Crum, interview with author, 15 February 2000.

16 Helmut Kallmann, letter to NG, 6 December 1988. NG's private papers.

17 John H. Yocum, 'Opera School's Work Pleases and Heralds Even Brighter Future,' *Saturday Night*, 28 December 1946.

18 NG, letter to Arnold Walter, 23 December 1946. NG's private papers.

19 Arnold Walter, letter to NG, 2 January 1947. NG's private papers.

20 *EMC*, 228.

21 Arnold Walter, letter to Felix Brentano, 15 May 1947. Uncatalogued records of University of Toronto, Faculty of Music.

22 Arnold Walter letter to Mrs Florence Easton, 2 June 1947. Ibid.

23 NG, letter to Arnold Walter, 28 May 1947. Ibid.

24 NG, letter to Arnold Walter, 3 June 1947. Ibid.

25 NG, letter to Arnold Walter, 23 June 1947. Ibid.

26 NG, letter to Arnold Walter, 4 August 1947. Ibid.

27 Bernard Shaw, *Music in London, 1890–94* (New York: Vienna House, 1973), 1:75.

28 Helmut Kallmann, *The Varsity*, 9 February 1948. COC.

29 Vincent Tovell, interview with author. 30 January 2000.

30 Arnold Walter, letter to Andrew MacMillan, 22 June 1948. University of Toronto, Fisher Rare Book Library Archives, RCOM A 75-0014, box 31.

31 Arnold Walter, letter to Felix Brentano, 26 June 1948. Uncatalogued records of University of Toronto, Faculty of Music.

32 Ibid.

33 Shelagh Goldschmidt, interview with author, 8 September 1999.

34 Ibid.

35 NG, letter to Arnold Walter, 11 July 1948. Uncatalogued records of University of Toronto, Faculty of Music.

36 Shelagh Goldschmidt, 8 September 1999.

37 NG, letter to Arnold Walter, 13 August 1948. Uncatalogued records of University of Toronto, Faculty of Music.

38 *Montreal Star*, 16 October 1952, n.p. COC.

39 Jon Vickers, telephone interview with author, 20 March 2000.

40 Jeannie Williams, *Jon Vickers: A Hero's Life* (Boston: Northeastern University Press, 1999), 37.

41 Carl Morey, interview with author, 30 January 2001.

42 Ibid.

43 Patricia Rideout, interview with author, 21 March 2000.

44 Schabas and Morey, *Opera Viva*, 31–3, and Kenneth W. Peglar, *Opera and the University of Toronto 1946–1971*, 12.

45 Ettore Mazzoleni, letter to R.H.L. Massie, 26 April 1951. COC.

46 Margaret Aitken, 'Between You and Me,' *Telegram*, 21 December 1949. NLC.

47 Margaret Aitken, 'Between You and Me,' *Telegram*, 30 November 1956. NLC.

48 Program for concert given in Massey Hall, Toronto, 11 September 1957. NLC.

49 Helen Beattie, 'Growing Up in Opera,' *Saturday Night*, 17 January 1953.

50 Editorial, 'Toronto Is Grateful,' *Telegram*, 23 February 1953.

51 Eric McLean, 'Toronto Opens Opera Festival,' *Montreal Star*, 6 February 1950.

52 Thomas Archer, 'Opera Festival Opens with Fine Performance of Singers, Orchestra,' *Globe and Mail*, 4 February 1950, 17.

53 'Festival Films,' *Scotsman*, 28 August 1951 (critic not named).

54 George Crum, interview with author, February 2000.

55 'Concert Artists Praise Audiences,' *Huntsville Forester*, 18 March 1954. NLC.

56 Canadian Broadcasting Corporation, 'Radio Times,' 1948 (no month or day).

57 Harry J. Boyle, Programme Director, Trans-Canada Network, letter to NG, 26 October 1948. NLC.

58 Iby Koerner, telegram to NG, 15 October 1953. NLC.

59 George Crum, interview with author, February 2000.

60 Jan Rubeš, letter to NG for Eightieth Birthday Book, 6 December 1988. NG's private papers.

61 Lois Marshall, letter to NG. Ibid.

5: Vision and Vicissitudes

1 Dr Bryan Gooch, interview with author, 30 March 2000.

2 John K. Friesen, interview with author, 29 March 2000.

3 University of British Columbia Notice of Appointment, 15 February 1950. NLC.

4 NG, interview with author, 2 March 2001.

5 NG, interview with author, 5 January 2001.

6 Gooch, 30 March 2000.

7 George Zukerman, 'Re: Goldschmidt,' personal e-mail to author, 17 May 2002.

8 Ernie Perrault, 'Famous Artists Make Local Festival Comparable to Salzburg, Edinburgh,' *UBC Chronicle*, 12:2 (Summer 1958).

9 Noreen Petty, 'Magic Flute in English Given at UBC,' *Vancouver Sun*, 13 July 1953.

10 Gooch, 30 March 2000.

11 Shelagh Goldschmidt, interview with author, 8 September 1999.

12 Norman Newton, radio review, written copy, 1950. NLC.

13 R.B. Middleton, employment manager, BC Electric Company, letter to NG, 3 August 1950. NLC.

14 Ada McGeer, 'Toronto Artists Score Triumph at Symphony.' *Vancouver Sun*, undated clipping. NLC.

15 NG, 'Mozart Festival 1956: An Idea for a Permanent Vancouver Festival of Music and Drama,' July 1954. John Friesen's private papers.

16 NG, interview with author, 14 May 2000.

17 John Kraglund, 'Director Forgotten in Opening Comment,' *Globe and Mail*, 21 July 1958.

18 Joan Sutherland, *A Prima Donna's Progress* (London: Orion Books, 1998), 66.

19 Leopold Simoneau, letter to author, 14 March 2000.

20 John Kirkwood, 'Conductor Steinberg Finds Opera Worth His Sacrifice,' *Vancouver Sun*, 29 July 1958. NLC.

21 John Beckwith, 'The Vancouver International Festival, 1958,' *Canadian Music Journal* 3:1 (Autumn 1958), 34.

22 Bruno Walter, letter to Walter Stresemann, 1957, quoted in Erik S. Ryding and Rebecca Pechefsky, *Bruno Walter: A World Elsewhere* (New Haven: Yale University Press, 2001), 386.

23 Janet Partridge, '"Style Show" at Festival,' *Vancouver Sun*, 13 July 1959.

24 NG, 2 March 2001.

25 Robert Creech, 'Nicholas Goldschmidt,' personal e-mail to author, 9 September 1999.

26 J.K. Friesen, 'A Report on the Relationship of the UBC Summer School of the Arts and the Vancouver Festival Society in 1959,' University of British Columbia, Department of University Extension, 16 October 1959. John Friesen's private papers.

27 John Kraglund, 'Orpheus and Eurydice Is Good Festival Fare,' *Globe and Mail*, 20 July 1959.

28 Howard Taubman, quoted in the *Globe and Mail*, 'Vancouver Opera Orpheus Rated Major League Calibre, 25 July 1958.

29 See letter from president of the VIF to festival members in which he notes that the 'festival deficit' for 1960 totalled $153,250, excluding grants and donations of $144, 272. Also financial statements 1958–64. NLC.

30 Ray Gardner, 'Vancouver's Bold but Shaky International Festival,' *Macleans*, 18 June 1960, 29 and 58.

31 Sir Kenneth Clark, *The Other Side of the Alde: In Tribute to Benjamin Britten* (London: Faber and Faber, 1963), quoted in Michael Kennedy, *Britten* (London: J.M. Dent, 1993), 69.

32 Joy Coghill, interview with author, 30 March 2000.

33 Jack Richards, 'Children's Play, "Noah's Flood" Touches All at Cathedral,' *Vancouver Sun*, 1 August 1960, 13.

34 Humphrey Burton, Canadian Broadcasting Corporation, Pacific Region, 'Critics at Large,' 27 July 1960. Written transcript in NLC.

35 Editorial, *Vancouver Province*, 25 July 1960.

36 Patricia Rideout, interview with author, 21 March 2000.

37 Burton, CBC, 27 July 1960.

38 NG, quoted in Douglas Collins, 'Peking Opera Gives Vancouver a Scoop,' *Globe and Mail*, 6 August 1960.

39 G.C. Andrew, letter to Nicholas Goldschmidt, Vancouver, 10 April 1957. NLC.

40 Les Wedman, 'Red Opera Group Invited to Defect,' *Vancouver Sun*, 8 August 1960, 1.

41 Desmond Arthur, 'Jam-Packed Theatre Rises to Cheer Peking Opera,' *Vancouver Sun*, 11 August 1960, 37.

42 Chenchunt Chint [*sic*], telegram to Nicolas [*sic*] Goldschmidt, 23 August 1960. NG's private papers.

43 Dilys Powell, quoted in 'Visiting Critic Astonished by Young City's Great Enterprise,' *Vancouver Sun*, 17 August 1960, 5.

44 Burton, CBC, 27 July 1960.

45 *Vancouver Sun*, 4 August 1960, 4.

46 Financial statements of VIF show a budget for 1960 of $428,039 and a net shortfall of $13, 859.

47 Coghill, 30 March 2000.

48 Mike Tytherleigh, 'Belafonte's a Hit – Last Time Here?' *Vancouver Province*, 21 August 1961.

49 Bruno Walter, letter to NG, 28 November 1961. NG's private papers.

50 General Sir Ouvry Roberts, letter to festival members, 10 November 1961. NLC.

51 Harold Weir, 'Worth It,' *Vancouver Sun*, 6 November 1961, 4.

52 General Sir Ouvry Roberts, statement to press, Vancouver International Festival, 21 November 1961. NLC.

53 David Watmough, *The Unlikely Pioneer* (Oakville: Mosaic Press, 1985), 43.

54 Zukerman, personal e-mail to author, 17 May 2002.

55 Creech, e-mail, 8 September 1999.

56 André Malraux, quoted by John K. Friesen, in Festival Vancouver 2000, Program Book, 4.

6: Celebrations East to West

1 Vincent Tovell, interview with author, 30 January 2000.

2 Norman A. Robertson, letter to NG, 29 August 1961. NG's private papers.

3 NG, 'A Report on the Possibility of an Arts Festival in Hawaii,' submitted to Canadian Pacific Airlines, 29 September 1962. NLC.

4 Chuck Frankel, 'Cultural Festival of the Pacific Considered for Isles in 1964,' *Honolulu Star-Bulletin*, 10 October 1962.

5 See various papers in NLC.

6 'Canadian Director Gets Belgian Raves,' *Toronto Star* (report from Canadian Press), 22 February 1964.

7 'Goldschmidt Wins Laurels in Netherlands,' *Globe and Mail*, 13 June 1966.

8 NG, interview with author, 16 October 2001.

9 Performing Arts Division, Centennial Commission, *Festival Canada: The Performing Arts Program in the Centennial Year of Confederation*, 15 November 1966, National Archives of Canada.

10 Wendy Dey, 'Centennial Choir: Dedicated Conductor, Loyal Followers,' *Ottawa Citizen*, 19 April 1967, 21.

11 Robert Cooper, interview with author, 28 May 2000.

12 'Unique Lesson for Students on History of Choral Music,' unidentified clipping. NLC.

13 Lee Edwards, 'Christ Church Cathedral Concerts: Stimulating Music,' *Ottawa Citizen*, 7 December 1970.

14 Ann Gamey and Barbara Eagleson, letter to NG, 17 May 1967. NLC.

15 Gamey to NG, undated. NLC.

16 Joy Coghill, interview with author, 30 March 2000.

17 Benjamin Britten, letter to NG, 31 October 1967. NG's private papers.

18 Coghill, 30 March 2000.

19 Mike Tytherleigh, CKWX Vancouver, 24 November 1967. Written transcript in NLC.

20 Jack Richards, 'World Premiere Lays Bare Tragedy of Canadian Society,' *Vancouver Sun*, 24 November 1967.

21 NG, 'Preface, Guidelines for Discussion,' Canadian Centenary Council, workshop no. 111, undated. NLC.

22 NG, interview with author, 1 May 2001.

23 Judith Skelton Grant, *Robertson Davies: Man of Myth* (New York: Viking, 1994), 445.

24 NG, interview with author, 14 April 2001.

25 Howard Taubman, 'The Arts beyond Expo,' *New York Times*, 17 November 1967.

26 Ibid.

27 NG, undated speech. NG's private papers.

28 Terry Crowley, 'The Founding of the Guelph Spring Festival,' in Gloria Dent and Leonard Conolly, *Guelph and Its Spring Festival* (Guelph: Edward Johnson Music Foundation 1992), 80.

29 NG, 'Shakespearean Festivals and Opera for Eskimos,' unidentified clipping sent from India to NG, compliments of the Office of the High Commissioner for Canada, 30 April 1968. NG's private papers.

30 Ibid.

7: For All Seasons and for All Places

 1 Mavor Moore, 'The Secret for Success at Festivals,' *Globe and Mail*, 9 May 1987.

 2 Barbara Little, interview with author, 6 April 2000.

 3 Murdo MacKinnon, interview with author, 14 August 2000.

 4 NG, 'Report on Activities of Director of Music,' University of Guelph, 1968. NLC.

 5 Ibid.

 6 Robert Missen, interview with author, 15 October 2000.

 7 MacKinnon, 14 August 2000.

 8 Ibid.

 9 John Cripton, interview with author, 20 August 2000. John Cripton became manager, on Niki's recommendation, of the Rebecca Cohn Auditorium in Halifax. He later was the first director of the Touring Office of the Canada Council and became a successful impresario.

10 Ronald Crichton, 'Guelph's Prodigal Son,' *Financial Times* (London), 10 June 1969.

11 John Kraglund, 'A Perfect Prodigal,' *Globe and Mail*, 5 May 1969.

12 Little, 6 April 2000.

13 Kenneth Winters, 'Victory at the Guelph Festival,' *Toronto Telegram*, 4 May 1970.

14 John Kraglund and Kenneth Winters, quoted in Dent and Conolly, 96.

15 Editorial, *Daily Mercury*, Guelph, 30 April 1970.

16 Little, 6 April 2000.

17 MacKinnon, 14 August 2000.

18 William Lord, interview with author, 10 October 1999.

19 Colin Graham, 'Goldschmidt Biography,' personal e-mail to author, 19 February 2000.

20 NG, letter to Jon Vickers, 7 May 1974. University of Guelph Archives.

21 NG, untitled, 1974. Ibid.

22 Tim Bray, *The Ontarion*, 17 May 1974, quoted in Dent and Conolly, 105.

23 John Kraglund, 'Vickers, Stubbs Soar at Guelph Festival,' *Globe and Mail*, 29 April 1975, 19.

24 MacKinnon, August 2000.

25 Stephen Godfrey, 'Marilyn Horne Wins Tough Battle with the Heat,' *Globe and Mail*, 23 May 1977.

26 Edwina Carson, interview with author, 14 August 2000.

27 Ibid.

28 Marilyn Crooks, interview with author, 14 August 2000.

29 William Littler, 'Derek Healey's New Opera an Interesting Technique,' *Toronto Star*, 9 May 1977.

30 Jamie Portman, 'Guelph Worked More Miracles with an Indian-Legend Opera,' Southam News Service, 10 May 1977. NLC.

31 William Littler, 'New Guelph Opera's Reach ultimately Exceeds Grasp,' *Toronto Star*, 11 May 1978.

32 John Kraglund, 'Psycho Red Strong Stuff,' *Globe and Mail*, 11 May 1978.

33 MacKinnon, August 2000.

34 Charles Wilson, telephone interview with author, 6 April 2000.

35 NG, interview with author, 24 June 2001.

36 Andrew Porter, 'Guelph Festival,' *Financial Times* (London), June 1986. Clipping in NG's private papers.

37 Michael Ajzenstadt, 'A Thriller at the Canada Pavilion,' *Opera Club Ensemble* (Vancouver) 12: 10 (June 1986). Clipping in NG's private papers.

38 MacKinnon, 14 August 2000.

39 Jakob Amstutz, letter to Murdo MacKinnon, 24 May 1974. University of Guelph Archives.

40 NG, letter to Jakob Amstutz, 24 May 1974. Ibid.

41 They included the percussion ensemble Nexus, Elmer Iseler and his Festival Singers, soprano Mary Morrison, harpist Erica Goodman, flutist Robert Aitken, cellist Gisela Depkat, pianists Monica Gaylord and Karen Keiser, and the Orford Quartet.

42 Vincent Tovell, interview with author, 30 January 2000.

43 See Dent and Conolly, 114 for more details of the Willan celebration.

44 Ernst Krenek, letter to NG, 13 May 1980. NG's private papers.

45 MacKinnon, August 2000.

46 Tim Porteous, interview with author, 30 March 2000.

47 See undated clipping from *Kitchener-Waterloo Record*. NLC.

48 NG, 'Report to the Canada Council: Visit to Vienna, 1 June–11 June 1981.' NLC. Quotations in the next few paragraphs are from this source.

49 William Littler, 'Robust Vickers Turns Songs into Dramas Full of Meaning,' *Toronto Star*, 26 April 1987.

50 Wes Blomster, 'Mozart Opera a Treat for Even the Most Jaded Ears,' *Daily Camera* (Boulder, Colorado), 26 July 1988.

51 Yehudi Menuhin, letter to NG, 26 May 1987. NLC.

52 Carson, 14 August 2000.

53 NG, letter to Peter Meincke, president, University of Prince Edward Island, November 1983. NLC.

54 NG, untitled report. NLC.

55 NG, 'Arts Communities: Industry and Individual Interested Parties in Proposed Affiliated Artists Program in Ontario,' report to Robert Sunter, Ontario Arts Council, 7 June 1974. NLC.

56 John Godfrey, interview with author, 19 October 2000.

57 NG, interview with author, 5 January 2001.

58 Creech, personal e-mail to author, 20 November 1999.

59 Naomi Lighbourne, interview with author, 15 September 1999.

60 Dave Robertson, 'The Collaboration Was Memorable,' *Sault Star*, 26 September 1983.

61 Letter to Joy Coghill, unsigned, from 'Jason the buck,' dated only 28, 1976. Copy in NG's private papers.

62 Nancy Acton, 'Re-enter Opera – by the Children's Door,' *Mid-Ocean News* (Bermuda), 18 February 1983. Clipping in NLC.

63 Carson, 14 August 2000.

8: Something up His Sleeve, and More

1 Glenn Gould, letter to John McClure, 11 June 1966, in John P.L. Roberts and Ghyslaine Guertin, eds., *Glenn Gould: Selected Letters* (Toronto: Oxford University Press, 1992), 92.

2 Glenn Gould, 'We Who Are about to Be Disqualified Salute You,' in Tim Page, ed., *The Glenn Gould Reader* (Toronto: Key Porter Books, 1990), 250–5 (originally published in *High Fidelity*, December 1966).

3 Zubin Mehta, letter to NG, 3 January 1983. NLC.
4 Edwina Carson, interview with author, 14 August 2000.
5 Moira Johnson, telephone interview with author, 14 September 2000.
6 Andrew Stephen, 'Is the Piano Your Forte?' *Sunday Times Magazine* (London), 18 August 1985, 14–20.
7 Ibid., 20.
8 Russell H. Gould, letter to NG, 31 May 1985. NLC.
9 NG, quoted in 'Something up My Sleeve.' Unidentified clipping in NG's private papers.
10 Leon Botstein, 'Of Thee I Sing,' *New York Times Magazine*, 28 November 1999. www.nytimes.com/library/magazine/millennium/m1/botstein.html.
11 NG, interview with author, 19 September 2001.
12 NG, administrative notes for choral festival. NLC.
13 Cathryn Gregor, interview with author, 16 September 2000.
14 The 1989 International Choral Festival Inc., minutes of meeting, 28 October 1988. NLC.
15 NG, letter to R. Murray Schafer, 12 May 1989. NLC.
16 Moira Johnson, interview with author, October 2000.
17 The Norfolk Singers, Simcoe, Ontario, letter to NG, 19 September 1989. NLC.
18 Ken Winters, 'The Fields and the Forests Resound Melodiously,' 'The Joy of Singing,' 1989 International Choral Festival Program Book (Toronto: June 1989), 54–5.
19 Robert Everett Green, 'Taking an Impish Attitude to a Solemn Mozart,' *Globe and Mail*, 12 June 1991.
20 NG, letter to Hamilton McClymont, 12 October 1989. NLC.
21 NG, in Paula Citron, 'How Niki Brought Wolfie to Toronto,' *Toronto Star*, 25 May 1991.
22 'Life of Niki,' 'Adrienne Clarkson Presents' (videocassette), Adrienne Clarkson, executive producer, Gordon Stewart, producer and director, Canadian Broadcasting Corporation, 1993.
23 Václav Havel, letter to NG, Prague, 19 May 1993. NG's private papers.
24 Urjo Kareda, 'A Choral Triumph of the Sensual,' *Globe and Mail*, 26 June 1993.
25 Elaine Mason, Faywood Arts Centre for Music Education, North York, letter to NG, 13 July 1993. NLC.
26 Douglas Roche, letter confirming previous arrangements, to James Fleck, 20 September 1994. NG's private papers.
27 Sir Peter Ustinov, honorary chairman of UNICEF, introductory statement in souvenir program, San Francisco, June 1995.

28 Arthur Kaptainis, 'Britten Work Is Opera for Everybody,' *Montreal Gazette*, 13 June 1995.

29 Robert Everett Green, 'UN Tribute Unites Audience, Players,' *Globe and Mail*, 12 June 1995.

30 Timothy Pfaff, 'Innocence of children Survives "Noah's Flood,"' *San Francisco Examiner*, 20 June 1995.

31 Joy Coghill, interview with author, March 2000.

9: 'Where is the song before it is sung?'

1 NG, interview with author, 10 June 2001.

2 NG, interview with author, March 2001.

3 Bruce Ubukata, card written to NG, 3 July 1989. NLC.

4 Carl Morey, interview with author, 18 October 2000.

5 Carl Morey, notes on occasion of presenting Nicholas Goldschmidt with Doctor of Music, University of Toronto, 13 June 1989. NLC.

6 Citation on the occasion of the awarding of the Degree of Doctor of Laws (Honoris Causa) to Nicholas Goldschmidt, York University, 17 June 1999. NLC.

7 Ludwig van Beethoven, letter to his nephew, Karl, quoted by NG, in address to Graduating Class, York University, 17 June 1999.

8 Lloyd Dykk, 'Having a Ball with Strings,' *Vancouver Sun*, 5 August 2000.

9 NG, interview with author, 27 July 2001.

10 In conversation with many individuals who contributed other information for this biography, the author asked for their assessment of the value of Music Canada Musique 2000. All responded positively, the general consensus being that the nature of the exercise will bring benefits for some time to come.

11 Robert Cooper, interview with author, 27 October 2000.

12 Joy Coghill, interview with author, 31 March 2000.

13 Teresa Stratas, fax to NG, 2 December 1998. NG's private papers.

14 NG, interview with author, 14 February 2002.

15 Shirley Thompson, remarks at Roy Thomson Hall, Toronto, 7 November 2001.

16 Isaiah Berlin, in Michael Ignatieff, *Isaiah Berlin: A Life* (London: Vintage, 2000), 295.

Bibliography

Amis, John, text, and Laelia Goehr, photographs. *Musicians in Camera*. London: Bloomsbury, 1987.

Beckwith, John 'The Vancouver International Festival, 1958.' *Canadian Music Journal* 3:1 (Autumn 1958).

Bing, Sir Rudolf. *Five Thousand Nights at the Opera*. New York: Doubleday and Company, 1972.

Burton, Humphrey. 'An Interview with Aaron Copland.' *BBC Music Magazine* 9:2 (October 2000). Interview based on transcript of original interview made for 'Mr. Copland Comes to Town.' First published in *The Listener,* 16 December 1965.

Centennial Commission, Department of Secretary of State, Festival Canada. The Performing Arts Program in the Centennial Year of Confederation. Ottawa. 15 December 1966.

'*Le Chef d'orchestre,* Cinema, Cinema.' Interview with Norman Latour. Jacques Valle, producer. TFO, 1987. Videocassette.

Copland, Aaron, and Vivian Perlis. *Copland 1900 through 1942*. New York: St Martin's/Marek, 1984.

Dent, Gloria, and Leonard Conolly. *Guelph and Its Spring Festival*. Guelph: Edward Johnson Music Foundation, 1992.

Elliott, Robin. *Counterpoint to a City: The First One Hundred Years of the Women's Musical Club of Toronto*. Toronto: ECW Press, 1997.

Encyclopedia of Music in Canada. 2nd ed. Ed. Helmut Kallmann and Gilles Potvin. Toronto: University of Toronto Press, 1992.

Frankenstein, Alfred. 'The Function of Criticism.' *The Voice of America Forum Lectures Music Series No. 3*. United States Information Service, 1959.

Friesen, J.K. 'A Report on the Relationship of the UBC Summer School of the

Arts and the Vancouver Festival Society in 1959.' University of British Colum-
     bia, Department of University Extension, 16 October 1959.
Gardner, Ray. 'Vancouver's Bold but Shaky International Festival,' *Maclean's,*
     18 June 1960.
Goldschmidt, Nicholas. 'Arts Communities: Industry and Individual Interested
     Parties in Proposed Affiliated Artists Program in Ontario.' Report to Ontario
     Arts Council, 7 June 1974.
– 'A Report on the Possibility of an Arts Festival in Hawaii.' Submitted to Cana-
     dian Pacific Airlines, 29 September 1962.
– 'Report to the Canada Council: Visit to Vienna, June 1–June 11 1981.' Ottawa:
     the Canada Council, 1981.
Grant, Judith Skelton. *Robertson Davies: Man of Myth.* New York: Viking, 1994.
History of Concerts and Performers. 2nd ed. Toronto: Women's Musical Club of
     Toronto, 1997.
Horowitz, Joseph. *Understanding Toscanini.* New York: Alfred A. Knopf, 1987.
Ignatieff, Michael. *Isaiah Berlin: A Life.* London: Vintage, 2000.
Jack, Adrian. 'Rudolf Serkin.' *BBC Music Magazine* 8:8 (April 2000).
Jacobson, Robert. *Reverberations: Interviews with the World's Leading Musicians.* New
     York: William Morrow and Company, 1974.
'June Callwood's National Treaures.' Jacqueline Barley, producer, Dan Robin-
     son, director. Vision TV, 1993. Videocassette.
Kennedy, Michael, *Britten.* Dent Master Musicians. London: J.M. Dent, 1993.
Lazarevich, Gordana. *The Musical World of Frances James and Murray Adaskin.*
     Toronto: University of Toronto Press, 1988.
'Life of Niki.' Adrienne Clarkson, executive producer, Gordon Stewart, pro-
     ducer and director. Adrienne Clarkson Presents, CBC, 1993. Videocassette.
Mazzoleni, Ettore. *Opera School Flying High.* Toronto: Royal Conservatory of
     Music, 1962. Pamphlet condensed from article in *Opera Canada,* February
     1962.
New Grove Dictionary of Opera. Ed. Stanley Sadie. London: Macmillan, 1992.
New Orleans Opera, <neworleansonline.com/perfart.htm>
Norman, Gertrude and Miriam Lubell Shrifte, eds. *Letter of Composers.* Universal
     Library. New York: Grosset and Dunlap, 1946.
Opera School. Gudrun Parker, director, Guy Glover, producer. National Film
     Board of Canada, 1952.
Ostrower, Gary B. *The League of Nations from 1919 to 1929.* Garden City Park, NY:
     Avery Publishing Group, 1996.
Page, Tim. *The Glenn Gould Reader.* Toronto: Key Porter Books, 1990. Originally
     published in *High Fidelity,* December 1966.
Peglar, Kenneth W. *Opera and the University of Toronto 1946–1971.* N.P., n.d.

Perrault, Ernie. 'Famous Artists Make Local Festival Comparable to Salzburg, Edinburgh.' *UBC Chronicle* 12:2 (Summer 1958).

Pleasants, Henry, ed. and trans. *The Music Criticism of Hugo Wolf.* London: Holmes and Meier Publishers, 1978.

Roberts, John P.L., and Ghyslaine Guertin, eds. *Glenn Gould: Selected Letters.* Toronto: Oxford University Press, 1992.

Ryding, Erik S., and Rebecca Pechefsky. *Bruno Walter: A World Elsewhere.* New Haven: Yale University Press, 2001.

San Francisco Conservatory of Music: A Brief History. <http://www.sfcm.edu/history/html.

Schabas, Ezra. *Sir Ernest MacMillan: The Importance of Being Canadian.* Toronto: University of Toronto Press, 1996.

Schabas, Ezra and Carl Morey. *Opera Viva: Canadian Opera Company, The First Fifty Years.* Toronto: Dundurn Press, 2000.

Shaw, Bernard. *Music in London, 1890–94. Vol. 1.* New York: Vienna House, 1973.

Sitwell, Satcheverell. *Liszt.* London: Columbus Books, 1955.

Stephen, Andrew. 'Is the Piano Your Forte?' *Sunday Times Magazine,* 18 August 1985, 14–20.

Sutherland, Joan. *A Prima Donna's Progress.* London: Orion Books, 1998.

Vaughan, Roger. *Herbert von Karajan: A Biographical Portrait.* London: Weidenfeld and Nicolson, 1986.

Walker, Frank. *Hugo Wolf: A Biography.* London: J.M. Dent and Sons, 1951.

Walters, Francis Paul. *League of Nations – History.* London: Oxford University Press, 1960.

Watmough, David. *The Unlikely Pioneer.* Oakville: Mosaic Press, 1985.

White, Eric Walter. *Benjamin Britten, His Life and Operas.* London: Faber and Faber, 1983.

Williams, Jeannie. *Jon Vickers: A Hero's Life.* Boston: Northeastern University Press, 1999.

Yocum, John H. 'Opera School's Work Pleases and Heralds Even Brighter Future.' *Saturday Night,* 28 December 1946.

Principal Archival Sources

Music Division, National Library of Canada, Ottawa

Holds the Nicholas Goldschmidt fonds in three sections:

1 1993–1, 61 folders, 5 boxes. Inclusive dates 1932–93, n.d.
2 Mus. 223 (1993–1) acc. 1993. 50 folders, 4 boxes. Inclusive dates 1951–93.
3 Mus. 223. (1993–1) 9 analogue audiotape cassettes, 3 analogue audiotape reels.

Archival, Rare and Special Collections, University of Guelph Library, Guelph, Ontario

Holds the Guelph Spring Festival Archives, 1968–85. 39 separate items containing files, programs, librettos, production notes, correspondence, minutes, contracts and other administration material, a photograph collection, and posters.

University of Toronto Archives

Holds historical records of Royal Conservatory of Music. Particular to Nicholas Goldschmidt years are acc. # 75-0014, boxes 30, 31, 48, 49, and 100.

Joan Baillie Archives, Canadian Opera Company

Holds material from the early years of the opera school and the first opera festivals. Includes correspondence, production notes, student lists, clippings, and programs.

Index